Dorot̶̶̶n

my

with love

S.F.R,

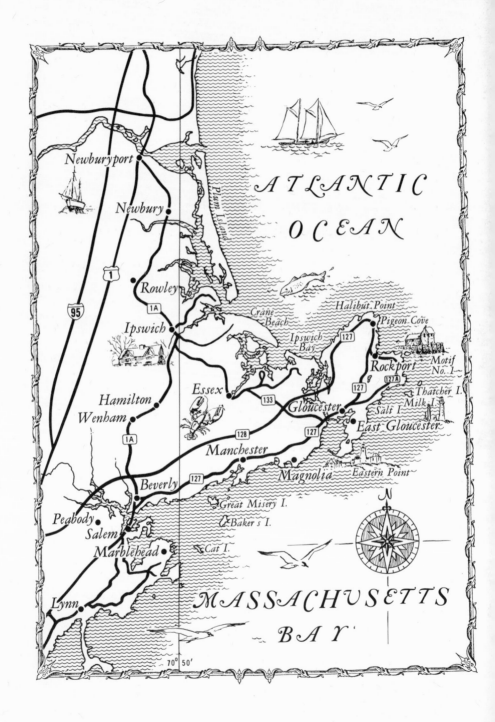

Cape Ann: Cape America

by
HERBERT A. KENNY

With line drawings by Tom O'Hara

J. B. LIPPINCOTT COMPANY
Philadelphia and New York

"Cape Ann" and the lines from "The Dry Salvages," "The Love Song of J. Alfred
Prufrock," "Marina," "Rhapsody on a Windy Night," and "Sweeney Erect" are from
Collected Poems 1909–1912 by T. S. Eliot, copyright, 1936, by Harcourt Brace
Jovanovich, Inc.; copyright, ©, 1963, 1964, by T. S. Eliot. Reprinted by permission
of Harcourt Brace Jovanovich, Inc., and Faber & Faber Ltd.
"Seascape at Evening: Cape Ann" is from Collected Poems by Horace Gregory.
Copyright 1951 by Horace Gregory. Reprinted by permission of Holt, Rinehart and
Winston, Inc.
Two stanzas are quoted from "Gloucester Moors" by William Vaughn Moody, pub-
lished by Houghton Mifflin.
The lines from The Maximus Poems by Charles Olson are reprinted by permission
of Corinth Books, Inc.
"Cape Ann; A View" is quoted from The Selected Poems of John Malcolm Brinnin
by permission of the author.
The quotation from Frame-up! by Dana Story is reprinted by permission of Barre
Publishers, Barre, Massachusetts.
"At a Gloucester Memorial Service" and "The Wind Is Alone" are from Suburban
Man by Herbert A. Kenny, published by The Monastine Press, Ozone Park, New
York, 1965.

*For Teresa
and the memory
of her Gloucester forebears*

❧ *Contents* ❦

﹩ *Acknowledgments* ﹩

I am indebted in greater or less degree to a number of persons, all of whom have my gratitude. To go into their titles and the extent of their contributions to me would take exaggerated space. I list them all with thanks and affection: Hubert Johnson, George Stevens, Peter Anastos, William D. Hoyt, Philip S. Weld, Mary Judith Coffey, Mary Gibran, Hyde Cox, Allan Davidson, Franz Denghausen, George Gloss, Carroll Sheehan, Joan Brown, Doris Connors, Paul Kenyon, Elliot Rogers, Maura Connolly, Barbara Erkkila, Joseph Garland, Irene Keegan, Josephine Rogers, Robert Taylor, Francis Burnett, Ralph Dexter, Margaret Ferrini, William Cafasso, Kitty Robertson, Harry Sagris, Louise Weiscopf, Mary Horton, Gertrude Goldsmith, Judge Edward Morley, J. Joseph Flatley, Mrs. Elsie Reed, the Reverend Leslie F. Yelland, and lastly, David McCord, for worrying about something he didn't do.

H. A. K.

Manchester

But you understand then why I can say that the center of things is here although we stand at the tip of the continent.

—Albert Camus, *The Fall*

Translated by Justin O'Brien
Copyright © 1956 by Alfred A. Knopf, Inc.

❧ *Introduction* ❧

The Commonwealth of Massachusetts ("state" is reserved for the lesser breeds without the law) has two capes, and the residents of one hardly speak to the residents of the other. As the inhabitants of John Bull's other island look on England, the natives of Cape Ann, also the smaller geographical unit, regard the denizens of Cape Cod as gross and commercial.

To the homeowner in the rocky fastness of the northern Cape, the very name of Cape Cod conjures up a vision of long lines of flatulent automobiles locked tail-to-snout like so many elephants, pulsating amid unendurable exhaust fumes and stretching for miles along undistinguished highways, flanked by neon signs flashing vulgar messages for intolerable roadside stands or garish motels with nauseatingly coy names, gift shoppes to make one's eyes poppe, all clustering like glassed-in ant colonies, with hippies sleeping on such lawn as can be found, homosexuals prancing through bitch-decorated antique shops, the whole lost amid marching sand dunes and tattered spinnies of tormented scrub pine and scorched by a relentless sirocco that only a Chamber of Commerce pamphlet could call a breeze.

In contrast to that, the average Cape Ann homesteader sees his home ground as a historic and shining region grouping picturesque New England towns famous for seventeenth- and eight-eenth-century architecture, blessed by the immutable sea, by meandering brooks and pacific inlets, the whole languid and lovely, and foreign to all except the most discriminating of tourists.

For this state of mind, there is, of course, no rationale, but there is evidence that discloses a discernible contrast. Route 28 through Cape Cod is becoming what the late Bernard De Voto called an "elongated slum." Cape Cod has turned too much the summer resort, and when people there boast of the antique charm of the bay side of the Cape, they are praising what is in fact the essence of the character of Cape Ann.

Now if Cape Ann was named for a Queen (the mother of Charles the First of England) and Cape Cod was named for a fish, the names have no relevance to what exists today. Cape Cod doesn't look like a codfish, and very few cod, relatively, are landed there. Cape Ann has as its heart the city of Gloucester, one of the great commercial fishing ports of the world, which on occasion, particularly if the wind is wrong, reeks of codfish. The fishing fleet from Gloucester still scours the Grand Banks, Georges Bank and the Banquereau, and its workers process more fish than any other city in the United States. Moreover, there is something regal about Cape Ann that Cape Cod seems to lack.

If one were to thrash about for the word that sets off one cape from the other, one might well seize on "integrity." If we accept that to mean an organized harmony of parts, Cape Ann has it. Cape Cod, geographically, is clearly marked off. Cape Cod Canal, which runs from Cape Cod Bay to Buzzards Bay, cuts off Cape Cod from the mainland of Massachusetts. Everything on the far side of the eight-mile canal, looking from Boston, is Cape Cod, although what the Cape Cod boundary was before the canal was cut through between 1909 and 1914 is a good question. Once you have crossed one of the great bridges at Bourne or Sagamore, however, and are on the Cape, you are not really into anything. Cape Cod is diverse but diffuse. Falmouth is as far from Provincetown as it is from Boston. Wellfleet is as different from Dennisport as it is from Brooklyn. The variety is there, but unity, excepting geographical unity, is lacking. Only the telephone company and the newspapers lump these towns together.

Now with Cape Ann things are the other way around. To be sure, there is a canal, called the Annisquam River, which runs from Ipswich Bay to Gloucester Harbor, and cuts from the mainland the town of Rockport and the greater part of the city of Gloucester, making an island that no one ever regards as such. The Cut at Blynman Bridge in Gloucester is so narrow that our Olympic broad-jumping champion could make it with two tries, and it really separates nothing. The foot traffic over the bridge is constant, and so is the boat traffic beneath it and through it. For the bridge is a drawbridge, which, summer visitors aver, spends more time in the air than locked in place. At the height of the summer season, motorists and mariners are pitted in a furious enmity over the raising and lowering of the iron span, but, of course, the mariner has the right of way and the conflict never gets beyond the cursing stage. In any event, the Annisquam River and Blynman Bridge do not mark the limits of Cape Ann.

Indeed, even the geographer is at a loss to determine where Cape Ann begins and ends. One has to draw an arbitrary line, or select an arbitrary line, and the best guide is the integrity, mentioned before, that exists among the various communities as a result of the comings and goings of the people who live in them. Beyond question the island that is composed of the greater part of Gloucester and the town of Rockport (bounded by Gloucester and the Atlantic Ocean) is indisputably Cape

Ann. Moving south along the coast, we find that we must include most of the town of Manchester, and moving in the other direction, we find that parts of the towns of Essex and Ipswich somehow fit into the business of being Cape Ann, along with a good piece of Plum Island, which spans four towns—Ipswich, Rowley, Newbury and Newburyport—and is approached on land by the last. So let us seize on a longitudinal line and hold to it. Let it be 70°47'30"w, which, fortunately for all concerned, is marked on the quadrangle maps of the area published by the U.S. Department of the Interior.

The whole of Cape Ann lies in Essex County. The entire area is redolent of the early history of the English colonization on North America. If one were to include, in an essay on Cape Ann, the cities of Beverly and Salem to the south, and Rowley, Newbury and Newburyport to the north, there would be no end to the texts one could recite. Rum and witches make good reading. Salem is several books in itself, and Newburyport at least one. The line 70°47'30"w does include Bakers Island, which is officially and historically part of the city of Salem, but it excludes the city of Beverly, which is sufficiently historic and lies between Manchester and Salem. Turning to the north, we find that the longitude we have selected includes Plum Island, much less definitely an island than Bakers Island, and part of the city of Newburyport, while it excludes Newburyport proper. Let us, then, make the concession to the irregularity of the coastline, and include Bakers Island and Plum Island in our discussion of Cape Ann, relegating Salem, Beverly and Newburyport to our discussion of its neighbors.

The city of Beverly lies contiguously southwest of Manchester, and beyond acknowledging its role in the historical growth of the Puritan colonies in the seventeenth century, and its supersocial section called Pride's Crossing (now somewhat less supersocial but still up there), we need pay little attention. Clinging to

Ipswich and Essex are the towns of Wenham and Hamilton, which have charm, innumerable upper middle-class homes and some lower ones, a claim on the late General George S. Patton, and the bucolic presence of the Myopia Hunt Club, where comely men and women still ride to hounds, but these towns can in no way qualify as part of Cape Ann no matter how their social elegance and leisured atmosphere importune.

We have thus included the city of Gloucester, indisputably the nucleus, the towns of Manchester, Essex, Rockport and Ipswich, and Plum Island (Newburyport) and Bakers Island (Salem), which is about as much as you can reasonably call Cape Ann. Gaze, then, at a map of Massachusetts (a word which in an Indian tongue may well mean "great hills," or "great hill shaped like an arrow") and observe the two capes. To the south is Cape Cod, like a great flexed arm, the biceps at Barnstable, the fist at Provincetown, the underpart trailing the ragged sleeve of Monomoy and other protuberances on Nantucket Sound, and the whole embracing Cape Cod Bay or the southern part of Massachusetts Bay. To the north, marking the northern end of Massachusetts Bay, is Cape Ann; but the more you stare at the latter's configuration, the less that can be made of it—although at times, having closed my eyes, I think I can see in that configuration the snout and mouth of a pig, or perhaps the profile of a goat. In any event, it forms in itself nothing very attractive, as does the boot of Italy, but is without cavil a cape with a magnificent harbor.

Samuel de Champlain thought it such, and when he sailed in about 1605, he called it "Beau Port." As early as 1543 the French had named Cape Cod "Malle-Barre," but Champlain called it "Cap Blanc" and let it go at that. When he brought his high-pooped ships past the headlands of Cape Ann fifteen years before the Pilgrims sighted Provincetown, the Indians came down to the shore to greet him and were wearing, it is reported,

Portuguese clothing. This should be no surprise to anyone who appreciates the lively traffic that existed between Europe and the New World in the sixteenth century. Basque and Breton fishermen, as well as Portuguese, sailed back and forth. Champlain undoubtedly had a map of the coastline, and if Cape Ann was on it, it was called the "Cape of St. Mary," or in Spanish, "Cabo de Santa Maria." Champlain called it "Cap aux Isles"; modern French spelling drops the "s" and puts a circumflex accent on the "I." There is no question what John Smith called it when he sailed about nine years later; he called it "Tragabigzanda" after a Turkish courtesan who had been kind to him. That name survives on a Gloucester street, as Beauport survives as the name of a curious museum. Soon after Champlain's visit, doughty English adventurers, as they called themselves, were drying fish on the shore of Cape Ann on a stage, as it was called, that they had misappropriated from some men of the Plymouth colony.

In any event, by 1642 Gloucester was enough of a community to be incorporated as a town; in 1892 it celebrated its 250th anniversary, and in 1942, its 300th. In 1874 it became a city, and 1974 will be its centennial year. We do not wish to confound the city with the Cape, however, and it is the Cape we are discussing. The city is so dominant, so significant, so historic, so dramatic, that it is only with effort one can resist its lure and give its neighbors proportionate consideration. Let us, then, try to keep the Cape in focus rather than the city. For just as Boston is more familiar around the world than Massachusetts, and conversely just as Cape Cod is more recognizable than any single community on it, so Gloucester, that charismatic city, has overshadowed the geographical concept of Cape Ann, and only by leaning into the wind can we tell the balanced story.

Let us, then, begin with the humbler towns, whose roots run deep in the soil of New England history, and whose gracious domesticities and natural favors have not yet been shamefully desecrated or destroyed by the Automotive Abomination or the Commercial Leprosy that disguises itself as Free Enterprise. The town meeting may yet save Cape Ann, for there is something about the rocks that lie beneath its soil and those the glacier piled on top of it that can enter into the soul of a man and make him as durable as the fishermen who have sailed to and from the Cape since before the arrival of Champlain, or the nameless wanderers who preceded him before the Indians had any European clothes to wear. As we approach Cape Ann from Boston (to which it might be said the Cape gave birth), we must try to see it not merely as one geographical feature of a historic state in quiet rivalry with another, a sort of north-south polarity, Boston's North Shore opposed to Boston's South Shore. We must try to see it as nothing less than the birthplace of English-speaking America, for this was the hook that caught the men who sailed from Europe to catch the fish.

Plymouth (with the extremely dubious claim of its rock) was a historical aberration. The men who settled it were not what they are in the mind's eye of the average American who is spoon-fed a phony history. Their achievements were accidents, and they died on the vine. They were misfits; "come-outers" who fled their native England to a Holland where they didn't fit either.

Their venture was ill-starred from the beginning. One ship, the *Speedwell,* had to turn back, being utterly unseaworthy. The *Mayflower* then had to be overloaded. The Separatists could not muster enough men of their own thinking to fill the bill, and so there were as many "strangers" as "saints" in the party, or more. The Mayflower Compact, that involuntary declaration, was a successful effort to keep both parties from fighting.

The company had not intended to land in New England and did so illegally. They behaved badly to the Indians from the start, stealing a supply of corn near Provincetown before reaching Plymouth. Only the courage of the hired crew of the *May-*

flower saved a shallop-load of the Pilgrims from drowning off Plymouth during a violent storm while they sat helpless on the thwarts. They suffered terribly from their lack of experience and foresight. They wouldn't have made it through the first winter at all if it had not been for the kindness of Indians, some of whom they had already robbed. They would not have been able to hold the land they took if plague had not cleared the coast of Indians shortly before they arrived (by happenstance) where they did. They were forced into Plymouth by lack of planning and time, and by the delays that attended their bungled departure from the Old World. In turn, it was not a "saint" who gave them the military striking force they needed to fend off their enemies but a "stranger," Myles Standish—probably the worst kind of "stranger" to them, a Roman Catholic.

Before the century was out, their colony was absorbed by the Puritans under John Winthrop, who had come over ten years later, but had come with foresight, determination, education, sufficient backing, and a higher set of ideals.

The Plymouth Colony captured the imagination of the nation because of several factors, again accidents of history—the suffering endured by its members; the presence of the historic women in the group (although William Bradford's first wife most likely drowned herself off Provincetown because of the torment of the passage over and the bleak prospect ahead).

A major factor, of course, is the romantic story attending the famous original, magnificent account of the Plymouth Colony, *History of Plimouth Plantation,* by Governor William Bradford —how it was lent by his descendants to the Reverend Thomas Prince, a historian, who kept it in his library in the Old South Meeting House in Boston (which is still standing); how it couldn't be found after the British redcoats, during the siege of Boston in the Revolutionary War, used the historic edifice as a riding school; how it turned up years later in the library of the

Bishop of London; and how its return to the city of Boston was effected only after long negotiations and finally by the importunities of a United States senator and a petition of scholars.

If man have no heroes, he must manufacture them. Historian C. Vann Woodward has written, "Myth-hungry and legend-starved, the Americans set about peopling the wilderness with folk-gods constructed from their own history. The tall tales and credulous minds of the American frontier were fruitful sources of myth. Popular leaders became folk legends before they were good and dead. Political hagiography preceded political biography in America and the two were sometimes confused."

That explains making Davy Crockett a hero, and it explains the slush of sentiment poured on the Pilgrims. "Mankind dearly loves a good story," says historian Allan Nevins, "and dearly loves to believe it true." The popular conception of the Pilgrims just isn't true. But William Bradford is real, and his journal is one of the great American treasures.

Bradford and his journal, however, now give the Plymouth Colony a reputation it doesn't deserve. George F. Willison has contended that the Pilgrim story was "wholly the creation of the 19th century." He overstates the case, but to understand the true development of New England and America and what it owed to English foresight, common sense, and strength of character, and what it owed to other stock, and to the Puritan ethic, and to the struggle with the wilderness and the frontier, one should try reading the history of America as if the Pilgrims had not existed and had not straggled into Plymouth and slowly strangled there.

If that is done, we can then see the true, straight line of discovery, growth and development, and at the base of that lies Cape Ann. For it was the strong-willed, strong-minded, highly organized, shrewd, independent, farsighted Puritans under Endicott, Winthrop and Bradstreet who founded the American colony which was to defy the crown, throw off the monarchical yoke, forge the charter of Harvard College, launch the first challenge to the union of church and state (which existed in Massachusetts into the nineteenth century) and draft the Constitution of the Commonwealth of Massachusetts, the matrix of the Constitution of the United States of America.

The role of Cape Ann was not central to all this, but it was basic. The *Arbella* sailed into the waters of Cape Ann in 1630 and first left its one thousand settlers at Naumkeag, which became Salem. They left there for Charlestown, and then, not having sufficient drinking water, crossed the Charles River to Boston. But Cape Ann was the hook that caught them. It was on Cape Ann that their advance agents set up, and it was to Cape Ann that their intellectuals repaired. It was fishermen on Cape Ann who fed them, and ships out of Gloucester which carried to Boston the catch from the sea that helped keep the Massachusetts Bay Colony alive. The Pilgrims in Plymouth never learned to fish, and when peltry ran out on them, they were helpless, so the Massachusetts Bay Colony took them over. Plymouth's chief contribution was this: For a short while it demonstrated that an English colony could survive in the New World. But if it had not been there, Winthrop and his Puritans would have come just the same, and would have been as successful as they were. If Winthrop and his Puritans had not come, however, the entire history of North America would have been altered.

David T. W. McCord, Oregon-born poet and essayist who has merged his blood and bones indistinguishably into the Boston mystique, has written that he finds New England to be the authentic version of America. The remark is profound and correct. It is strong enough to bear a refinement, and that refinement is this: New England is indeed the authentic version of America, and Cape Ann is the authentic version of New England. In it we have a microcosm of the United States of America, its growth and history. Cape Ann people today are doing what they were doing when Champlain arrived—they are fishing. It was fish that brought the first Englishmen to America; and it was not money alone that led the people of Massachusetts to call the cod sacred and to hang its replica in the House of Representatives of the General Court and honor it. It was a profound understanding of the meaning of America that led the General Court to mount in its sacred chambers a replica of the codfish and not a replica of Plymouth Rock.

"Humble the subject and homely the design; yet this painted image bears on its finny front a majesty greater than the dignity that art can lend to graven gold or chiseled marble. The sphere it fills is vaster than that through which its prototype careered with all the myriad tribes of the great deep. The lessons that may be learned of it are nobler than any to be drawn from what is only beautiful; for this sedate and solitary fish is instinct with memories and prophecy, like an oracle. It swims symbolic in that wider sea whose confines are the limits set to the activities of human thought. It typifies to the citizens of the Commonwealth and of the world the founding of a State. It commemorates Democracy. It celebrates the rise of free institutions. It emphasizes progress. It epitomizes Massachusetts." So wrote in eloquent anonymity some agent of a legislative committee of three assigned to prepare a history of the Sacred Cod. The passage is not rodomontade, not mere rhetoric; it is a key to the history of English-speaking America. Nothing is a surer symbol of it all than the cod; and no place is associated more directly with the cod than Cape Ann.

In its towns we find paradigms of the end of feudalism, the sensible American modification of the class society, evidences of the results of the emigration to the West, the slow and sad elimination of handicrafts and the artisan from American life, the rise of electronics, the eternal struggle of the artist against the corruption of commercialism, the persistence of the antiaesthetic strain in American life, the great mixture of the races, whose mature strength still lies ahead, the theological search for egalitarianism, the continuing war against poverty, the decline (and curious vitality) of the small farm, the flight from the city to the country—in brief, all the marks of social development in the United States are to be found on Cape Ann.

Romance makes history. Cape Ann's early role was humble and obscure—its romance came with the schooner and the heroic men, the titans, who sailed that ship—but its contribution was basic, vital, continuing, profound. It is no accident that great poets and great painters have seized on Cape Ann, that Anne Bradstreet wrote there in the seventeenth century, and T. S. Eliot in the first half, and Charles Olson in the second half, of the twentieth century; that Winslow Homer came to the Cape, and John Sloan; that Fitz Hugh Lane immortalized it.

Cape Ann was and is unselfconscious. It doesn't know where it stops and starts. James B. Connolly, the great chronicler of its larger-than-life fishermen, said of them, "They don't know how good they are." The same could be said of Connolly, who was a modest man. What I am attempting in this book is simply to tell Cape Ann how good it is, and to suggest how it might measure itself historically. Where it starts and stops, there is no telling, because its spirit has crept into the blood stream of the United States of America, and that country—which doesn't know how good it is—may yet, by seeing itself straight and seeing itself whole, be an example to the world.

≥ 1 ≤
The Killarney of America?

Setting out from Boston for the North Shore and Cape Ann, our worthy fellow traveler, distracted by the ignominies endured at some airline terminal, moves through an area lush with history. If he departs the capital by the Mystic River Bridge (officially the Maurice J. Tobin Bridge for a former Secretary of Labor) he will see on his right "Old Ironsides" (the *Constitution*), hero ship of the War of 1812, and farther off, the slender white tower of the Old North Church. From that tower Paul Revere was signaled to alert the Minute Men to initiate an earlier and somewhat more satisfactory conflict. The word "Mystic," by the way, is from the Indian word "Mustick" and has no transcendental or psychedelic overtones. To the left of the bridge rises the gray granite obelisk commemorating the Battle of Bunker Hill, which, as every schoolboy once delighted to learn, was misnamed, since the hill was called Breed's Hill, and Bunker Hill lay beyond.

Farther on the left is the Chelsea Naval Hospital, and high on a hill to the right a Soldiers' Home, reminders that war debts are paid in other than taxes, and cruelly so. Moving along the broad divided highway, Route C-1, we and our imaginary companion are leaving the major scenes of the Revolutionary War behind us and are approaching Essex County, which lent its name to the Essex Junto, a cabal of virulently anti-Madison folk

who indulged the hope of an American defeat in the War of
1812, the most unpopular war in the history of the country, the
war in Vietnam notwithstanding.

Nowhere was that war with Britain more unpopular than on
Cape Ann and its environs, for it ruined American shipping, and
particularly New England shipping. Treason and secession, or
threats of them, scorched the air, and even the governor of the
Commonwealth treated with the enemy. But Cape Ann men
fought in that war, built ships to fight in it, and rejoiced in the
triumphs of their fellow townsmen. They died in it and were imprisoned during it; and they were happy to see its end.

From Chelsea with its infirmaries, we move to Revere, named
for the patriot (whose father spelled it Rivoire), a municipality
celebrated because of a dog track, a two-mile stretch of beach,
a sleazy midway and a scattering of gangsters. From Revere
(birthplace, by the way, of Horatio Alger, Jr.), our explorer motors past Malden, part of which the late Elliot Paul immortalized in *Linden on the Saugus Branch*. From Malden we enter
Saugus, whose Marion Starkey has written the most popular and
penetrating account of the infamous Salem witch trials (*The
Devil in Massachusetts*), and where public-spirited citizens have
reconstructed the first ironworks in America. The inspiration for
the erection of the original came from a Cape Ann pioneer, a
miracle of seventeenth-century enterprise.

After clearing Saugus, cutting through Lynnfield, and ridding
ourselves of Peabody, a most unattractive tannery city whose
loveliest hill has been blighted by a sprawling shopping center
and clustering apartment houses, our traveler and we tool
through Danvers (on the left), where the seventeenth-century
witchcraft manifested itself, and Salem, far on the right, where
the perfervid trials took place, and then move into Beverly,
which boasts of itself as the birthplace of the American navy.
Thus we come at length to the fringe of Cape Ann.

Two features—one of them astonishing, one of them developing—mark the approach. Driving along Route 128 on the hottest of summer days, with a green strip on both sides most of the way, one is suddenly conscious of a marked drop in the temperature. The change is so abrupt, so vivid, one has the sensation of passing through some invisible curtain, which on one side is oppressive and on the other blessedly cool. One is conscious also that the topography is altering. Bold, startling outcroppings of brown and gray granite have burst through the rolling grassy banks on both sides of the divided highway. Large islands of rock rise up so that the median strip has to widen to allow for them.

We are moving onto the promontory that has withstood the ravages of the sea since the retreat of the glacier ten thousand years ago. These outcroppings are the bones of the giant whose shoulders bore the prodigious pressure of the glacier, and have fended off for thousands of years the relentless questings of the ocean. These are the stones that laughed at time. From these tawny, ocher, gray, chocolate, jagged, impassive miniature mountains, tempered in the ancient womb of the world, and extruded in unimaginable parturitions to the surface and the sky, a man could draw a miracle of strength, enough character to defy a king and build a new nation. Secrets lie in the granite, the ancient secrets of the rocks which are divined not by poets and sculptors only but will yield themselves to any man who can sit in silence and acknowledge his soul.

For what must be remembered about Cape Ann that is central is not the presence of the sea, which is unforgettable, or the genius of granite and gneiss that lies beneath the forests and the meadows and the lawns, and is too easily forgotten, but the sempiternal conflict between the two—the sea and the rocks—which gives the area its character and symbolizes precisely the contentious condition of man, forever aspiring, forever stubborn.

On this highway which we travel stands the highest point on the Cape, modest enough by any standard but signal against the low littoral that encircles it. Mount Ann, it is extravagantly called, and is certain as a symbol as it is pretentious as a peak. To climb it (you walk up), however, is to gain a sense of time. Thence all elemental things can be seen: the road itself, which in its prehistoric beginnings was an earnest of brotherhood; the sea, from which we have crawled to greatness and over which our forebears moved when wild beasts held the shore; forests, which hid us from predators and gave us materials to build our shelters; the farms which nourished us; the placid animals that have carried us and fed us; the towns where we learned tolerance; the cities where we were taught to sell or swap our surpluses and bargain for a fair reward for our skills and talents. On Cape Ann, a microcosm fighting to remain unspoiled, we can find all these things, but at their base are the sea and the rocks and men scrambling over both, sometimes drowning in one and dying on the other, but ultimately making both serve. On Cape Ann enough wilderness is left to help a man remember that there are reasons in nature, on sea or land, why he should always be, if not afraid, thoroughly respectful.

For one thing, the glacier that was here may someday start back. Ten thousand or more years have passed since it retreated, but the character of Cape Ann is what it is because of the glacier. Singing Beach in Manchester, where bikini-clad women and men in madras shorts romp on broiling August afternoons, was once buried beneath an ice cap at least 2,000 feet thick. This was the fourth such glacial escarpment to crawl over northern New England. Glaciers form when the winter's snows are not completely melted in the summer; the snow line moves south and behind it layer on layer of snow combine, recrystallizing into ice, the whole growing on itself to incredible heights. When the pressure of ice reaches a certain intensity, the ice at the bottom is squeezed forward and the glacier advances.

Glacial action, combined with volcanic action, altered and realtered the structure and face of Cape Ann until the softer rock was crushed or scraped away and only the semi-immutable remained. As the glacier retreated, leaving a rocky wrack behind, nature's holy process of life brought soil, vegetation, and mammals back to the land, freed at last from the sterile empery of ice. Cape Ann is what geologists call a terminal moraine. The glacier moving south over Canada carried with it an accumulation of rubble and debris, some of which it left on Cape Ann when it retreated. Amid this rubble are "erratics," great single stones seen standing in majestic isolation on a stretch of sandy shore, or like monstrous sheep on some hillside or meadow.

The retreating glacier, having worked over Cape Ann like a titan's rasp, and having deposited everywhere rocky rubble called till, set the course of history for the inhabitants of the Cape. It was destined not to be farm country; and its enterprising invaders automatically turned to the sea. Not that there weren't farms. There were. Indeed, the Cape boasts the oldest farm in continuous operation in English-speaking America, the Appleton Farms in Ipswich. But the farm's plow found new rocks each spring; and the stone walls of till that were piled by hand and mended each spring, as Robert Frost's poem so vividly conveys, were more the result of clearing the soil than of seeking to set a boundary. The soil was stubborn; the sea was fruitful; the outcome inevitable.

The outermost reach of Cape Ann is an island, separated from the mainland by the Annisquam River, which is not a river but a tidal inlet, sea water flowing from Ipswich Bay to Gloucester Harbor that on some ancient maps was called Cape Ann Bay. The Annisquam River did not always connect the two bodies of water. When only Indians roamed the Gloucester shore, the island was attached to the mainland at the harbor, or south, end. Imaginative colonists made a cut to create a canal which was later turned over to the care of the Commonwealth. On one occasion a great storm closed it up and it stayed that way for a while, but eventually it was reopened and a bridge was thrown across it. When the gasoline motor began to move ships with a certainty sails and wind could not guarantee, the Annisquam River became a short cut home for the fishing fleet, and the "cut," as it was called, was deepened and walled with stone.

The island at its widest is about 4 miles across, from the banks of the Annisquam River to craggy Loblolly Point on the easternmost Rockport shore. In length, the island runs 8 miles from Halibut Point—the northernmost tip of Cape Ann—to Eastern Point, which is the southernmost tip of a teatlike peninsula, a miniature Florida, that hangs from the main body of the island and forms one side of the great harbor. Halibut Point, by the way, is not named for the fish that helped make Gloucester famous, but is a corruption of the phrase "haul about," for it was there that the sailing vessels rounding the tip of the Cape had to shift their tack to continue their course.

The Annisquam River is an estuary, a great salt inlet, almost a mile wide at one point, with islands and marshes and sand bars in it, and minor inlets running off it, also extravagantly called rivers—Jones River, Little River, Mill River—although all are salt water. Some of them are fed by small brooks, but the water in them is salt moved by a tide that rises and falls as much as 8 feet—rises and falls in them all, creating in the central stream, at predictable hours, powerful currents that can make sailing difficult and swimming dangerous. The river is lined with summer cottages and many year-round homes. Fishing vessels move through it winter and summer in steady traffic, but in the summer the pleasure craft, gaily pennanted, gaily painted, make it one of the liveliest and loveliest of waterways.

So many inlets, bays, and broad reaches of water lie before the spectator on any height around the river that it was not a wild fancy for some early real estate promoter or poet to call it the Killarney of America. The phrase, however, is never heard today. A railroad drawbridge crosses the Annisquam to bring commuter trains of the Boston and Maine Railroad into Gloucester, and Route 128, down which we have driven from Boston, crosses it on a bridge with sufficient clearance over the water to permit a 65-foot mast to go through. The third bridge over the river is the one at the cut at Gloucester Harbor, Blynman Bridge, named for an early settler whose ancestors' name might have been Blindman. The Cape Ann natives had a gift for corrupting one word into another, sometimes into a recognizable but utterly inappropriate word, and sometimes into a word whose original meaning might be lost forever except for the diligence of antiquarians. An example of this occurs in the Annisquam (itself a corruption) River, at the beach, a small one, near the red-brick Gloucester High School. The beach is called Dunfudgeon, and is very popular with young children and mothers with infants. The name, however, is a contraction of "done fudging." Early boatmen heading north in their sailboats from Gloucester Harbor through the cut on the Annisquam River had to pole or fudge them against the current, since they lacked motors, until they reached a spot where the inlet became wide enough to permit them again to hoist sail and tack toward their destination. The spot where they were "done fudging" was the beach. All sailors are "done fudging" today. Sailboats are not permitted through the cut unless they have auxiliary motors. Small outboard motorboats should go through with caution because the wash of water churned by the wake of a larger boat can create a rip tide between the cut's granite walls which might capsize them.

Between the cut and the river entrance at Ipswich Bay is a multitude of features—the Annisquam Yacht Club, whose sailboats flutter in and out of Ipswich Bay throughout the summer; a shipyard; a marina; several sandy stretches where the swimming can be excellent; innumerable floats before cottages; and several islands: Ram, Pearce, Rust and Oak, not all truly islands, and not all habitable, but with some lovely summer homes, and Hangman's Island, where several pirates were dispatched in 1724. On the river, too, is a glue factory, which no longer makes glue but merely processes and packages it. Spreading American affluence is changing the nature of Cape Ann.

The portion of the city of Gloucester which is cut off from the mainland by the Annisquam River is far from all there is to Cape Ann, although the name has been used for the island only or parts of it. Much of the city of Gloucester is on the mainland, and has differing topography. In the town of Manchester are woodlands, salt marsh and beaches. Between Manchester and Gloucester lies Magnolia, now altered from a fashionable summer resort to a suburban hamlet whose beach is in Manchester and whose post office is in Gloucester.

Magnolia for a few decades was a resort that each summer brought eminent families from all parts of the East. A railroad station in nearby Manchester was named for the village, and carriages and later motor cars lined up to receive men returning from a week of business for a week end of family relaxation. The Oceanside was one of the mammoth rambling wooden hotels where the affluent took a room, rooms, or a suite by the week or by the summer. All, all is gone. Magnolia is making the shift-over to a suburb sitting on a majestic cluster of rocky shore line, harassed on one end by a rash of pathetic small homes that should never have been built. The Oceanside burned to the ground. The trains no longer pause at Magnolia station on their way to Gloucester.

Inland lies West Gloucester, a bucolic area slowly shedding some remaining Tobacco Road vestiges, where scholars and writers have been moving in and buying property to front their picture windows on the kaleidoscopic stretches of marshland running to the sea. West Gloucester retains enough of country isolation and backwardness to have a spiritualist colony, a farm or two, and lonely houses set in woodlands accessible only by footpaths or gravel roads slowly growing over with relentless vegetation.

The road through West Gloucester leads to Essex, a town of low hills and a winding estuary, and beyond Essex is Ipswich, the largest in area of the Cape Ann communities, a town a-growing, with plenty of farmland left. The prevailing wind is from the west, and its average velocity is 10 to 12 miles an hour. In winter the mercury has dropped lower than 10 degrees below zero, and in summer it has topped 100 degrees. Those are rare extremes. The sea, as always, is a powerful tempering influence; and while it can be savage it can also be kind.

Cape Ann is yachting country. In Manchester, the Manchester Yacht Club, which marked its 75th anniversary in 1967, maintains its clubhouse and floats not too far from the harbor shore where Masconomo—the local sagamore, as shown on the town seal—rowed out to greet the first settlers. Each town has its yacht club, each harbor is filled with moorings, and room is at a premium. The Eastern Point Yacht Club stands on the shore of Gloucester Harbor, maintaining a quiet dignity in the face of a brazen introduction of catamarans into local waters by a local mariner who argues that if the purpose of sailing is to see how fast one can go with sail only, why not go as fast as one can with sail only?

The resistance to multihulls (the general name for catamarans, trimarans and proas) is as stern on Cape Ann as it is elsewhere. Philip S. Weld, publisher of the *Gloucester Daily Times,* brought to Cape Ann the largest (and fastest) catamaran on the East Coast, a handsome craft with two 30-foot fiberglass hulls in tandem, bolted together with steel pipes or tubes, raising a 40-foot aluminum mast and a prodigious spread of Marconi sail. For deck, taut dacron was stretched between the hulls—as tough as woven steel. With speeds over twenty knots, Weld's catamaran, known as "Poseidon's Chariot," would cut didos around the plodding schooners, yawls and racing sloops of Cape Ann. But the masters of the monohulls (as the multihullers like to call them) scorned the instrument he was riding, and a youthful but grizzled columnist in Weld's own newspaper referred to him disdainfully as a man "who likes to go to sea on a trampoline." The history of the monohull is too strong in the mystique of Cape Ann. Weld, as a result, had a trimaran built for him in England, and in 1970 was the only American entered in the famous race around the British Isles, a demonstration in itself that Gloucester sailors are still challenging the seas even in the bleak era of oil.

All the other customary conveniences and exercises one looks for in beach resorts are on the Cape: tennis courts, golf links, motels, hotels, rooming houses, summer cottages for rent, and year-round homes to let. There are gift shops and restaurants, some pitched at the very edge of the wharves. There are roadside stands; there's a popcorn man; and there's a man who sells catnip. All the appurtenances of summer colonies are at hand. Yet Cape Ann is not an area that is dominated by its summer colony aspect, as is Cape Cod, but a section of the country that is itself, year-round, self-sufficient, productive, and above all historic.

Perhaps it has yet to come to an understanding of its own significance, but it is building toward that, and a number of things are helping it to do so: the recent mounting concern with ecology and the preservation of our natural inheritance, the twentieth century's interest in Americana, the advance of scholarship which has taken to classifying and scrutinizing the accumulations in our historical societies and local libraries, the contribution of retired citizens to the recording and collating of local history and folklore, the widespread interest in local artists, and, for Cape Ann, the body of work of its late poet laureate and historian, Charles Olson.

We examine the region to find a microcosm of the United States of America, the end of a mild feudalism and the growth of an egalitarian society, the struggle between art and kitsch, the disappearance of the artisan before mass production, the end of the age of sail and the onset of the gasoline engine, the shock of immigration and the gradual absorption of the immigrants, the cultural deepening of the area because of those foreign cultures, the fight against continuing pollution of the earth, sea and air, the eternal vigilance required to preserve the character of the communities from real estate developers and the countryside from the excrescences of utility companies, the never-ending effort needed to provide good government, good schools, and stable homes. All these are to be seen on Cape Ann, and seen here uniquely because it is the one place in America one can observe them from the first decades of the seventeenth century down to the present. Thus it is that, standing on Mount Ann and surveying the land around, we realize that we are surveying the United States of America, and can perhaps from such a vantage point come to a better understanding of it.

≥ 2 ≤
Manchester

You come to Manchester as through a sea of trees. It is as if a vast expanse of waters parted, after the manner of the Red Sea, and you, the Israelite, motored down the middle over a divided highway along the black carpet of asphalt, curving gently, or rising and falling slowly, with walls of green on either side, still perhaps, or surging in the breeze, but for all the world a veritable ocean of leaves, now dark, now light, maple, oak, beech and birch, and yellow willows. The conifers are outnumbered here by their deciduous brothers but are nevertheless an important factor, dark and silent by contrast, for it is late summer. The ash is decorated with crimson clusters to furnish a flush of color, and the aspen is dancing to indicate that there is a breeze. On either side of the highway, granite breaks through the soil to remind you: this is the great headland.

Manchester is a seashore town of single-family houses (there is a modest modern apartment house, however), a sort of miniature Darien, Connecticut, eschewing the vulgarities and garishness of the latter, sequestering its most opulent estates behind orchard and copse. It is 32 miles from Boston and, if you must know, 245 miles from New York City. The town is small in area, about 7 square miles, and has a shore line about 12 miles in length on Massachusetts Bay. A dozen golden beaches perforate the grim, granite coast that gnarls its way from Beverly to Gloucester. Facing the south, and offering ideal protection against the northeast storm, is the long pouch of Manchester Harbor, surely one of the loveliest harbors anywhere. To enter it at sundown, when the quiet waters reflect the modulating fires of the sunset until the flames extinguish themselves in the purple shadows of a summer night, is to sense and savor the ineffable glory of a maritime Valhalla.

In 1630 the *Arbella*, out of Cowes, England, and six other ships sailed into the harbor. On the first day out, one of the seamen had got into the rum and had to be confined, but otherwise it was an easier crossing than the *Mayflower* had had. The *Arbella* was the second ship to bring women colonists to the New World, and among its passengers was that magnificent woman Mistress Anne Bradstreet, who was to win immortality as the first English poet of the New World. Aboard with her were her husband, Simon Bradstreet, who was later to be governor of the colony and defy the King, and her father, Thomas Dudley, who also was to be governor. What was most significant was that the *Arbella* had aboard the charter for the Massachusetts Bay Colony, and this was the first charter to come to the New World. Previously the charters had remained in England, thus giving the motherland a tight rein on the settlers. That the Massachusetts Bay Colony had its charter in New England, and that that charter did not say where the directors should meet, was to give the colony an independence of action and of spirit that led directly to the War for Independence. That it was aboard the *Arbella* can be credited to the wisdom of the company's commander, John Winthrop, a titanic figure in colonial history.

Under his leadership, the city of Boston was founded and named, and the spirit of independence nurtured against the day when the colonists would be called on to fire the shot heard round the world.

The men of the *Arbella* did not come as vagabonds, in the manner of the Pilgrims. They came after planning and with considerable foresight. There were forerunners on hand to meet them, who had come over from Naumkeag to welcome them. They all gathered on the shore to celebrate. The town of Manchester, wilderness that it was at that time, nevertheless had a name. It was called Jeffries Creek, after William Jeffrey or Jeffries, a carpenter who had been sent over earlier to help build the fish stages where the cod were dried before being shipped to England. The advance agents of the Dorchester Company, as it was called, had ingratiated themselves with the local Indians, and when the *Arbella* arrived, Masconomo, chief of the Agawams, paddled out with attendants to board the flagship and welcome the colonists. It was June, and the weather ideal. Among those who went ashore was Simon Bradstreet, who later, by designation of the General Court of the Massachusetts Bay Colony, would be assigned the task of setting the town boundaries of Manchester.

The men of the *Arbella* knew what to expect when they put into Manchester Harbor. The year before, almost to the day, the *Talbot* had dropped anchor in those sheltered waters, and the Reverend Francis Higginson, who was aboard, noted in his journal that they had come "to a fyne and sweet harbor, seven miles from the head of Cape Ann (in this harbor twentie ships may lie and easily ride the rein) where there was an island near, wither 4 of our men went with a boat, and brought back ripe strawberries, gooseberries and single sweet roses." The *Talbot* arrived on Saturday and stayed until Monday, when she, as would the *Arbella* the following year, went on to Naumkeag. The Reverend Mr. Higginson does not mention the Indians. John Smith years earlier had seen them in astonishing numbers on the shore, but between his observations and the arrival of the *Talbot* and the *Arbella*, the great plague had destroyed them by the thousands.

Masconomo was lucky to have survived, and more than likely looked to the white man as an ally against those tribes farther inland which had not suffered such devastation.

In 1630 when Masconomo went aboard the *Arbella* (and stayed all day), he was probably able to greet the new arrivals in their native tongue.

He had had two or three years' experience (if not more) with white men on the shore. In 1626 the names of William Allen, William Jeffrey and Richard and John Norman were already associated with the settlement. They were, no doubt, part of the crew assembled by Roger Conant, who was waiting in Naumkeag to receive John Winthrop. The first settlers in Manchester, however, had not sailed into Manchester Harbor but had come ashore about three miles east at Kettle Cove, today called Magnolia Beach, or perhaps at Black Beach, an indentation on the shoreline shaped like a purse, "foul at the head" as the Coast Guard charts read today, but lovely enough to have been chosen for a *Holiday* magazine photograph a few years back as one of the most exquisite spots on the New England coast. Which of the two coves they chose is disputed. The name "Kettle" may well come from a later settler who is said to have built a house nearby, or perhaps from the fish weirs or kettle nets that were used to trap the raging schools of mackerel, and which even today, 350 years later, are still anchored to the rocky shore and to a nearby island called Kettle, and harvested by licensed haulers.

The *Arbella* went on to Naumkeag and warped into the harbor (let the landlubber consult his dictionary) the following day, and John Winthrop recorded in his diary:

"Tuesday, 10th June, the wind continued all day a gale from the south, and yet we bore all sail and at four o'clock p.m., made land, called 'The Three Turks Heads.' Tonight we could see the trees very plainly, and had a fine fresh smell from the shore. The next day we stood to, and as the wind would bear, on Saturday we stood in towards the harbor, and by the aid of some shallops we passed through the narrow straight between Baker's Island and another little island, and we came to anchor within the harbor. Our friends came down from Salem, and many of our Gentlemen returned with them at night, were supped on good venison and beer; but most of them, disliking their lodgings, returned to the ship. In the meantime most of the people went on shore on the other side of the harbor, where they were feasted with strawberries and were like as merry as the Gentlefolks at their venison and beer. Sunday, Masconomo, the Sagamore of the tribe, with another Indian, came on board and bade us welcome, tarrying with us all day. On Monday the wind coming fair, the ships proceeded to Salem where the planters landed. Here they found about ten houses and some Indian corn planted, which was good and well liking."

Spelling was a sportive thing in those days. Even familiar English words won an orthographical variety that remains astounding to our conformist age. Indian words offered opportunity for virtuosity. John Winthrop spelled Masconomo as we spell it today, but in other records it is found as Masconomco, Masquenomco, Masquenomenit and Maskenomett. Small wonder the Cape Anners called him Sagamore John and let it go at that. Small wonder we find them a few decades later proposing a "grammar chole." If a visitor to the Cape wants to touch the electricity that lies in historical continuity, let him remember that there are houses standing today that were a-building before Sagamore John, not finding the first settlers—alas—quite the noble people some historians deem them, went to the happy hunting ground, where he didn't have to submit to the humiliation of having to ask the town fathers if he might keep a rifle. They did let him, and gave him some acreage. He died in 1658, according to one historian, "poor, disheartened, and friendless, as a ward of the state, [and] found peace in death and was buried on Sagamore Hill in Hamilton" (then part of Ipswich). He wasn't at peace for long. A rowdy young man dug up his body and walked around with the skull on a pole. His final grave has not been marked for us.

The boy was punished for his act of desecration. The early settlers showed a decent respect for the dead, even dead Indians. Indeed, that sensitivity eliminated archeological activity. If the early settlers accidentally dug up some aboriginal bones and artifacts, they quickly reburied them. They didn't hesitate, however, to level the funeral mounds the Indians had built for their dead, which is a pity, for one of them was 150 feet in diameter and 8 feet high, conical in form and surrounded by a moat. We have some knowledge of the aboriginal funeral customs, however. Some of the Indians were buried upright, others flat with their heads toward the west and their faces raised toward the east, hoping for the light and, presumably, the resurrection.

Indian graves must have abounded on the coast when the first settlers arrived, for the plague brought by the white man, called the yellowing disease—perhaps smallpox and perhaps diphtheria—ran for five years and devastated the tribes. One tribe alone, the Massachusetts, it was said, was reduced from thirty thousand fighting men to three hundred, so virulent was the visitation. The Indians never recovered. When John Smith sailed along in 1614, the shore was noticeably populated by Indians. In 1626 they were comparatively few in number. In a 1761 census of Manchester, there was one; today, none. Descendants of the first settlers abound, however, particularly the Allens, and the names Archer, Williams, Knight, Bennett, Norman, and Sibley can still be found on shop signs and business letterheads.

In his *History of Manchester, 1645–1895*, the Reverend D. F. Lamson, close in spirit to the first settlers, writes:

"It is difficult, after the lapse of two centuries and more, with the slight materials at our command, to draw a full-length portrait of a Manchester man of the 17th century. But from what we can gather from brief records and occasional letters that have come to us, and from the few traditions that still linger, we shall not be far wrong if we conceive of him as in the main a religious and God-fearing man, one who ruled his household well, a faithful husband and true friend, honest in all his business transactions, strenuous in his attachment to his religious and political beliefs, somewhat narrow and wholly uncultivated, but possessed of strong native character, and not ill-fitted by heredity and training to act his part in life." A somewhat romanticized view, since the chances are not dim that the William Jeffrey or Jeffries for whom the settlement was first named probably suffered the same fate as his pen pal Thomas Morton and was hounded out of town. In any event, he left with little trace, having shown too much or too little character to remain, and went off to Ipswich.

The good Parson Lamson was somewhat Weemsian in his appraisal, which continues thus:

"From a general knowledge of the men and women of the time, we may fairly judge what Manchester men and women— caeteris paribus—must have been. They were of average material of which the early New England colonists were made. They were neither great-minded founders of empire nor mere commercial adventurers. They were not religious separatists like the men of Plymouth, nor revellers like the men of Merry Mount. No doubt there were differences among them as there are among their descendants; and, perhaps, whether conscious of it or not, most of them were actuated by somewhat mixed motives. There was on the part of man, no doubt, the desire to seek, 'A faith's pure shrine' but there was as certainly on the part of many, the desire to better the conditions of living. It is always safe, however, to estimate men by their works; and, judging the tree planted on 'Cape Anne in Newe Englande' by its fruit, it must have been of sound, sturdy stock, its juices nourished by the best soil of English nonconformity in the times of the Stuarts."

If the works of the men of Manchester may be judged by their taking to the slave trade then and the pollution of Gloucester Harbor today, we may need another factor in the formula for measuring that fruit. The Old Testament code was a hard one, and applied properly could be a profitable one, encouraging as it did industry and frugality, albeit with a loss of charity and even simple philanthropy. The slave trade was at first forbidden. But the Reverend Mr. Lamson offers us the following table of prices which gives us several insights into life in the town in the time of Cromwell:

1657–1661

Negro Boy	20 pounds	Swine	20s
Cow	3	Cord of Wood	1s
Horse	10	Yoke of Steers	10
Ox	5	Otter Skin	10s

This is ten years after that magnificent document *History of Plimouth Plantation, 1620–1647* by William Bradford. He gives us no such practical merchandising tabulation, although there is more business in his book than there is theology. All this raises an interesting historical point—the question of the key to a true understanding of American history, when such an emphasis is placed on Plymouth while its predecessors and contemporaries are so slighted.

Generations of children have grown up with the wrong idea of America because Plymouth rather than Cape Ann is taken as the paradigm for the beginnings of America. There is no living continuity between the Plymouth of yesterday and the Plymouth of today. Even the rock is said to be a fake. The Pilgrims were not a major sect in England, nor are they in America today; they were Separatists (today members of the Assembly Brethren), honest, God-fearing people utterly out of their element when they arrived at Plymouth. The presence of women made it the second permanent English colony in the New World, and the town still celebrates Thanksgiving Day with pageantry, reverence and fun, but Plymouth still is not thickly populated. A lovely town with vast areas of open land, it does not have a good harbor and there is no river; so in the settlement of New England it was soon outstripped by the Puritans and absorbed by Boston. The idea of a new world burgeoning from there doesn't fit the picture.

Cape Ann, on the other hand, began with men taking fish from the sea. It also began with a quarrel; with a threat of firearms and an imposition of force. It began with one group of entrepreneurs jumping the claim of another and getting away with it. There is something unhappily American in that tradition, but something very vital as well. The pageantry of its beginnings also had shady characters moving in and out, for it was concerned with building a business, not a theocratic, community; and business bears more of the American tradition.

But back to Manchester. Catching fish, curing fish, building boats, skinning otters—and a seal or two, no doubt, since they still come into the shallows when the weather's the way they like it—occupied the people of the town. A few lobstermen still put out today, and some fish traps are slung from the shore and the islands, but Manchester today harbors a less stable society, a multiplex of financial men, brokers and bankers, corporation lawyers, and bond salesmen, realtors and trustees, financial advisers and one gentleman who calls himself an "imagineer." There are as well electronic experts and engineers, a distinguished composer, an editor or two, and, moving in and out of the summer property, sculptors, novelists, artists and publishers. Such is the tone of the town. These people fill the harbor each summer with their sailboats, motor cruisers and yachts. They lounge in their skin preservatives on Singing Beach, a half-mile stretch of pinkish, coarse sand which, when properly scuffed by the human heel, squeaks distinctly enough to give the beach its name. With an area of 7.9 square miles, Manchester is the second smallest of the towns under our scrutiny. It has 4,386 residents (latest census), does not contain much land for further development, and is rather well governed through that instrument known as the New England town meeting which, unfamiliar as it is to the rest of the country, had better be described.

Under the system, all registered voters can take part in the town meeting. The presiding chairman is called the town moderator, and he must have a sound grasp of parliamentary procedure, a quick hand with the gavel, an unruffled nature, and a ready speech. He presents to the body an agenda, called a warrant, previously publicized, the items on which are known as articles. The majority vote rules. The vote in the main follows the recommendations of the finance committee which, in harness with the moderator, has prepared the articles, voted recommendations among themselves, and determined on a plan of presentation. It is very simple for any voter of the town to challenge from the floor any article on the warrant. Thus do the townspeople work out their financial destiny in the purest form of democratic governance, setting their budget for the coming year and determining their real estate tax rate.

Innumerable amusing anecdotes come from the exchanges of a New England town meeting, and Manchester is no exception. Few of the stories rise above being "in" jokes, requiring for appreciation an understanding of the nuances of the town affairs. Manchester claims to be, however, the town where the supreme town meeting anecdote has its provenance. The story takes differing forms in different towns, but concerns generally a man who was protesting the purchase of a new pump for the fire department. He denounced the acquisition at length and as his rhetoric hotted up, cried out in condemnation,

"Why, I can piss farther than that pump can throw water."

Down came the moderator's gavel.

"You're out of order," the moderator shouted.

"Yer damn right, I'm out of order. If I wasn't out of order, I could piss twice as far."

The town is run from year to year between town meetings (usually held in March) by three selectmen (in some towns, five), who are elected by popular vote. There are other town officers, however, whose quaint titles seem singularly outmoded, but whose offices nevertheless retain powers of public service. Among these are the fence viewers, the pound keeper, the field drivers, and the measurer of wood and bark. If two neighbors dispute about property lines, and the engineers they hire cannot agree, the fence viewers will determine where the line is, and the only recourse from their decision is an appeal to the land court. In the day of the automobile, the field drivers are rarely called upon to round up stray cattle, but if they do, they turn them over to the pound keeper. When the beast—be it dog, cow or horse—is driven into the pound, the pound keeper takes over. The measurer of wood and bark can be called on to tell you if you have received a full cord, and the measurer of lumber can tell you whether the wood you purchased has been cut to proper measurement. They are not too often called upon, but elected they are, each year, and serve they do. And each year, other town officers make a "perambulation of the bounds."

The town meeting is distinctively New England and grew out of the role of the congregation of the early Puritan churches in New England. The members of a church ran each colony or settlement, and at first they alone voted. This practice was subsequently modified, and at length all property owners voted; later, all males over twenty-one years of age; and finally, with female suffrage, all citizens over 21. Democracy does not spring up overnight, and frequently the form is there before the fact.

To scrutinize the history of the town of Manchester is to observe the extinguishing of the last ember of feudalism in New England.

For many years Manchester was a fishing village, and in the eighteenth and nineteenth centuries it won a reputation for woodworking and cabinet-making. The veneering process was invented in the carpentering shops of Manchester but, never having been patented, was soon a common production method everywhere. The woodworking was no doubt an outgrowth of shipbuilding on Cape Ann, for New England's ship carpenters became the best in the world. Woodworking, cabinet-making, the hand-making of musical instruments, and the designing of furniture were town businesses until well into the twentieth century, and many families today are proud possessors of Dodge chairs, sturdy in construction, artistic in design, and unique in character, not too unlike Chippendales. The decline of wooden ships eliminated the demand for skilled work, and Manchester found itself transforming to a feudal barony of absentee landlords who visited their great shore-line estates only in the summer.

Richard Henry Dana, the author of *Two Years Before the Mast,* in the late nineteenth century is credited with being the first such, and Dana's Beach still bears his name and is still private. The trend he started continued unabated until the market crash of 1929, the New Deal and the virtual disappearance of the servant class. The graduated Federal income tax which came in under Woodrow Wilson (ironically, the only President

ever to stay in Manchester) had indeed begun to trim the sails
of the happy economic voyage of the American moneyed aristocracy, but it was the crash that sounded its death knell.

The watershed from one era to another, so vividly seen in
Manchester, but common to many communities throughout the
East, can be best exemplified by the career of Charles Walker,
known by townies and friends alike as "Chalker" Walker, perhaps from the chalk board of the stock market, perhaps from an
upper-class accent which sounded to the ears of the workers on
his estate as if he had a hot potato in his mouth.

Chalker Walker was by popular acknowledgment the richest
man in Manchester, summer or winter, and that was saying a
good deal. He had a massive granite and wooden mansion on
ground high enough to give him a view of the ocean, from
which it was set back a mile. It rose three or four floors, and the
upper floors in the wings had innumerable rooms for servants,
each no bigger than a monk's cubicle. In the 1920s he was planning to raze this structure and build something even more elaborate. But that was only part of his plan. He had sketched out
an expansive domain, a great estate called Highwood, on which
there would be a dozen or more buildings of the most solid construction, along with parks, gardens and his own polo field. A
mark of distinction in Massachusetts was—and is—possession of
automobile registration plates with low numbers, without the
letters of the alphabet included. Mr. Walker had 101, 202, 303,
404, 505, 606, 707, 808, and 909. That record was not matched
by any millionaire in Massachusetts. It not only indicated
wealth; it indicated a certain longevity of possession of wealth.
It was impressive enough to win more than a nod from J. Pier-
pont Morgan, whose sister, as it happened, lived in Manchester
less than a mile from Walker's home. In fact, Morgan's *Corsair*,
a sleek, black yacht, palatial and with a reputed crew of forty

hands, was a not infrequent visitor to the historic harbor. Walker's financial presence was not unequal to that of Morgan.

The story is told that when the stock market crash came, Walker's attorney drove down from Boston and presented himself on the Walker doorstep at Highwood, only to be told by the butler that Mr. Walker was at dinner and was never disturbed while at dinner. The lawyer insisted; the butler demurred; but at length the insistent urgency of the visitor was too much for the imperturbability of the servant. Walker was notified and confronted the lawyer in an anteroom, to be informed that he had lost $29,000,000 in the market.

"That is no reason," Walker responded, "to take a man from his dinner. I will see you in the office in the morning." Walker survived handily, but the feudal demesne never developed. The old mansion remained. Building plans were scrapped. The hundreds of craftsmen who had been bustling around Highwood with the celerity of worker ants vanished. On his death, his effects and furnishings were auctioned off, the land was sold for real estate developments, the proposed polo field, now called Walker Road, became a nest of single-family houses, the cellars of which are usually flooded in springtime, a situation to which polo ponies might be indifferent but, alas, not people. After his death an architect's drawing of the magnificent conception of the multidwellinged estate hung on a kitchen wall of one of the few outbuildings that had been constructed, a sad memorial to a sweeping dream. A number of architecturally exciting if smaller houses now stand on Highwood. The age of feudalism is past.

For the brief years feudalism reigned, the town meeting operated in something like the rotten borough style. The constituency of the town was made up of the rich along the shore, the servants who lived with them, the gardeners and other attendants who lived in their own homes inland, and merchants and others in the town who provided, as individual entrepreneurs, services for both classes. Ten per cent of the people paid 90 per cent of the taxes, and, generally speaking, the worker, captive though he was in a way, was infinitely better off than his counterpart in any city, or factory workers anywhere in the world today. Manchester has always been a beautiful town to live in. While 10 per cent of property owners paid 90 per cent of the taxes, the tax money was, of course, dispersed in the town meeting not by the persons who paid it, but by the majority of the residents of the town, who were, in turn, dependent for their livelihoods, in the main, on the property owners who paid the taxes. Not unnaturally, the gardener who, on the town floor, voted extravagant expenditures to kick up the tax rate might find himself out of work the month after the town meeting. Since the majority were themselves homeowners, however, there was no disposition to waste money. The majority of their descendants vote Republican today. Puritan frugality is still a virtue in New England. It was not until the public education fever seized Manchester, as well as other Cape Ann towns, that tax money was spent without intense discrimination. Manchester today spends $622 per public school pupil, compared to Gloucester's $441, and besides has the highest percentage of children in private schools of any town on the Cape.

Sending one's children to private schools while, at the same time, still paying town taxes (50 per cent of which goes for the schools) is a sort of public benefaction. Manchester has not benefited particularly by the public benefaction of its wealthy residents, as have other towns in Massachusetts. T. Jefferson Coolidge, whose fortune came from the United Fruit Company and its exploitation of the banana, whose son was to serve the United States as an Undersecretary of the Treasury, and who traced his ancestry back to Thomas Jefferson, donated to the town the building in which its library is housed.

The largest benefaction ever bestowed by one of its residents went not to the town but to the faraway city of Boston. The benefactor was George Robert White, a manufacturer who made his fortune from real estate investments and the sale of Cuticura soap, still available at your corner drugstore, although not so popular as it once was. Dark gray and unattractive in color and odor, it was believed to have special therapeutic properties, and women conscious of their epidermis bought it religiously.

Mr. White, the story runs, found himself moved by a spirit of public service (not, happily, uncommon among the wealthy) and placed in escrow $5,500,000 to bestow on the town of Manchester for public works beneficial to the citizenry. He asked as a small *quid pro quo* that the selectmen build a road directly from the railroad station to his home, which, some felt, would have disfigured the charm of the harbor or the adjacent property. There was a disagreement and, in a fit of pique, Mr. White turned and put the money at the disposal of the city of Boston, whose mayor at the time was no less an undesirable recipient than James Michael Curley, controversial hero-rogue whose portrait was drawn brilliantly in *The Last Hurrah,* by the late Edwin O'Connor. The legend will not die, although aging town officers and even the more youthful Judge Edward Morley, former town counsel, declare that no record or oral testimony can be found to document the story. The monumental fact remains that Mr. White gave the money to Boston, and the fund, to this day, is the largest such at the disposal of the city fathers. When a man of such fortune and liberality dies, it is not without a sense of excitement that a private safe of his is discovered by the new owner of his house, and opened after great difficulty and with great expectation. It was found chockablock full of Cuticura soap.

No Chalker Walkers or George Robert Whites grace Manchester today. Prouder names with tidier (but sufficient) purses range along the shore. At one time the shore line bore the name Embassy Row, and with justification. United States ambassadors and ministers of lesser rank or embassies from foreign nations seeking relief from the malarial heat of Washington, D.C., cluttered its shores.

Such a reputation may well have been a factor in bringing Colonel Edward House to Manchester as a summer resident and President Wilson as his guest. Crowds gathered when Wilson played golf at the Essex County Club, which boasts eighteen of the finest holes in New England, albeit somewhat antique with narrow fairways and small greens. Yet it has championship yardage. J. Joseph Flatley, erudite town moderator for many years in Manchester, was a moppet at the time, tagging along beside the visitors and members watching the President play. When Wilson's two iron put a golf ball far into the rough, it was the future town moderator who retrieved it. He was too young to make the most of it. Strong men wrenched it from him before he could return it to the country's chief executive. "I never knew," he remarked recently, "whether they were secret service men or merely job applicants."

Wilson was the only President to put up in the town. William Howard Taft, while President, attended church services in Manchester while vacationing in adjacent Beverly. John F. Kennedy before he was President was a visitor. Presidents aside, residents of the town recall with pride that Christian A. Herter, a regular summer resident when Secretary of State, rode in the July Fourth celebration.

Like many other New England towns, Manchester still honors the Fourth of July, and gives it ceremony. The traditional bonfire was built of barrels, railroad ties, and scrap lumber and other combustibles; fireworks decorate the night air with their showers of color, both a private display at the Essex County Club to which the townspeople throng and a public barrage at

Masconomo Park (named for the Sagamore)—each very satisfying, with figurative set pieces and their climactic cannonades. Hundreds watch from the cockpits of their sloops or the thwarts of their launches as the fusillades explode and glare over the harbor waters. Alas, the war against air pollution has extinguished the bonfire.

Not in relation to the sea only has Manchester a native charm. Recently Otto Preminger, the well-known motion picture producer, selected it for the making of the film version of *Tell Me That You Love Me, Junie Moon*, a moving novel about three patients discharged from a hospital, one disfigured, one a paraplegic, and one suffering from a progressive neurological disease. The scene of the story is a small town, a rather ideal small town. Preminger and his art director, Lyle Wheeler, searched Canada and the United States for an unspoiled town. "Most of them," Wheeler explains, "have a great highway running through the center which disfigures them, cutting them in half, or dominating the landscape. Others have permitted gasoline stations, garish signs and other abominations to clutter them up."

Manchester was chosen even though the town in the story is an inland town. Preminger's cameras had to turn their backs on Manchester's loveliest asset, its shore line, water front and harbor. The townspeople were flattered, naturally, to have their town selected for the reasons it was selected, although there are always those who would rather have motion pictures made somewhere else. There is, of course, no movie house in the town.

❧ 3 ❦
Essex

The town of Essex is monumental in the history of shipbuilding in America. Otherwise, it is an undistinguished New England coastal town, dim in definition, sleepy except on summer week ends when its restaurants and marinas and antique shops are crowded. It is a rural town where farmland abounds and a great hatchery supplies thousands. One drives to it from Manchester over a bucolic backwoods road, alongside Cedar Swamp, past Agassiz Park, past a gentleman's manicured farm and newly constructed houses of the sort Frank Lloyd Wright called "little breeding stalls" and onto the main street. Or one can approach the same main street over a more populated, equally tortuous road from the city of Gloucester. From the north one enters Essex through Ipswich, from which it separated 150 years ago.

Driving along Main Street, popularly called the Causeway, since it runs along lowland, parallels and crosses the Essex River, one is immediately struck by the garish, ill-built roadside stands, shacks and restaurants, with customers' automobiles entering and leaving the highway, or parked beside the restaurants or clam shacks while their owners dine and watch the innumerable small boats moving to and from their moorings. Sadly, the smell of frying fish and clams, heavy with the aroma of boiling fat, has replaced the delicious odor from wooden

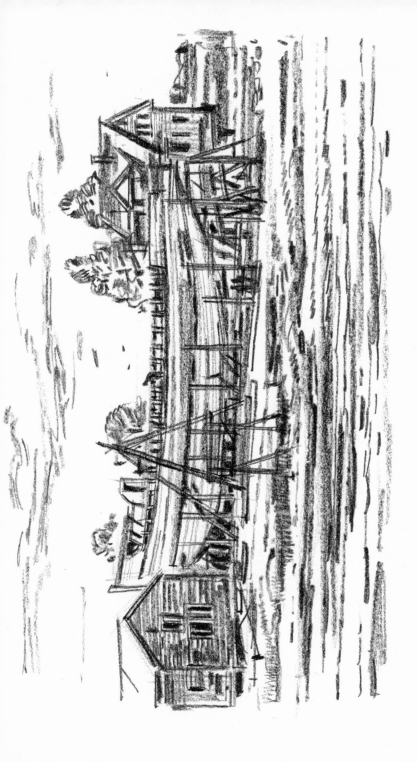

shavings and scraps of pine that once made a carpet under the feet of workmen in the shipyards standing where the restaurants are today. Instead of the sound of the adze shaping a keel, the whine of a buzz saw or the list of a plane shaping a spar, one hears the flatulence of automobiles, the put-put-put of inboard engines, the snarl of outboard motors as small craft nuzzle each other in and out of the river. Essex's day of glory is gone.

The town is a small town, and in many ways a hick town. A hillbilly flavor rides about some of its rural areas which you do not find in Manchester or even in Ipswich, although it is matched in West Gloucester, which adjoins Essex. The people of Essex have been farming since the early seventeenth century, and they hope to go on farming for some years. They are wise enough to resent suburbanization, and to seek to secure for their children the idyllic aspects of their rural community. There are fewer than 3,000 persons in Essex; 2,502 in the 1965 census, about 176 to the square mile. Essex has 14.18 square miles of township, roughly twice as much as Manchester. The town has twice as many Republicans as Democrats, which indicates the historic interest in the tariff walls that were raised to protect the fishing industry for which the town supplied the ships, as well as the natural conservatism of rural people, and here and there, the customary preference of the very rich for the Grand Old Party. It also indicates the lack of a sizable intellectual community such as tempers the Republicanism of the town of Manchester and is generally the mark of East Coast upper middle class towns and villages. Essex has a good deal of inbreeding, more than other Cape Ann communities, although, heaven knows, there is enough in all of them. Newcomers to such communities are warned, "Careful whom you denounce someone to, they are probably related."

A town joke in Essex has it that any stranger coming into the town has only to say to the first man he meets, "Good morning,

Mr. Burnham," and he's likely to be right. If "Burnham" doesn't work, "Good morning, Mr. Andrews," or "Good morning, Mr. Story," is sure to. There are more Burnhams in the telephone book (per capita) than there are Browns in the Dublin, Ireland, or Sullivans in the Boston directory. Nothing better has been or will be written on this facet of the town's character than the delightful chapter in *Frame-up!*—itself a charming book by Dana Story, he who is heir to and master of the town's most famous shipyard, where, alas, ships are no longer built, but only repaired. He has won literary repute as chronicler of the town's great tradition.

After pointing out that it is not unusual for a small New England town to have four or five basic names which occur again and again, Story acknowledges that Essex excels in this matter. "As might be imagined, the large number of people with the same last name made things a little confusing to the outsider or the newcomer to town. Natives weren't much bothered because they had been brought up in it and had a little system which designated the various individuals. It was simple. All you did was call a man (or woman) by his first two names, or his first name and middle initial, or his first name and father's first name, or his first name and his father's nick-name, or even by his name and where he came from. This, of course, was if he happened to have a regular Essex name but moved into town from somewhere else. You automatically knew last names by virtue of having lived here all your life.

"Thus," he continues, "we had John Prince, Frank White and Sam Lewis (Story—no relation); Henry Clarence, Charlie Gus and Frank Ellis (Burnham—no relation); Lucy Zack (Burnham —so-called because her father's name was Zaccheus); Charley Sam (his name was Burnham and his father's name was Samuel); Frank N. (Burnham), Lewis I. (Andrews), Cy Israel (Andrews) or George Hamilton (Story—so-called because he came to Essex from Hamilton). Then, just to make things interesting, we had Fred M. (Burnham), Fred K. (Burnham); Fred Ephraim (Andrews), Eddie James (Story), and Johnny Frank (James). Imagine what it was like when girls married into families of the same name. It often happened. Lots of people who have moved to Essex in recent years have lived there quite a while without knowing that some of those to whom they spoke every day had real names quite different from those by which they were commonly called."

Then there were nicknames such as Hatcher and Handle, obvious for a couple of brothers one short and one tall; Hock and Spit, West Gloucester brothers; and one which must forever stand all by itself—Head-Him-Off-Around-the-Goose-House. One unsuccessful candidate for office in Gloucester was known for years as "Seventy-Seven," because that was the number of votes he got in an election. In Manchester, one young athlete was known as "Sleepy Jim," and his brother, by a strange transfer, or perhaps not so strange, was known as "Little Sleepy." Somehow water-front cities and towns breed curious nicknames, and as William Hazlett pointed out in a brilliant essay, nicknames can be serious business. But enough of that—on to the great chapter of Essex history, now, unhappily, closed, and forever.

Essex was formerly called Chebacco Parish, and was settled in 1634. Goodman Gradstreet and William White are reputed to have been the first settlers, and the first thing they probably did was dig clams and the second thing was go fishing. The town does little fishing today, but clams are still dug, are succulent and famous, and are served proudly in various dishes and with care in the town's restaurants. Indeed, when the Essex Sesquicentennial Committee had a commemorative medal struck, a clam digger was depicted on the obverse, and the shipbuilding industry on the reverse. On the town seal, the shipbuilding industry is depicted, of course.

The men of Essex were building ships before 1656, for in that year there was already a sawmill in the town. As we shall see, John Winthrop, Jr., no doubt helped with that. Throughout the seventeenth and eighteenth centuries, Essex was part of the town of Ipswich, as Chebacco Parish, or simply, Chebacco, which sometimes, for convenience or through ignorance, was spelled Jebacco. Not until 1819 was it incorporated as a town. In 1668, the town historians recount, the town of Ipswich granted an acre of land on the Chebacco River (now the Essex River) for the building of vessels. In that year there were three sawmills in the parish, and they had been there for at least ten years. There were wood and water and stout good will.

Obviously, shipbuilding had grown apace and was being put on an organized basis. Within two hundred years the industry came to its apogee, for in 1852 there were no less than fifteen shipyards in the town, and in the year from November, 1851, to November, 1852, sixty vessels were built. These were not rowboats. The Essex yards built the fastest fishing schooners ever constructed, as well as wooden freighters of hundreds of gross tons, and ships to carry granite to the world, ships as solid as their cargo. The largest of all was the *Vidette,* a steam collier 191 feet long and 34 feet wide, with a 17-foot depth of hold, and a gross weight of 810 tons, a proud ship built for an Essex man, Lamont G. Burnham, who founded the still prospering Metropolitan Coal Company of Boston.

Standing today on the Causeway in Essex, and gazing at the Essex River, about 50 feet across, tidal water at that, with mudbanks and little depth, one wonders how the shipwrights ever got the boats to the sea. It wasn't easy. Tugs towed the big ones, of course, and sometimes had to wait for three high tides before they wound the 5 miles of serpentine stream through gleaming salt marshes to attain at last the broad reaches of Ipswich Bay. Even there, the perils were not past; sand bars threatened, and high seas and wind from the wrong quarter could beach a towed boat in a matter of minutes.

A marked determination in our early New England forebears grasped life by the throat (which is also the purpose of poetry, Robert Frost said, with New England insight). Just as the farmers had to clear the land of rocks and timber before they could farm (some of the stone walls still mark off Essex fields), so the shipbuilder had to navigate narrow streams and outwit low water to get his boats to sea.

Shipyard records show documentation on more than 3,300 ships built in Essex yards, but since the records do not begin until 1785 and many yards kept no records, Dana Story, the best authority, believes half as many more must be added to the written record. A good many small boats must have been crafted between 1634, when the first settlers came, and 1668, when the town meeting set aside a common acre for shipbuilding. And how many after that until bookkeeping became part of the trade? Lumber was plentiful, the sawmills were bustling, the first settlers were all joiners and carpenters and men of the sea and the techniques were older than Noah. Indeed, the building of a wooden boat had not changed essentially since the Flood, and the design must have been devised by the first man to swim on his back, think of his spine as a keel, his ribs as ribs, and his chest as a deck.

Moreover, the land in Essex never lent itself to farming as much as the land farther north in Ipswich and Andover did, and it is not surprising that the first settlers of Chebacco, like the first settlers of Gloucester, preferred fishing to farming. It is a measure as to where the heart of things lay that this small town gave its name—its earlier name to be sure, but its name nonetheless—to a type of boat as familiar to the ship-minded as a galleon or a dugout. A Chebacco boat is of distinctive design, pointed at both ends, with two masts, displacing about ten to twelve tons, and calculated specifically not merely for fishing, but for fishing in the waters off Cape Ann, which can grow choppy to turbulent very quickly. The Chebacco boat was decked over fore and aft, with open space amidships where the fishermen, with hand lines, stood to fish and drag the catch aboard. The two masts it stepped were about the same height; and while it is generally conceded to be the forerunner of the schooner, it is, like the schooner, an indigenous ship, perhaps even more so than the schooner, now that Holland challenges the claims of Gloucester to be the birthplace of the latter— although Gloucester certainly gave it its name.

The Chebacco boat gave way to a vessel with the unlikely nickname "pinkie." The name has in this age been pre-empted by the semiliterate for the little finger of either hand, but in the early eighteenth century the pinkie was a hard-riding, stout fishing vessel. The name arises from the ancient English word "pink," which meant to thrust, stab or perforate. The pinkie had a niche or pink in its high-riding stern in which to crutch the boom of the aftermast. It was much the same as a Chebacco boat, similarly rigged, but about twice the size. Both carried foresail and mainsail but no jib, although after the schooner rig was devised the pinkies swung over to it. The Essex yards not only created the Chebacco boat (although it must be remembered all are modifications of what went before); they also built the best of pinkies. And the best of the schooners.

Of the latter the most famous was the *Gertrude L. Thebaud*, which was built at the Arthur D. Story shipyard in Essex in 1929–1930, with an eye for racing. Louis Thebaud, a wealthy New York summer resident of Gloucester, put up $45,000 of the $60,000 cost. She was built for speed. When one thinks of her, one immediately thinks of Gloucester, out of which port she sailed with a Gloucester captain and a Gloucester crew, or mainly so, for with them in one of the last races was Sterling Hayden, the motion picture star, a bona fide seaman who had trained on square-riggers. Although the general public may think of the *Thebaud*—or the *"Gerty"*—as a Gloucester vessel, the residents of Essex, knowing where she was built, claim her for their own. Well they might, for she was the fastest of them, although fated never ultimately to wrench the International Cup from her Nova Scotian rival the *Bluenose*, the Pride of Lunenberg.

In one race, the *"Gerty"* sailed a 1⅞ mile leg at a speed of fifteen and a half knots, which (according to that most partisan and unreliable historian of the fleet, James B. Connolly) included time lost when Captain Ben Pine luffed her across the finish line to give news photographers ample opportunity to photograph the schooner at her best. But her greatest feat, an epic in the history of schooner sailing, came in the fall of 1930. On October 12 (sacred to the memory of Columbus) she rounded Eastern Point breakwater in Gloucester Harbor at 11:30 A.M. before a wild northeaster, headed north under Captain John T. Matheson, at 4:00 A.M. of the 13th sighted Sable Island, the graveyard of fishing ships, and at 6:00 P.M. went past Chesbucto Head into the harbor at Halifax, Nova Scotia. The 400-mile run had taken her thirty and a half hours, a record. She had averaged better than thirteen knots, and over one hundred of those miles, sailing them in seven hours, better than fourteen knots. Her great rival, the *Bluenose*, had taken thirty-five hours to go from Lunenberg to Gloucester. The *Thebaud* lost the 1930 races in Nova Scotia waters to the *Bluenose* but returned to Gloucester in thirty-four hours.

The *"Gerty,"* like the other famous Essex schooners, had been towed through that meandering tidal river from Main Street, be-

tween the overhanging mud banks, past Bull Island, heading
north, and then, turning east, between Cross Island and Co-
nomo Point, past Tommy Island, and into what are actually
Gloucester waters, for the town lines join in midstream, before
going between Castle Neck (which is Ipswich) on the port bow
and, on the starboard, Two Penny Loaf, crowning the northwest
end of Wingaersheek Beach, which is Gloucester. Our boat is
then in the bay, but the sand bars mentioned before threaten for
more than half a mile out. The pleasure craft that thread the
river today and put-put through the channel do not have the
draft of the Chebacco boats, the pinkies, the schooners or the
freighters which were nursed through that narrow passage in
glorious procession to make Essex world-famous in the nineteenth century. Piloting is a skill in itself, as meticulous as boat
building, and there was an age when such an approach to a port
was a defense not only against enemy warships but against pirates, at one time all too frequent in New World waters.

Once brought to sea, the boats were taken to Gloucester,
where they were rigged. There was a time when one out of
every eight American boats was Essex built. Essex, as Chebacco
Parish, prospered so that it scorned the mother town, Ipswich,
which, following the American Revolution and again the War of
1812, declined. Sand bars sealed up Ipswich's access to the sea
just as they would the great port of Salem. The people of Chebacco Parish didn't like paying so much tax money to Ipswich.
At the annual town meeting, when sectional interests ran high,
they were outvoted. When Chebacco Parish broke away, like so
many other communities, its citizens chose for it a name drawn
from the English community that had sired their ancestors.
Essex became Essex. Today the economic situation is reversed.
Ipswich has grown more prosperous than its offspring. The marinas, the restaurants, the roadside stands selling "lobster in the
ruff" (God forbid) and antique shops, each with its cultists, give

the town what income it has. Like other Essex County towns, it is becoming, slowly, a bedroom for Boston, and a number of its residents each morning take the Boston and Maine railroad coaches from Manchester to the State capital.

The historic days when it was a force in New England's maritime industry are past, and cannot return. Wooden boats have become less and less common as fiberglass, plastics and aluminum take over, not the sort of thing that can be fabricated in a small town. Mass production, the mold, the machine-made, assembly-line products, have swept the artisan aside, and, probably, not a man today in Essex could wield an adze or broad axe —certainly none who could have wielded them with the old magic. "Those Essex ship carpenters," Gloucester's Ben Pine once said, "could carve you a violin from a solid block of wood, using nothing but an adze." They were artists, and their products had such individuality, such idiosyncratic style, so much baraka, to use the word Robert Graves made famous, that seamen thought of those boats as they thought of their wives, as living, breathing, lovable things, something a man might die for as well as happily live aboard.

To mark the watershed from past to present, the climacteric when the world turned from the day of the proud artisan to the day of the indifferent mass-producing robot, no better moment can be chosen than the 113th town meeting of March, 1932, when the town paid tribute to its greatest shipbuilder, A. D. Story. The meeting was called to order on March 7. According to the *Gloucester Daily Times*, "Lester Tompkins, chairman of the board of selectmen, then offered a motion, 'Out of respect to the late Honorable Arthur Dana Story, one who has been a respected citizen and a constant contributor to the best interests and welfare of this town, I move that his name be honored by ceasing deliberations at this time, and that this meeting stand adjourned until Friday evening, March 11, at 7:30 o'clock, and I further move that a committee of five be appointed by the moderator to draw up resolutions on the death of Mr. Story and that these be spread on the record and a copy be sent to the family of the deceased.' This was unanimously voted. This was the first time in the history of the town, as far as can be recalled, that a town meeting had been adjourned on account of the death of a private citizen."

The resolution read: "Arthur Dana Story—Born Oct. 11, 1854, died March 5, 1932, native, lifelong resident and lover of the town of Essex, and its people; for nearly 60 years creator of the most advanced types and construction of the finest fishing vessels to sail the seven seas; devout in his support of the religious life of the community; a leader in the civic affairs of the town and enjoying the confidence and respect of the leaders of his part in the State and the nation; of striking integrity in both his personal and business dealings; descendant of the Pilgrims who landed at Plymouth Rock in 1620; a splendid example of the courage and persistence of the men and women of the historic pilgrimage; quiet but forceful; stern and austere in appearance but warm-hearted and affectionate in action. Arthur Dana Story exemplified to the last degree, not only the spirit and life of his early ancestors, but that rapidly disappearing type in the community 'New England Gentleman of the Old School.' " The dreadful cliché on the end cannot hide the nobility of the man and the lost nobility of his trade.

Before its beginnings as an independent municipality, in the days when it was still Chebacco Parish, the town had another distinguished citizen, not a fisherman but a fisher of men, the Reverend John Wise, minister, scholar and rassler, a big man who was strong enough to pick up a man of like stature and deposit him on the other side of his front-yard fence. Wise was born in Roxbury, which is now Boston's Harlem, and baptized there on August 15, 1652. He attended the free school in Roxbury, one of the first in the New World, and then Harvard University, from which he was graduated in 1673. He was destined for a noble appellation—the "first Democrat in America."

Before being called to Chebacco, he had preached in Connecticut and had served as chaplain to colonists marching against the Narragansett Indians. It was 1680 when he came to Chebacco Parish, and he remained there until his death on April 8, 1725, almost a century before the parish broke off to form the town. Today his home, a charming dark brown seventeenth century dwelling, still stands; privately occupied, it is the town of Essex's lone historic shrine, if we exclude a church with a Paul Revere bell.

If "taxation without representation" was the touchstone or war cry of the American Revolution, Minister Wise was the father of such protest. His moment came when Governor Edmund Andros, sent by King James to restore monarchical prerogatives among the truculent colonists, sought to impose a tax on the independent members of the Massachusetts Bay Colony in particular. These brazen colonists had even failed to answer a letter from the King, and all along had been ignoring his Navigation Acts. When Edward Randolph, one of whose relatives, named Robert Mason, had a claim to the territory of the colony, was named Collector of Customs for the Port of Boston, it was obvious that trouble was afoot and the Crown meant the colony no good. The Mason claim to the colony land was being pressed with vigor, and was particularly pertinent to Cape Ann, for it fell full within the boundaries claimed by the Mason family.

While the claim (which finally came to nothing) was agitating Cape Ann, Randolph verbally attacked various members of the General Court (which is still the name given the legislature of the Commonwealth of Massachusetts). The upshot of the contest between Randolph and the liberal wing of the General Court was an order of the English Court of Chancery vacating the famous charter that John Winthrop had brought with him from England. Cape Ann, along with the rest of the Massachusetts Bay Colony, was made over to the King of England. The colonists, exhausted by King Philip's War and having no strong party in England to support them, had no recourse but to acquiesce, sullenly. Joseph Dudley, son of Governor Thomas Dudley and brother to Anne Bradstreet, was named governor of the "dominion," and a council of eighteen replaced the General Court. Before 1686 was run, Sir Edmund Andros replaced Dudley as governor, and promptly imposed a new tax. The colonists were enraged but again felt they had no recourse. Andros had brought British redcoats with him to enforce his edicts. Manchester, Salem, Newbury, and Marblehead went along with the new order; others began to mount resistance, and looked for a rallying point. It came in Ipswich, and from Chebacco Parish, which is now Essex. The selectmen of Ipswich met and voted not to raise the tax unless there was a vote of the general assembly.

The Reverend John Wise spoke against the tax and urged resistance. At that moment in history, Ipswich was the second community in size and influence in the colony, exceeded only by Boston, and resistance at Ipswich was resistance indeed. A warrant was issued for Mr. Wise, charging that he "did particularly excite and stir up His Majesties subjects to Refactoryness and Disobedience contrary to and in high contempt of his Majesties Laws and Government here established." Two of Wise's Chebacco parishioners stood with him. Other Cape Ann residents were imprisoned along with them, including Samuel Appleton, the local hero in the war against King Philip. Appleton remained in jail for five months. Mr. Wise was not confined that long. He was found guilty, jailed for twenty-one days, then sentenced. He was fined fifty pounds and had to post a thousand-pound bond that he would keep the peace. He was released but

denied the right to preach. A month later, however, Andros allowed him to resume that ministerial office. But time was on Mr.
Wise's side. Within two years, Prince William of Orange landed
in England; James fled; Andros was deposed; the old charter
was restored; and Simon Bradstreet was governor. Wise was
then chosen as one of two representatives from Ipswich to reor-
ganize the General Court. His service to the cause of freedom,
however, was not yet over.

In 1705 Increase Mather, who had been president of Harvard
College, attempted to organize the clergy and usurp for a central body some of the functions previously left to the individual
churches, which were, of course, supported by public taxation.
Mr. Wise saw in the Mather scheme the danger of a tax-sup-
ported hierarachy and a reactionary church constitution. In
1710 he published *The Churches Quarrel Espoused,* and his co-
gency in argument and his literary style ended the movement.
Mather's stock had not risen in the intervening years, partly as a
result of the witch hunts in Salem.

"The first human subject and origin of civil power," Wise
wrote to make history, "is the people, for as they have a power
every man over himself in a natural state, so upon a combina-
tion they can and do bequeath this power unto others and settle
it according as their discretion shall determine; for that this is
very plain, that when the subject of sovereign power is quite extinct, that power returns to the people again. . . . The formal
reason of government is the will of a community yielded up and
surrendered to some other subject, either or one particular person, or more. . . ."

It was no surprise to those who had read him closely that his
language turned up in the Declaration of Independence. It is
something to remember when one drives past his house with its
quiet dignity, and to remember with even more vitality when

one is standing amidst the fried-clam fumes on the historic Causeway, for it is fair to say that much of that rugged independence still stirs the people of Essex.

For example, take Franklyn E. Goucher, who as a youth started clamming in Essex and forty-four years later is still going strong. Goucher was born in Gloucester, but his family took him to Essex while he was an infant; after a sojourn in Salem, the family returned to Essex. It was during the depression of 1930, and the economic circumstances of the family were such that Franklyn, at fourteen, had to get out and hustle. Clamming was an obvious way for an Essex boy. For Goucher it became a way of life, bringing him an independence that any man might envy. He shakes his head sadly when he thinks of the regulation, the uniformity, thrust on his fellow man by the developments of today's society.

Goucher can talk about clamming for hours on end, elucidating the details of the tackle and gear of the trade, why one should use a light outboard motorboat in winter and a heavier one in summer, what sort of boat is best and what sort of sheer it should have. He smilingly dismisses automation.

"They haven't made a machine yet that can shuck a clam," he says.

In Essex there are about a dozen regular clammers, although Goucher on occasion employs two dozen clammers. The Essex clams are still the best. The clams one buys frozen and already fried are clams dredged out of the depths of Long Island Sound, and not the soft-shelled clams that delight the gourmet. The supply of Essex clams varies from year to year, and there are never enough to supply all the restaurants. Goucher goes on supplying them as best he can, checking the clam flat daily, shucking the harvest at day's end. It's an individualistic business, older than shipbuilding on the banks of the Essex River and an excellent example of the type of enterprise that time will not change and only America's mad pollution practices can end. Whatever its future, its celebrated practitioner, Franklyn Goucher, is an ideal type of the independent citizen of Essex.

≫ 4 ≪
Ipswich

The most neglected town in the history of English-speaking America is Ipswich. It is unfortunate that today Ipswich is thought of mostly as the home of John Updike, the novelist, and perhaps as the prototype of Tarbox, the fictitious town of his celebrated or salacious novel *Couples*. It is likewise unfortunate that all the persons who have read his *Couples* have not read his other novels, particularly *The Centaur*, or better still his brilliant literary criticism. He has, moreover, done much to restore high verse to its proper place as a true precinct of poetry. We mention Updike because he is the most notable literary figure in Ipswich today, chief heir to the distinguished literary tradition of the town.

Ipswich, originally Agawam spelled with one or two g's as the spirit moved, was the intellectual center of the Puritan commonwealth mustering on the New England littoral in the middle of the seventeenth century. The town sparkled intellectually and literarily; it bristled with graduates of Cambridge University, the cradle of Puritanism. It deserves more adulation than Plymouth or the colonies of Virginia, for it was the first community in the English-speaking world to produce a poet of stature, or to feel sufficiently at ease with itself to rebuke the intellectual community of the motherland. As much as any other community, and far more than most, it spawned the War for Independence, which cost it dearly, for its shipping ceased, its intellectuals went elsewhere, and much of its best blood went west to colonize Ohio. Heading that migration was America's first covered wagon, Conestoga claims to the contrary.

The depression in Ipswich, aggravated by the loss of the enterprising citizens who went west, left the town too poor to tear down and rebuild. The "make do" that resulted finally paid off. The old homes, preserved and repaired, became a national treasury. Ipswich today has more pre-Revolutionary houses than any other town in English-speaking America, and is, happily, inordinately proud of them. The finest of them is the John Whipple House, an elegant example of a seventeenth-century wooden dwelling, with leaded glass casement windows, brick fireplaces to delight the heart of any antiquarian, a very rare hand-carved ogee molding, and furnishings of the period. Wallace Nutting, whose hand-colored photographs were a rage some decades back, pronounced the Great Room of the Whipple House "probably the best in the country." The house was built by John Fawn in 1640, but Elder John Whipple was soon the occupant, and the Whipples lived there for two hundred years. It was enlarged in 1670 and again somewhat after 1700. The Ipswich Historical Society took it over in 1898 and restored it, adding a touch of genius: a seventeenth-century garden.

The pioneer mother was also the doctor for the family, and a knowledge of "physicke" was essential to her role as mother and medicine man. The garden at the Whipple House was designed by Arthur A. Shurcliff, who supervised the Governor's Palace Garden at Williamsburg. Mrs. A. W. Smith, who had been president of the Massachusetts State Federation of Garden Clubs, planted the garden, including in it a salute to Anne Bradstreet, the poet, who wrote, "Give Thyme or Parsley wreath, I ask no bayes." The garden contains the chief flowers and herbs a Puritan mother had need of. "But besides all the remedies which she had brought from England," Mrs. Smith has written, "or gleaned the use of from the Indians and with which she treated her family for everything from worms and fevers to the loss of eyesight and toothache, she must also extract from her garden all the simplest household aids. Cleansing agents, dyes, insecticides, air purifiers and all her lotions and cosmetics must come from her flower beds. In the event of a call from Samuel Sewall, she could pick a fresh stalk of burnet for him to stir in his beer. On her garden she was dependent to meet such hurried demands as to staunch a wound, lay out the dead, or counteract the bites of snakes or mad dogs. She must grow all her seasonings and flavorings, all her tonics, all her green salads which were such a help against scurvy. Her attic beams must hang with drying herbs, her herb chest must be always stocked.

"The 1683 inventory of the Whipple House lists, on the shelf beside the Great Bible and other books, five bottles of clove, gilliflower, three bottles of rosewater, two bottles of mint water, angelica water and strawberry water." The building and its setting are all charm, from its clamshell walk to its steep-pitched thatched roof. Owing to its relative isolation from the main highways and expressways of a speed-minded age, the Whipple House attracts only three to four thousand visitors a year, the other historic Ipswich houses less. Among these are the Emerson-Howard House, the Waters Memorial, the Colonel Nathaniel Wade House, the Hovey House, and the Polly Dole House, this last lately sold by author Updike. There is also the handsome John Heard House, which is not pre-Revolutionary but nineteenth century, a monument to the Orient trade and the clipper ships.

Ipswich, with 33.21 square miles of territory, is in area the largest of the communities which contribute to Cape Ann. Part of it lies on the Cape; part does not. The people of Ipswich today would, if polled, undoubtedly not consider the town part of the Cape, but unique and sufficient unto itself. Because of the activities of the Reverend Mr. Wise when Chebacco Parish was part of Ipswich, the town seal proudly calls the town the "birth-place of American independence," and lets it go at that. From the days of its settlement in 1633 (although archaeology tells us the Indians were there before Christ) when the intellectual cream of the Puritan crop was sent to the site to build their homes, down to the present, the town can boast a proud intel-lectual tradition, no small part of which is the annual series of concerts and recitals at the Crane Estate, high above the waters of Ipswich Bay; the presence of editors, publishers, authors, composers; a coffee shop that provides rock entertainment; a movie house; seminaries; and the fact that its inhabitants get more newspapers per capita than those of any other town in the Commonwealth.

The town of Hamilton, like the town of Essex, was once part of Ipswich but broke away. It was known as the Hamlet, and it was from the Hamlet that the first covered wagon went west, heading for a New Frontier, the development of a continent and the building of the nation. To this town from that built-up West, seeking the sea and the sense of security that comes from retrac-ing to one's roots, came the master of supreme American gadge-try, the man whose family put the United States so far ahead of the rest of the Western world in the matter of plumbing and central heat that even Europe has yet to catch up—Richard T. Crane of the Crane plumbing fixtures and valves. It was he who created the magnificent Crane estate, which crowns a great drumlin along the shore and stands opposed to the seventeenth-century houses in the river valley. There is a contrast there that is close to the heart of America's meaning.

The Crane estate and the Whipple House represent two dis-parities, and, if the present generations have sense enough to make the best use of both, not merely their physical properties but also their mystiques can ornament American life. Public-spirited citizens are laboring on behalf of both, but too large a portion of the mass is indifferent. Here, as in Gloucester, as we shall see with startling clarity when we examine that fulcrum of Cape Ann, the public does not appreciate what it has been given. The Federal Government, thanks to the vigorous representations of farsighted residents of Ipswich, has thrown a protective arm around the historic landmarks of the town. The performing arts are left unaided, however, and the Castle Hill concerts on the Crane property have had a marginal existence for fifteen years. To a man in a helicopter, Castle Hill, the great house of the Crane estate—aside from the town's natural wonders, the beaches, the salt water marshes, the classic drumlins, the predatory sand dunes—would be the town's most obvious landmark.

The estate is now known as the "Richard T. Crane, Jr., Memorial Reservation," and of it the Trustees of Reservations, a typical New England organization of private citizens incorporated for the public welfare, writes that the reservation "represents one of the several unique and memorable landscapes of the Commonwealth of Massachusetts. It contains a remarkable conjunction of New England scenery: the three-mile Castle Neck peninsula, a wild and mysterious region of shifting sand dunes, thrust into the Atlantic; the woody heights of Castle Hill and Hog Island, smoothly molded drumlin hills rising from the beach; the vast expanse of the Essex marshes; and the tidal meanders of the Castle Neck and Ipswich Rivers. The dunes, stirred by winds and waves, have moved restlessly for centuries and bound one of the finest sand beaches north of Cape Cod. The marshes are another world of billowing green and gold grasses, unique in size and character."

The report continues, "Castle Hill, with its Georgian Great

House and gardens, is a monument to traditions of excellence in architecture and landscape design and to another, and perhaps, more gracious era." What we have here is a beautiful brick Georgian house crowning a smoothly sloping hill which fronts a magnificent bay. The house was not the first built by Crane. The first to rise on the hill was of Italian design with an Italian sunken garden which remains. But Mrs. Crane changed her mind about the first house, so it was razed and the Georgian palace reared in its stead. Within the house is a library, the woodwork in which was brought over intact from the castle of the Earl of Essex, including rare examples of Grinling Gibbons wood carving. The rear of the house opens on a parterre which looks down the Grand Allee, 150 yards of lawn flanked by a classic Greek statuary. On either side of the steps leading from the parterre are two great griffons carved by the late Paul Manship, one of America's and Cape Ann's most celebrated sculptors. To the right as one descends the steps is another slope of lawn, stretching like a great green fan from the apex of the hill to the road circling up to the house. Beyond the road lies the beach and beyond the beach the bay. Great throngs have come to the estate and its gardens. Thousands have stood or sat on chairs or the lawn in the Grand Allee to hear Louis Armstrong, Duke Ellington, Joan Baez, the Kingston Trio or Dave Brubeck, while smaller audiences have filled the temporary chairs in the Italian garden to hear classical performers such as Lorin Hollander, Helen Micheliades, Rudolf Serkin, the Budapest String Quartet and other small musical groups, or to see Jean Van Destine or Geoffrey Holder and their thrilling dance groups. As head of the Castle Hill Foundation, which operates the estate on a nonprofit basis for the Trustees of Reservations, David Crockett has to struggle constantly with a deficient budget.

The popular practice (although not sufficiently popular) has been to arrive at Castle Hill from 6:30 P.M. to 7:30 P.M. on a

late summer Friday or Saturday night with a picnic lunch—a
bottle of Rhine wine or a chilled Liebfraumilch, some Double
Gloucester, Liederkranz or Cheddar cheese, crab meat or lobster salad, stuffed eggs, sandwiches, grapes, cookies, or whatever
—and dine overlooking a Maxwell Parrish landscape, greens-
ward walled by trees, descending to Ipswich Bay, with Annisquam Light signaling in the distance, sails dotting the water,
late bathers like toy figures on the beach, and overhead, the
birds. It is to live as man was intended when Eden was still
practicable, and all nature alive and man utterly receptive.
Having picnicked, seated either on the lawn or at white circular
tables, the picnickers down the lees of their wine, dispose of the
detritus in trash cans, return their baskets to their automobiles,
and then descend to the Italian garden, where, with the moon
intensifying its light in its proper place, music sounds better
than it could in any concert hall where the acoustics are superior. In the garden, the stage bears in memoriam the name of a
local composer, the late John Alden Carpenter. Another local
composer, Samuel L. M. Barlow, whose summer home is
Gloucester, was for many years the master of ceremonies whose
urbane curtain speeches were one of the pleasing features of the
evenings. What Cape Ann has here is another Tanglewood, far
less significant, but more intimate, and, for location, equally
worthy and indeed superior. It is astonishing, in view of the
modest prices, that the concerts are not crowded each weekend.
Bad luck on the weather, and a widespread but thoroughly mis-
taken notion that something frightfully social taints the concerts,
are two of the factors that have hurt attendance.

Several attempts have been made to bring the Crane estate to
full public use. On the grounds, and particularly relevant to a
town that with justice calls itself the Birthplace of American Independence, is the Museum of the Constitution and Freedom, in
which exhibits trace the sources of our constitutional rights and

privileges back to King John of England, brought to heel by the barons who forced upon him the Magna Charta. The exhibit contains not only numerous reproductions of key documents but some interesting originals. It doesn't win the visitors it should. An art school was set up in the Great House but failed to flourish. A noble attempt to bring the New England Conservatory of Music, one of the nation's distinguished music schools, to Castle Hill as a regular summer venture collapsed because both the foundation and the conservatory lack sufficient money. The conservatory's presence made for musical triumphs, but financial loss.

About Castle Hill, however, there is something dynamically and dramatically unique, so that it should always remain a public attraction and a public opportunity. A discussion of its wildlife, its natural riches which attract naturalists and photographers from all over the world, must be reserved for another chapter. It is, by the way, stocked with deer, and poachers are not unknown. The beach is the most popular feature of the estate, and throughout the summer the parking space is choked with automobiles and the beach filled with color by families down for the day. In the days when the Cranes were living in the Great House, the beach was private and admission was by ticket only. These were issued to friends by the Cranes, and they were proud possessions. Without one, visitors found the gate barred. Even President William Howard Taft was denied entrance by an obedient youthful gatekeeper who was impressed neither by the robust presence nor the title.

Besides coming to an appreciation of Castle Hill, the town has a lot of growing to do. Like Gloucester, it, above other communities on Cape Ann, can lay claim to the magic of the American melting pot. To Ipswich in the nineteenth century came Greek and Pole and Celt to work the mills and live in uneasy symbiosis with the descendants of the early English settlers and the perennial adventurers from the Maritime Provinces who, like the European immigrant, sought a better existence than their native precincts offered. Living residents can remember the immigrants coming in by trainloads, Polish peasants, heads covered by babushkas, their few possessions in neckerchiefs tied to sticks, eager to get the jobs in the lace mills which the Yankees spurned, mills that made the town's name momentarily famous. The town had a tradition of lace-making. Even as John Hancock smuggled madeira wine past the British customs officials (one historian has called him the colony's great bootlegger), so Ipswich settlers smuggled machinery into the colony despite British laws that sought to keep lace-making a monopoly of the motherland. The Puritan ethic always wavered a bit when profits were in sight. No doubt John Winthrop, Jr., had a hand in the matter.

When the French claim to Agawam (fairly solid) drove the Puritan masters of the Massachusetts Bay Colony to sending settlers to the area to cultivate and to hold, the volunteers were, like so many volunteers in a cause, seen as more noble than mercantile, a cut above the mass—and the mass of Puritans in the Massachusetts Bay Colony were a pretty high-level cut to begin with.

Among those first settlers were Simon Bradstreet, later to be governor of the colony, and his wife, Anne Dudley Bradstreet, daughter of Thomas Dudley, a man who was also to be governor of the colony. All three were passengers on the *Arbella*, the flagship that had put into Manchester a few years before. Anne, as mentioned earlier, was to become forever famous as the first poet of the New World writing in English (it must be remembered that the Spanish were ahead in everything). But husband Simon, although less well known, was a four-square man in his own right, and his connection with Ipswich was to become significant in the history of the colony because he would be governor when the colonists restored the colony's independence and

marched Governor Andros out of town. As we have seen in the
chapter on Essex, the intellectual inspiration, the moral backing
in the repulsion of that reactionary movement toward reasserting
ing absolute monarchy, came initially from the town of Ipswich
and is commemorated on the town seal.

Such a heroine as Anne Bradstreet deserves an accolade in
passing. As a teen-age bride she left England to go by an un-
comfortable and dangerous passage from a comfortable and
pleasant life in England to a wilderness that held not the promise of well-being but the prospect of drudgery, discomfort and
peril. She was ever the pioneer, physically and intellectually.
Shortly after her arrival in Salem, she left for Charlestown. She
left Charlestown for Cambridge and Cambridge for Ipswich and
then Ipswich for Andover, where she died at the age of sixty
years.

She had mothered eight children, and had kept her book of
pensées, which, today, vulgar and sophisticated and superstitious as the country has become, we can still read with profit.
She wrote her poetry in a primitive village in moments snatched
from a regimen which, hard as it was on women in such a century and under the Calvinist shadow, must have been close to
intolerable for such a person as she, raising her children, often
in fear of Indian attack, each day marked by a backbreaking
routine. That all her children but one outlived her is a measure
of the depth of her devotion as a mother, for the seventeenth
century, and particularly the seventeenth century in New England, suffered a steep infant mortality.

Had she been born to a broader culture than the Puritan con-
viction, she might have ranked with Emily Dickinson as a poet;
just as Miss Dickinson likewise might have risen to unimaginable heights had her base been broader, for her charm does not
spring from her reiteration of the rhythms of the Common Book
of Prayer and her off-rhymes, but from a sensitivity of soul that

was unique. Mistress Bradstreet, with the French Protestant Du-
Bartas as her model and mentor, dissipated or inhibited her natural gifts by a rejection of the benefits of the Incarnation. Her
poetry is a poetry of the mind and the imagination, not one of
the concrete and particular world around her. How she has de-
prived us by not having recorded her observations of what was
before her eyes, morning, noon and night. She deals with the
coins of semantic cliché. But let us be thankful for what she did
write, true and wonderful woman that she was. Consider her
poem to her husband:

> If ever two were one, then surely we.
> If ever man were loved by wife, then thee;
> If ever wife were happy in a man,
> Compare with me, ye women if you can.
> I prize thy love more than whole mines of gold,
> Or all the riches that the East doth hold.
> My love is such that rivers cannot quench,
> Nor ought but love from thee, give recompense.
> Thy love is such I can no way repay,
> The heavens reward thee manifold I pray.
> When while we live, in love lets so persever
> That when we live no more, we may live ever.

Although the poet John Berryman has won international praise
for his later poems, his "Homage to Mistress Bradstreet" remains, for me, his best work. No woman in American history has
won such a tribute from such a poet, and perhaps it is fair to
say no woman deserved it more. Appropriately, her complete
works have been reprinted within the past decade by a Cape
Ann publisher, Peter Smith of Gloucester, another tribute to her,
since the publication was as much a labor of love as it was one
of profit.

It is a proud thing for Ipswich that not only can it claim
through Mistress Bradstreet the first poems of the New World
(although William Bradford of Plymouth tried his hand at

verses) but also the first distinguished prose work—*The Simple Cobler of Aggawam* by Nathaniel Ward, written in 1645. The Reverend Mr. Ward, while serving in Ipswich, was outraged by —of all things—the latitudinarian views of Oliver Cromwell, who, fearing that the Puritans, already splitting into sects, would destroy their own successes by factionalism, had called for a spirit of tolerance in England, if only among Protestants toward Protestants. Mr. Ward, who, like John Winthrop, Sr., and others, hoped to establish in America the perfect and pure Protestant state (with the ultimate aim of transferring the same to England), saw Cromwell's tolerance as flaccidity and rang out his appeal for a pristine orthodoxy.

He wrote the book under the pen name of Theodore de la Guard, a translation of his first name into Greek and his last name into French. To the title *The Simple Cobler of Aggawam in America,* he appended the subtitular explication, "Willing to Mend His Native Country, lamentably tattered both in the up-per-Leather and Sole, with all the honest Stitches he can take." He then added on the title page, "It is his Trade to patch all the year long, gratis," and "Therefore I pray Gentlemen keep your Purses," and more. It was a day when every noun, as in German, was capitalized. The forced joviality of the metaphor was intended to make the polemic more winsome to the brethren it berated.

Ward was born in England and was to die there. He attended Emmanuel College, Cambridge, "the nursery of Puritanism," and was educated as a lawyer. Before he turned to the ministry, he had practiced law. Like many another cleric, he had been harassed by Archbishop Laud and his pursuivants, dismissed from his rectory, and so had emigrated to Massachusetts. He went immediately to Ipswich; it was the place for an intellectual. Because of his erudition and his legal training, he was called upon by the General Court of Massachusetts Bay Colony to assist in the preparation of a legal code for the colony, "the first code of laws to be established in New England." They were enacted in 1641 and were known as "The Body of Liberties." John Winthrop gives Ward the credit for them.

They were, in effect, a "bill of rights" and improved upon the justly honored common law of the motherland. One of them read: "*Everie* married *woeman* shall be free from bodilie correction or stripes by her husbande, unlesse it be in his owne defence upon her assalt." The old English law had declared that a man might punish his wife with a "reasonable instrument." One cannot resist speculating how much the presence of Anne Bradstreet in Ipswich, where Ward knew and admired her, had to do with the forging of that enlightened clause.

Six years later Ward's *Simple Cobler* was published. One critic says of it: "The book is amusingly digressive: There are satirical thrusts at women's fashions and some neatly turned couplets. . . . It remains a landmark in American letters, for its homely style, interwoven with apt and erudite metaphor, surpasses in vigor anything in Colonial literature written within the author's lifetime." Ward returned to England to end his days, but his presence contributed significantly to Ipswich's brief spring years of illumination, and there is little doubt that the spirit engendered in Ipswich helped make the man.

Ministers played a major role in the Puritan theocracies of colony and town, and three ministers of Ipswich have given it major historical distinction. We have mentioned Mr. Wise and Mr. Ward. The third is the Reverend Manasseh Cutler.

The Reverend Mr. Cutler was a chaplain in the Revolutionary Army (as Wise had been in King Philip's War) and returned from the wars to Ipswich to take up his ministerial duties. The Ipswich town meeting of 1772 found the citizens backing the people of Boston in their resistance to British impositions. Following the Boston Tea Party of December 16, 1773, it convened again to announce that the "citizens of this town have received real pleasure and satisfaction from the noble and spirited Exertions of their Brethren of the town of Boston, etc. . . ." In Ipswich, as in Boston, there was a good deal of smuggling in violation of the British laws. It was a bustling business along the New England coast. When the Revolution came, Ipswich, like the other towns of Cape Ann, did its share. It was not Tory country.

The Revolution, however, was followed by a depression, and the town became far from prosperous. The war had driven Ipswich fishing vessels from the seas, for the British fleet utterly commanded the coastal waters until the French came over. When the war was over and the British had been defeated, England closed the West Indies ports to American shipping and thereby cut off Ipswich's flourishing trade. Debts hung heavy on the Commonwealth of Massachusetts and on every town and on almost every citizen. Unrest was ubiquitous. In the western part of the state, Daniel Shays, with Irish irritation, initiated his rebellion, and Ipswich men were mustered along with troops from other communities to put it down. Money became scarcer and scarcer. Lotteries were resorted to for repairing bridges over rivers and for building roads, including the road from Manchester to Gloucester.

The soldiers of the Revolutionary Army were owed back pay, and to placate them bounty lands in the West were offered them. Citizens in Boston and environs formed the Ohio Company of Associates to take advantage of the offer and solicited fellow veterans to join in planning a new settlement in Ohio, where the land was fertile and the climate said to be mild. The Reverend Manasseh Cutler, then minister in Ipswich's Hamlet parish (now Hamilton, named for the first Secretary of the Treasury), had long dreamed of moving west with his growing family. In March, 1786, the Ohio Company planners got together, and invited Cutler to join with them. He was nominated one of three directors and in 1787 was sent to the national capital, then in New York City, to negotiate purchase of the land. He brought the matter off with some skill and a bit of bluff. In the Ordinance of 1787, Congress made available about 5,000,000 acres in all, of which 1,500,000 acres went to the Ohio Company. The actual price the men had to pay was less than ten cents an acre. The project hurried along, and the day of departure came.

A large covered wagon was built with black canvas cover. Painted on the sides was the legend "Ohio, for Marietta on the Muskingum." Armed and provisioned, the company set out, Mr. Cutler's son, Jervis, included. The elder Cutler did not follow for six months, but it was he who was the moving force, and the pioneer company set out from his home. The fact that that company went from a town of such a libertarian tradition became subsequently significant for the history of the United States. The independent spirit of Ipswich and the state of mind that had somehow nagged it to greatness in the Body of Liberties drafted by the Reverend Mr. Ward, and in the animadversions of the Reverend Mr. Wise on the origins of authority and democratic government, came to the fore. Slavery was excluded from the new territory, and hence from the State of Ohio, and the erection of that barrier against the spread of slavery subsequently became decisive in the history of the country.

The emigration from Ipswich was the beginning of a titanic movement. It is not too much to say that besides the independent mind Ipswich developed, which is deemed typically American, it also developed the nomadic spirit which is also typically American. We are a nation of wanderers. The Bradstreets went from Ipswich to Andover seeking even better farmland, although Ipswich was the best north of Boston. The younger John Winthrop ventured on to Connecticut. The Reverend Mr. Ward went back to England. With Mr. Winthrop to Connecticut went eleven others, all original settlers of Ipswich.

They had built a community to admire. In the second year of its settlement they had changed the name from Agawam to Ipswich. They had delighted in the farmland, and in the clams found along the shore and famous to this day. The rivalry between Ipswich and Essex on which town produces the better clam is not wholly factitious. As we have said, Ipswich today boasts the oldest farm in America in continuous operation, and some Ipswich clams are still shipped over the road to Boston markets.

John Winthrop, Jr., is too often forgotten despite his contributions to the Massachusetts Bay Colony, overshadowed by his father. But he was a man in his own right, formidable, knowing. He was only twenty-seven years old when he was selected to head up the new town. He had come to the New World the year after his father, and had brought with him a library of one thousand books. His bent was not along theological or political but along scientific lines. He was a member of the Royal Society, and corresponded with Sir Christopher Wren, Isaac Newton, and Robert Boyle, surely an indication of the range of his interests. He was a scholar and a practical one. He built the first saltworks in the colony in 1638, mined the schists of Cape Ann to get graphite, and built the first ironworks in Saugus, one of the towns we motored through to reach Cape Ann. He negotiated the purchase of Ipswich and adjoining Chebacco from the Sagamore we have met before, paying him twenty pounds. In the document the name is spelled Musconominet.

One could trace the descendants of the Ipswich settlers forever. The late Sherman L. Whipple, one of the great trial lawyers of the State, sprang from the Whipple family of Ipswich, and Ralph Waldo Emerson also traced his ancestry back to the town. Culture as well as business ran thin after the Revolution and the War of 1812, which didn't help any New England port. In the nineteenth century, poetry became mannered, but Edward Gilbert Hull wrote in Ipswich and charmed his times. Eliza Boyle O'Reilly, daughter of the famous John Boyle O'Reilly, loved Ipswich, and wrote some memorable lines at the turn of the century, entitled "Lines at Ipswich."

> Long banks of drifted sand shut out the sea,
> White fossil waves piled up in barren state;
> No life lives here; a buried orchard tree
> But makes the dreary scene more desolate.
> As one who in a sleep unfortunate,
> Fain would escape some fast-pursuing fear
> Yet cannot move,—so strains a traveller here.
>
> The friendly ocean, longing for the fields,
> Whose rustling groves it hears beyond the sand,
> Silently up the peaceful river steals
> And lays its arms about the dune-locked land.
> Around this hillock, here where oaks command,
> The sea-born waters lure, and swallows fly
> Backward and forward, flitting endlessly.
>
> And skimming o'er the inlets, each can see
> His mirror image in the tranquil streams,
> And breathlessly he dips, as if to be
> At one with it. . . .
>
> But as I mused, a sportsman in the marsh
> Scattered a shot, and swift away then sped
> The frightened scudding swallows, at the harsh
> Discordant sound. One drooped his eager head,
> Fluttered and fell into the water—dead.
> And then I wondered what that swallow found
> Within the stream it loved to circle round.

The landscape looks much the same as when Miss O'Reilly observed it. The hunter is still there during the season, but the swallows are protected. They are threatened in another way than by buckshot. Real estate developers are eying Ipswich as a lecher eyes a woman. Its open spaces are catching the eye of John Doe as they caught the eye of John Smith. Utility companies yearn to send power lines overhead. Steely-eyed, enterprising men long to open marinas wherever there is open water. It is not impossible that Castle Hill will be turned into a summer colony like Little Neck and Great Neck, two minor drumlins which have long been covered by summer cottages and camps, and now are acquiring an increasing number of year-round residences.

The antique charm of Ipswich appears again in the summer colony Little Neck, for the place is run as an autonomous region by a group of self-perpetuating trustees known as Feoffees, pronounced "feefees." Feoffees are persons who own a fee or a fief, which is an estate of land held on condition of homage to a superior. In this case the town of Ipswich is the superior, and the Feoffees in this case have been operating since the seventeenth century, an institution unique in America, proudly maintaining the old English name. The Feoffees collect the taxes from the inhabitants of Little Neck and turn them over to the town. Such is one inheritance from the seventeenth century. Another antiquity is the oldest stone bridge in America, the Choate Bridge, still sound, and until very recently unmarked.

A project is now under way in the town to provide suitable markers for all historic homes and sites, with the manual arts class of the high school cooperating. Meanwhile, Dr. William D. Hoyt of Rockport, a dedicated scholar, is compiling and indexing old and valuable town records with the ultimate aim of having them microfilmed. The records are considerable. There is a two-volume history of the town, each as fat as a dictionary. While the records are thus being taken care of, the Ipswich Historical Commission has negotiated an agreement with the Department of Housing and Urban Development in Washington,

D.C., to preserve the aesthetics and authenticity of the old houses of Ipswich. The houses remained, of course, because during the lean years after the Revolution the people of Ipswich did not have the means to raze them and build larger, vulgar houses. The depression was a benison. The plan is now to preserve them forever. The agreement is in reality a pilot project, unique in the United States, "to demonstrate the feasibility of protecting buildings of historic significance by means of covenants with home-owners under which outstanding architectural features would be specifically safe-guarded." The program will be funded by the Department of Housing and Urban Development and the Ipswich Heritage Trust.

Another historical treasure is the Appleton Farms, still in the family, still bundling hay. The owner, Francis R. Appleton, Jr., heir to the English king's seventeenth-century grant that began the farm, is the end of his line, unhappily childless, but concerned about the future of the spacious countryside he owns. He has willed it to the Trustees of Reservations.

Ipswich has pretty well guarded itself against the real estate developers, but its open spaces are threatened. Indeed, there is no keeping up with the money-hungry predator with no regard for the ecology of a region. Only recently, the town found itself in a strenuous battle to prevent a New Hampshire man from pursuing plans to dredge millions of tons of sand from the shoals and beaches of Ipswich for construction elsewhere, with no concern for the destructive effects on the shellfish population, the spawning grounds and the possible erosion of magnificent Crane's beach through exposure to heavy seas. The town successfully repulsed the assault.

Slowly all Cape Ann is learning that the struggle to preserve its natural inheritance as well as the brilliant legacies from its forebears will require, even as liberty, eternal vigilance.

≱ 5 ≰
Rockport

When you think of Essex, think of shipbuilding. When you think
of Rockport, think of granite. No town of comparable size in
America has given as much granite to the world. The headlands
of Cape Ann which are Rockport are composed of little else.
The word "granite" comes from the Italian word "granito,"
which means grainy (as opposed to Italy's clear marble), for
granite is a mixture of feldspar, quartz and other minerals which
give it varying colorations. Rockport's granite, of a rare sort, is
of high quality and fine grain and is still being exported. Rather
indicatively, it is used today mostly for tombstones. When the
town broke away from Gloucester early in the nineteenth century and declared itself a separate municipality, it almost voted
to call itself Granitetown. Rockport was a happier choice.

Since Rockport is the tip of the Cape, the very cap of the
Cape, it was common for people to say—Cape Parish or Fifth
Parish being cumbersome—that they lived "on the cape." Indeed, "Cape Ann" was also seriously considered as a name for
the fledgling town when it took its wings in 1840. It had become
a separate parish in 1753. In 1840 it was 150 years old if we take
Richard Tarr as Sandy Bay's first permanent settler. He came
from Marblehead with his wife and two children, Richard and
John, and their descendants are still with us. Tarr built himself

a log cabin and settled down. He had to wait ten years for another permanent settler to arrive, and in the interim, presumably, fed himself and his family by rod, gun and some farming. The second settler was more enterprising. He promptly went into the lumbering business, and having built himself a sloop from the oaks of Sandy Bay, shipped timber to Boston to build its wharves, including historic Long Wharf.

The first settlers were a hardy breed. Ebenezer Babson, one of their number, cornered a bear in the tide, slew it with his hunting knife, and skinned it on the spot, turning an exigency, Yankee-fashion, to profit. The spit of land where the fight is believed to have taken place is to this day called "Bearskin Neck," once an artists' haven, now threatened by an excess of quaintness and an acne of artsy-craftsy shops.

A century was to intervene before the Fifth Parish of Gloucester, made up of Sandy Bay and the more northerly section known as Pigeon Cove (which was settled earlier), were to wake up to the wealth of magma stone beneath the thin layer of topsoil already bursting upward to confront the sky like the bones of a buried titan. To be sure, a gristmill was early established, and its builder must have been happy to have at hand granite for the grinding stones.

Many mooring stones had no doubt been cut over the earliest decades, for Sandy Bay was more easily attained by water than overland. But the isolation of the tip of the Cape did not keep its inhabitants ignorant of the issues of the day. The men of the Fifth Parish served with distinction in the Battle of Bunker Hill, June 17, 1775, under Captain John Rowe. Long hair was the custom for young men in those days, at least in such rural corners as Sandy Bay; and it is interesting to note that as the men went off to the wars, they cut off their tresses to leave them with their wives, sweethearts and mothers, a practice not unknown to the hirsute young men of today who find themselves about to be drafted. William Parsons and Francis Pool died on Bunker Hill; the rest of the company returned.

History intruded again on the town in the War of 1812. The story cannot be better told than in the words of Dr. Lemuel Gott, who gave the Centennial Address in 1853:

"In 1812 the United States declared war with England, but, its results to this place were not like those of the old war. Then our country was in its infancy, contending with a gigantic power, for a free and independent existence. Now, she is herself a giant and able to repel aggression. Our fishing interests, with some little interruption, proved highly profitable and the mass of the people obtained a comfortable living in peaceful pursuits, but some for purposes of plunder and more rapid gains embarked in privateering. But what little wealth was thus acquired was, in most cases, dissipated by habits of extravagance and vice engendered by the war spirit. One privateer owned in Salem, named *Cadet,* commanded at first by a Capt. Evans, and manned in part from here, cruised around this coast. She was afterwards commanded by Capt. David Elwell of this place. The Capt. was said to have cleared twelve thousand dollars; the crew, several hundred. They never came to an open engagement, but occasionally boarded some vessels and took some prizes. During the war, a number of our men in other privateers and others in merchant vessels found their way, before the war closed, in the prisons of Halifax and some few in Dartmoor prison, England.

"In the latter prison were Benjamin Colby, Joseph Bailey, and one from Folly Cove. Some were in Chatham prison on the Thames, [among them] William T. Abbott. Those in Dartmoor prison were there at the time of the shooting of the prisoners. It was said the prisoners complained of their bread, which is supposed to have aroused some ill feeling. They are accustomed to exercise themselves by playing ball. One day the ball went over the wall into the barracks. The soldiers there did not return it as usual; when some of the prisoners threatened to break through the wall. They were commanded to desist, by the soldiery, but declining, a fire was opened upon the prisoners and seven were killed and a large number were wounded. Our men were retained in prison some six months. This was in 1815.

"The leading citizens of the place, soon after the war was declared, formed a Committee of Safety to have the oversight of affairs. The English privateers occasionally ran into the bay and molested the coasters which had run in under the land for protection. At one time, 1813, one privateer fired upon the inhabitants. The people returned the fire from Bear Skin Neck and the old wharf, with a long six pounder, carrying a shot through her from stem to stern, when she crawled off. Finding that our coast was, from its exposed situation, to suffer from the enemy, the inhabitants deemed it advisable, in 1814, to erect a fort on the neck. This was done by subscription at a cost of about six hundred dollars. The fort was mounted with several cannon, making a somewhat formidable appearance, so much as to attract the attention of the British cruisers. It was regarded by them as a government fort. The English frigate *Nymph*, lying in the offing Sept. 8th of this year about midnight sent three barges in to reconnoitre and, if things appeared favorable, to make an attack. The fort was manned by nine men or more detailed from a company of about sixty-four who were drafted to protect interests principally located at Gloucester, at Stage Fort, and commanded by Captain Benjamin Haskell of West Parish. The soldiers had eight dollars per month; those quartered here had their barracks at the old house, then standing where the Union Store now is, till the watch-house was built. The English were piloted into Long Cove by one of our townsmen, Capt. David Elwell, by command of the enemy who had captured his boat for this purpose. Three barges landed twenty men. Elwell led the way to the fort. The watchman on duty was said to be asleep. The men who were stationed at the fort were taken prisoners and put aboard the barges. The enemy spiked the two cannons and threw them off the breastwork, then set fire to the watch-house and left. One of the barges with twenty men came around to the old dock, fired at a sloop's mast, then started out. The meeting-house bell beginning to ring an alarm, the barge while passing out by the end of the pier fired at the meeting-house and lodged a shot in one of the steeple posts. This discharge started a butt in the bow of the barge, which caused the crew to pull for the rocks at the back of the pier. Thirteen of them were taken prisoners; some of them were rescued from drowning, by being taken out of the water. The remainder (except one who escaped in a float to the back beach and ran into the woods) passed over to Long Cove, took a fishing boat belonging to James Parsons and William Lurvey, and went off to their ship, about daylight, in the fog. The prisoners were well cared for by the Committee of Safety, in the old house of James Tarr, standing then where the house of Deacon Thomas Giles now stands, near the Great Hill. At evening they were marched to Pigeon Cove, the one in the woods till now joining them, and they were sent on board the frigate in Capt. Daniel Wheeler's boat, the captain having previously sent word by a vessel he had captured, that he would willingly exchange men of ours and release some Americans whom he had on board.

"The captain sent our men back and some others and also gave up the fishing boat to James Parsons, and from that time while stationed off the coast he gave the fishermen liberty to fish unmolested. Among the prisoners sent back on exchange were the nine from the fort, Capt. Elwell and two Salem men. While the English prisoners were in custody here, orders came from Salem to the Committee of Safety to surrender up the prisoners but our people judged it best that they should be exchanged for

Americans and they thought that this course would conciliate the Captain and prevent further trouble, which proved to be the case. The other barge, I would further say to complete the history of the affair, that left the fort, on hearing the firing of the barge in the dock, at the meeting-house, rowed into the bay but was driven back by the three persons firing small arms at them. This barge returned the fire with a six-pounder; three shots were exchanged; no one was injured. The sunken barge was raised and given to the owner of the stolen whaleboat, Ebenezer Davis, and was in use for years and I believe a valuable boat. She was well built and copper fastened. The small arms, pistols and cutlasses were divided by the Committee of Safety. The cannon of the sunken barge is yet retained as town property and is fired on great occasions.

"About this time during the war, the frigate *Leander* came in near the Folly Cove and fired several shots and attempted to land for the purpose of watching a small craft which was there. The people mustered to prevent their landing. The Company from this village, called the Sea Fencibles, about sixty men, marched to the scene of expected conflict, with a nine-pounder and two six-pounders and small arms, the old Revolutionary soldiers going with them. The Gloucester militia were also on hand, Col. James Appleton commanding. When they arrived they disputed the landing of the barge. Then a flag of truce was sent in but the Colonel replied in a letter that they could not allow their landing for any such purpose as proposed, and that he did not fear their threats. The frigate soon after stood off."

Would that the Norman invasion of Harold's England had been as fastidiously reported! But what a picture our Centennial orator gives of the times. Sandy Bay was still the Fifth Parish of Gloucester, but the community was about to come into its own. The quarry business was soon to burgeon. As early as 1800 a millstone had been shipped to Newburyport, and no doubt others had been supplied to gristmills closer to hand, as well as those on the Cape. Josiah Norwood (his cabin still stands) and his son, Josiah, Jr., would sell millstones and mooring stones which were "cut as called for." In 1823 Nehemiah Knowlton drilled out four hundred to five hundred tons from a ledge and advertised granite for sale for "cellar and underpinning stones." Outside interests, attracted by Knowlton's enterprise, came to Pigeon Cove to exploit the natural resources. The chief name here is William Torrey, not a native, who had learned his trade in Quincy, which is even more famous for its granite.

The Federal Government was building Fort Warren on one of the islands in Boston Harbor, and the colonel in charge appealed to Torrey for stone. Torrey, who had rightly appraised the granite of Cape Ann, opened a pit at Sandy Bay, and from there, and from another at Folly Cove on the Gloucester side of the town-line-to-be, supplied granite until 1842 to the harbor forts, the Charlestown and Portsmouth navy yards, and to other Federal projects. At the height of his business success he had shares in six sloops, all stone freighters, and supplied stone freighters from Quincy and Vinalhaven, Maine, both famous for their granite.

Granite became in demand everywhere for building jails, for piers, for street paving, for curbstones, for factory foundations. The industrial age was at hand, and the steam that was to sink the schooner and the clipper ship brought prosperity to Rockport. The Custom House tower in Boston, long the tallest building in the city, was built with Rockport granite and is said to be the tallest building in America without a steel frame, raised by simply piling granite block on granite block. By 1848 the granite industry was doing better than $150,000 a year. In 1853 came mechanization. A steam engine was introduced into the Wetherbee quarry to pump out the deep cuts that filled up with rain and spring water. The work of pumping had hitherto been done by hand, as was much of the hoisting, although cattle were also used to hoist as well as to haul. Labor was imported for years. Stout men from New Hampshire and Vermont, where quarrying was familiar, were housed and fed and paid by the season. When one company attempted to bring in Irish laborers from Boston during the Know-Nothing period, about mid-century, the boarding house that was to receive them was blown up more than once with gunpowder charges. But the Irish laborers came in nevertheless. In 1857 the second steam engine was imported for quarry work, and about the same time others were put aboard the sloops *John Brooks* and the *Hard Chance,* stone freighters, which with their sister ships carried granite north and south, to New York and New Orleans and even San Francisco, to Providence and Portsmouth and Boston and to Maine. In 1882 the Rockport Granite Company alone had five sloops registered in its name to carry granite from the granite piers of Rockport to the world, and several miles of railroad tracks to get the granite to the ships. All that is gone.

John Kieran, sports writer, naturalist, and genial human encyclopedia, who fled Manhattan for Rockport, puts it this way in his autobiographical memoir *Not Under Oath:*

"Rockport was well named. Before steel, reinforced concrete, aluminum and glass put granite out of the building business, the local quarries were the most famous and busiest in the country. The great pits, now filled with water and maintained as private ponds or swimming pools, furnished the granite blocks used in the construction of banks, libraries, churches, museums and halls of ivy all across the United States in the old days. The rock from Rockport went into the solidity of the huge locks of the Panama Canal.

"Silent they lie now, those pits large and small that once were loud with the din of steam drills, creaking derricks, puffing locomotives and exploding dynamite. Concrete crushed the quarryman just as ruthlessly as the automobile ran over the village blacksmith. Except for one lone quarry that turns out—cut by flame now—curbstones for streets and headstones for burial lots, the Stone Age of Rockport is over. A few houses of native granite and occasional bits of fine stonework in the form of doorsteps or garden walls are all the visible relics of a lost art and a vanished industry."

The granite taken from the Johnson quarry by a Providence company is cut in prodigious blocks and shipped by truck to Rhode Island to be finished. Finns, brought in because of their skill in stonecutting, and despite their radical politics, have turned contractor, stone mason, schoolteacher, author and clerk. Everywhere in Rockport and Pigeon Cove are white clapboarded houses on elm-shaded or maple-lined streets, all with carefully tended back yards, or manicured lawns that run down to the sea. The rims of the quarries are crowned with cottages, and the spring water that fills the deep cuts makes prized swimming pools, privately owned, some shared by families, others the sequestered rendezvous of tanned and naked boys diving from the high ledges into the clear, cool depths of fresh water, which is, in almost all cases, warmer than the Atlantic currents at the beaches the town boasts, few in number despite its length of coastline.

The folds of granite, the geometric edges left by the saws, the shades of color given by the mixing of minerals in the granite or by rusting machinery, are tempting subjects for a painter's brush. So is the sea. So are the ships, today mostly pleasure craft, but with a good percentage of lobster boats. So are the tackle and gear of the fishermen and the shacks (now converted to studios and shops) where they stored their gear at day's end before they walked back to their gardens and their homes. Rockport was fated to be an art colony. Gilbert T. Margeson was the first artist to come in and set up a studio. He had to moonlight, and so he sold artists' supplies, ran a stationery shop, and even turned his hand to telegraphy. That was in 1873. Others soon followed.

For the first three decades of the twentieth century, the artists streamed into Rockport each summer. More and more took up permanent residence. In 1929, prosperous like everyone else, the artists, through the Rockport Art Association, then about eight years old, bought the Old Tavern on Main Street, once the home of Captain Josiah Haskell, sometime a public house operated by Caleb Norwood and agglutinated with additions. The original structure was built in the late eighteenth century, and it has style. The Art Association refurbished the rooms and walls to receive paintings for exhibition and built an additional gallery in the rear. The Association made the town more notable for its art than for its granite, and most people today, thinking of Rockport, think "art colony" before they think "granite town." Macadam, cement and steel have replaced granite for highways, piers and buildings. Oil on canvas is immortal, *ars longa, lapis breva,* or to put it another way, *Sic transit gloria saxi.*

The sea leads men to fish and the fish lead men to the by-products—glues, fertilizers, cat food—made from the gurry. Sailing ships drive men to manufacture the necessaries for outfitting them. Thus in Rockport men were quarrying mooring stones soon after they found a harbor. *Saga of Cape Ann,* coauthored by Harvard professor Melvin Copeland and one of the Cape's distinguished naturalists, Elliott Rogers, tells how moorings were made in the wilderness, so to speak, before men were able economically to fashion iron to their will. They drilled a hole through the center of an enormous stone, and then uprooted an oak tree, having sawed through the bole. Next they thrust the bole through the hole, which, having been cut to size, received the bole but would not permit the dangling roots to go through. The mooring line was tied to the bole, and stone and bole thrown into the waters of the haven. The oak, always submerged, would last for years. The blocks were big enough to anchor the *Arbella*. If any ship was wrenched from such a mooring, it was not because the anchor dragged, but because a line snapped. The sea, then, not only led to fishing; it also led to quarrying. But the ships required sails and line, and that led to weaving. The Rockport Steam Duck factory was built of Rockport refuse granite (which in 1847 cost fifty cents a ton delivered), and in 1848 machinery was brought in from Taunton, Massachusetts, a town which is famous for its iron foundries and which still, in the speech of the man on the street, clings to the old English pronunciation of its name—Tahnton. In 1849 the factory was producing duck sheeting, twine and yarn, thirty tons of which in one order went to a company in Essex to make fishing line for the fleets of Gloucester. Batting was also made from the waste cotton of the mill. In 1883 the mill burned down in the biggest fire in the history of the town.

The duck factory was not the first factory in Rockport. Long before that an isinglass factory had begun operations, using the air bladders of the fish that were brought ashore. The word "isinglass," which came to be associated with a type of translucent mica, etymologically has nothing to do with "glass" but is most likely a corruption of the German word "hausenblase," meaning "sturgeon's bladders." A semitransparent gelatin used as a clarifying agent in cider, beer and jellies, it was a red-hot item in the days when Grandmother preserved the summer's fruits against the cold winter days, and Grandpa wanted an ale that sparkled when held to the light. The last isinglass factory on Cape Ann was torn down less than a decade ago. The sounds (air bladders) of hake and cod were excellent for making isinglass, and the business prospered. That, too, has gone. Ebenezer Pool, the antiquarian (there were as in Essex a number by the same name), has told in his journal (on which all Rockport and Cape

Ann historians rely) how the sounds were ground between iron rollers similar to those used by brewers, two men to two rollers. The factories are all gone, except the Cape Ann Tool Company, and it runs, fortunately for its neighbors who want to sleep, only sporadically.

If there is a historical resonance between Rockport's young men with long hair going off to war, and cutting their hair off for the sake of George Washington (who preferred a wig), there is a much more pertinent bit of Rockport history in this age of ours which is deemed to flaunt the laws even to violence.

Seaports are traditionally hard-drinking centers, and Gloucester and Sandy Bay in the nineteenth century were no exception. This can occasion an understandable reaction, and as early as 1814 some citizens of Sandy Bay protested publicly at the abuses of the law being winked at in Gloucester. The following year, a temperance society of sorts was formed in which the members solemnly swore "to abstain from an excessive use of ardent spirits . . ."—showing in the word "excessive" a true Yankee sense of qualification or hedging. This group dissolved, but in 1841 Rockport citizens formed a local chapter of a national total abstinence society. This lasted seven years. Even after it folded, the interest in the temperance movement continued. A new organization seemed to spring up each time one died.

The abuses continued, of course, and one lady, by name Hannah Jumper, had a good deal to say against ardent spirits, and proved herself an ardent spirit indeed. The most violent result of her protestations occurred on July 8, 1856, when two hundred men and women, with the women far outnumbering the men, marched through the town, armed with hatchets, to raid one place after another where liquor was being, or had been, sold illegally or even legally. If the shops or houses were closed, they forced the doors and "once within the premises," the historians say, "seized casks, demijohns, jugs and bottles that contained the bane of their happiness and emptied their contents into the street occasionally making use of the hatchets (with which they were liberally supplied) to hasten the flow of the hated liquid." The official history does not record, but tradition has attested, that young men and old knelt in the streets to lap up the fire-water. In all, the women raided thirteen places, quite illegally, marched to the main square, congratulated themselves and went home. There is no evidence that the local authorities were courageous enough to interfere at all. Hannah Jumper, credited with instigating the action, did not participate, according to William D. Hoyt, curator of the Sandy Bay Historical Society. Some of the victims instituted legal action.

A witness for the defendants testified: "There were many men there, and almost all the women in Rockport—all who could walk or move on crutches. All the men appeared to be approving, except the rumsellers; I heard no objection. The selectmen, the ministers, deacons, policemen were present; none of them forbade what was done, but all was peace and harmony. They appeared to be very happy, and the shouts came up from the gentlemen. The justices of the peace were there; everything that could walk. We determined to carry it through and destroy all the liquor."

The women were twice brought before the courts, and twice acquitted. When the storekeepers brought an action of tort against them, their defense attorneys contended that the women were "abating a public nuisance." The jury found for the women. It was, as today, a case of the aggrieved taking the law into their own hands rather than waiting for the slow processes of justice to work through the public law enforcement agencies. Today's militant extremists have some historical precedents.

Rockport, perhaps not so curiously, is still dry today. Residents must buy their liquor elsewhere if they want it on their tables, and must journey to Gloucester if they want to belly up to a bar. As it so happens, a good deal of wisdom lies in the exercise of what the law calls local option in the prohibition against the sale of liquor in the town. Because it is a most desirable summer resort, only a little more than an hour away from Boston by major highways, and because it is an art colony, the usual number of barrooms, taverns or saloons, or even restaurants selling liquor, could turn the town into a honky-tonk, kick up the accident rate, and leave it with a reputation as unpalatable as that of Provincetown on the tip of Cape Cod. As it is, some of the finest food served in the northeast corner of Massachusetts is served in Rockport, where the restaurateurs realize that their reputation depends not on the strength of their drinks but the expertise they show in their cuisine.

As it is, Rockport is made hideous in midsummer by the week-end traffic. The narrow streets were made for fishermen in their rubber boots to walk home; they curve and turn and narrow as they go. Route 127 is a loop of highway around Cape Ann, ringing Rockport completely, and as charming a drive as one could find when the weather is right and the road not crowded. But on a Saturday or Sunday afternoon in the summer season, no resident of Rockport except the feeble-minded would dream of taking his automobile into town, or perhaps even walking there. The "trippers"—those motorists down for the day —crowd all the shops and galleries; their automobiles take up every available parking space, pre-empt the parking meters, and foul the air. When it is not crowded, Rockport is one of the loveliest of villages to walk through, to visit, to dine in, to photograph, to inhabit.

The Rockport Art Association, with a large membership not only of artists but of patrons, associate members and supporters, serves almost as a civic center, for years ran an all-too-popular costume ball, and now runs each Christmas a truly moving and magnificent pageant, in which the Nativity of Christ, with an-

gels, wise men, shepherds, and animals, is re-enacted in solemn
procession through the streets, with readings along the way
from the Evangelists. It is a unique commemoration of the season. The R.A.A. as an association has served the town well, although there is a question as to how well it is serving the holy
cause of art.

Experimental painting has long been discouraged in Rockport, and to thumb through the catalogues of the annual shows
(1970 is the fiftieth annual) is to see the same tired old subjects
treated and retreated *ad nauseam*. Conventional representational pictures are the specialty of Rockport, and one result has
been that the avant-garde, the vigorous, the powerful have fled
to Provincetown or other parts where expressionism is not considered a dirty word, or acrylics regarded with horror.

White-topped breakers crashing against the gray and brown
rocks of the Cape Ann shoreline, green-hulled draggers tied up
at the Gloucester wharves, a lobsterman hauling his traps or
standing on the shore by a dory in his sou'westers (although
dories are seldom seen today), a dragger churning home with
gulls fluttering above it, boats on the ways, perhaps being painted
or calked, a wrecked boat on the beach, low tide, high tide,
summer surf, winter surf, various edifices of Rockport or
Gloucester, the eternal bouquet or basket of fruit, the usual
portraits—such is the fare. Not that some of it isn't good; some
of it is very good. But a number of artists cannot get their best
work past the juries, and the Rockport Art Association has yet to
run a show where the members are permitted to show whatever
they damn well please, rather than having their offerings fil-
tered through a jury which year after year manages a majority
vote that loves the traditional, cannot discard the ordinary, and
is overwhelmingly kind to the common. Rothko would get nowhere here; or Munch, or Dali, or Motherwell, or Magritte, or
Ben Nicholson. No assemblage has ever made it, and a collage

is a rarity. One wonders how much the painting scene in Rockport has been dominated and colored by necessity of economics —of having to hold the level of painting to the taste and pocketbooks of the kind of people who drive to the beach for a day and buy a painting as an afterthought because to do so isn't anywhere near so expensive as they expected.

The Association was warned long ago by one of their own number, Parker Perkins, "Paint the dollar sign and you're done for." But paint the dollar sign too many of them do, pictures that they know the banks and restaurants will want to hang, pictures that will not have colors so loud the R.A.A. judges will pass them over lest they end up with an "uneven" wall, pictures that have sold before and will sell again.

The symbol of Rockport's art world is a red-stained fisherman's shack set on a granite pier jutting into the harbor, a readily observable landmark and a tempting subject for a post card. Painted innumerable times, perhaps more than any other building in America, it is known far and wide as "Motif #1," a name given it many years ago by a distinguished artist and teacher of art, Lester G. Hornby, who, confronted with a painting of it by one of his pupils, reportedly cried out, "What—Motif #1 again!" In 1923 Charles Boardman Hawes published *Gloucester, by Land and Sea,* and Hornby illustrated it with one water color as a frontispiece and a number of highly skillful pencil sketches. The water color shows two men reclining beside Motif #1. Ten years later a float representing the famous shack rode off with the prize at the American Legion's National Convention. It is the signature of the town—seen in silhouette in every other advertisement, offered in oils and water color at every other gallery. No wonder the art colony was once told that if it wished to take art seriously, the first thing it should do was to burn down Motif #1.

Like many another New England town, Rockport has a sturdy

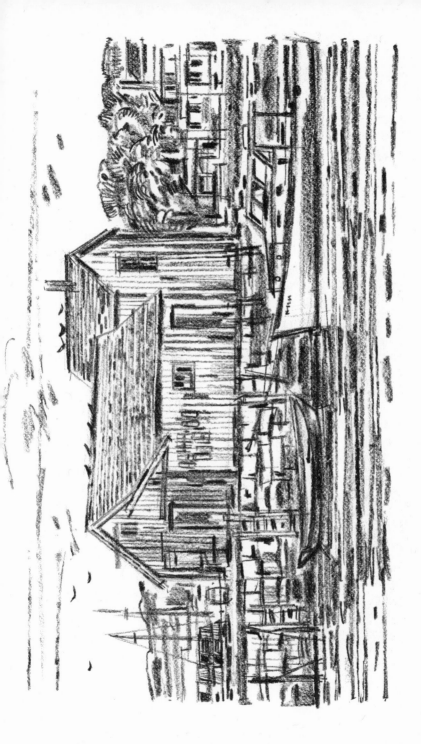

conservative disposition that does not like change, innovation or instruction. When the Reverend Frank Potter, an Episcopal priest, erudite and interested, began a series of exhibitions, seminars and lectures on the relationship of art and religion, he finally left in discouragement. One of the whispered complaints against him was that he brought too many paintings by non-R.A.A. people to his walls, and paintings that were too far out. Another attempt by a retired educator and psychiatrist to get a cultural center operating in an unused Coast Guard building foundered on similar apathy and resentment. Rockport is content to be as it is, and its artists to seek the spiritus eternitatis only in the traditional forms.

Charles Olson, the late distinguished poet and an authority on Cape Ann, scorned Rockport's conservatism, referred to the town as a "Frigid Provincetown," and suggested cutting it adrift from the Cape and letting it float away. Equally significant is the fact that the greatest painters who have painted on Cape Ann have found their inspiration not in the Rockport art colony or Rockport's headlands but in Gloucester Harbor, Gloucester streets and Gloucester ships. To name a few: Fitz Hugh Lane, Winslow Homer, John Sloan, Marsden Hartley, Childe Hassam, Gordon Grant, and Stuart Davis, men who have put their names into the major histories of American painting.

The Association has the avowed purpose of encouraging and promoting "the development and appreciation of the graphic arts and sculpture in Rockport and the Cape Ann area through free exhibitions, practice groups, lectures and classes," and has been fulfilling that purpose to a degree for the past fifty years. Under Harriet Matson, curator, and John C. Pettibone, an assistant, the operation is marked by courtesy and efficiency. Two hundred exhibiting artists are in the membership, which sets the condition that they have painted, sketched or worked in Rockport for a brief period of their careers. Six—Henry Gasser,

Aldro Hibbard, William Meyerowitz, John C. Fellew, Umberto
Romano and Stow Wengenroth—are members of the National
Academy of Design, but Hibbard, one of the founders of the Association and in every sense a grand old man, is the only one
whose studio remains in Rockport, and his brushes more often
than not turn to New Hampshire's hills and Vermont's maple
sirup country. Meyerowitz, one of the major figures on Cape
Ann, is in Gloucester. Umberto Romano was in Gloucester at
the Rocky Neck colony, which is more openminded, but he fled
that for Provincetown. Four associates of the N.A.D.—Harry
Ballinger, Tom Nicholas, Jerri Ricci and Don Stone—are Rockport figures. Of these, Stone, working in traditional representational forms, is showing strength enough to infuse them with
spirit that elevates and gives a name to things. Some artists in
Rockport—Joseph Jeswald, for example—have turned their
backs on the R.A.A., but manage to find satisfactory reception
both at home and afield. What members of the prestigious National Institute of Arts reside on Cape Ann are in Gloucester or
Manchester.

The fiftieth year is a climacteric for a man or an organization,
and the Rockport Art Association in its second beginning may
find a new direction, encourage all the aesthetic expression its
members are capable of, and bring the art critics motoring ea-
gerly to Cape Ann's old Fifth Parish rather than straining their
texts to smother a "ho-hum."

What has hurt in part is the economics. Fifty years ago when
Harrison Cady, that amusing, talented and delightful man
whose drawings of Peter Rabbit fixed that character's image in
the minds of several generations, came to Rockport, rents were
low, the shops in the town were meant to serve the people of
the town and not lure in "trippers," and the rural aspects of the
town were more evident than they are today. A young artist
seeking to find his medium and his milieu could live cheaply,

work undisturbed, and find fellow artists to chin with—for artists are gregarious people, much more so than poets or novelists. But the very publicity they gave the town, by emphasizing its beauty in their work, has brought to the town a continuing flow of elderly persons seeking a pleasant seaside place to retire and live out their retirement in an atmosphere of relaxation and an ambiance of beauty. The result has been a rise in rents. The artist cannot afford to live in Rockport and experiment unless he has a private income or sells very well. The economic grip doesn't permit him to find his own milieu, his own strength, but drives him into following in the footsteps of someone else who has prospered albeit with banalities. The artist ends up painting not what he sees, but what someone else has seen and put on canvas and sold. Hence the dreadful *déjà vu* that descends on a visitor taking in all but a few Rockport galleries.

⇗ 6 ⇖

"Cape Ann-side" Towns

To the west of the arbitrary line we have selected as the demar-
cation of Cape Ann lies a string of towns and cities which ancient travelers casually might well have included under the appellation "Cape Ann-side." All of them were at one time
seaports, all built ships, all have distinguished maritime histories, and if sand and silt have choked their rivers and closed
their harbors to major shipping, they all shelter and mother
small craft today and luxuriate in their past.

At the northernmost point of our concern is the Merrimack
River, spelled with a *k* in one place and without it in another.
On its south side at its mouth stand Newburyport and the northern tip of Plum Island, the bulk of which today is a wildlife
sanctuary and all of which we shall leave to another chapter on
nature and the islands of Cape Ann.

The roll call of the cities and towns as we move south from
Newburyport is Newbury; Rowley; Ipswich (the greater part of
which lies west of our line); Hamilton, its offspring; Wenham
and Beverly, both of which were once part of Salem; and then,
like a great anchor at the end to stop the whole from floating
out to sea, historic, storied Salem and once rowdy and raffish,
but now fashionable and yacht-minded, Marblehead, two sepa-

rate communities which, simple geography would designate, should be one.

This buffer of municipalities, much of it even richer in history than the heart of Cape Ann, has within its precincts some of the lordliest estates, the most beautiful architecture, the loveliest pastureland, meadows, parks, rivers, streams, lakes and ponds to be found in America. A five-foot shelf of books could be written about Salem alone, and Newburyport would lend itself to three or four volumes.

These two cities, one the oldest in Massachusetts and one the smallest (in population), have much in common besides bracketing, as they do, Cape Ann on the north and south. In area they are about of a size, Newburyport having 8.3 square miles and Salem 7.99 square miles; each is about one-third the size of Gloucester, which sits almost equidistant between them, and which, while it never had their prosperity, has stubbornly retained its character.

Salem was settled in 1626 by Roger Conant, a salter, whose ninth child was named Exercise (which tells us a good deal about the Puritan mind). It was incorporated as a town in 1630. Here was formed the first Congregational church. Until 1764 Newburyport was part of the town of Newbury, but even as Essex prospered away from Ipswich, so Newburyport prospered away from Newbury. Shipbuilding did it, with the Merrimack River a supply line for oak and pine. Both Salem and Newburyport had good harbors, both of which were abandoned with the advent of steam, neither having sufficient depth for steel bottoms. Newburyport had only 7-foot clearance at low tide, Salem little more.

In 1775 both cities were famous for shipbuilding, both stood on the Boston Post Road, and both were served by the stagecoach. Both were famous also for the privateers they sent to sea in the Revolution and later in the War of 1812. Before the Revolution both prospered as seaports, serving England and English ports to the north and as far away as the West Indies, and both suffered as a result of British shipping restrictions afterward. Both did their share of smuggling. Both revived after a decade of depression, and both were hurt again by the War of 1812 Like all American ports, following the Molasses Act they were smuggling centers, particularly Newburyport, which manufactured and still produces rum, and good rum, too. Both of them were swept by conflagrations, Newburyport in 1811 when five acres were leveled and Salem one hundred years later. Both were badly hurt commercially by the Erie Canal and the Middlesex Canal, which took freight away from East Coast shipping and from Post Road transportation, since a horse could draw along water one hundred times the weight it could haul in a wagon. Both cities were famous for centuries, and still are, for the ships and houses they built. John Paul Jones's ship the *Alliance* was launched in the Merrimack; *Cleopatra's Barge*, the gorgeous first ocean-cruising yacht in America, was a Salem product. Between 1681 and 1741, 107 ships went down the ways at the rum capital on the Merrimack. For a long time Newburyport had been exporting more barrel staves to the world than any other American port. It was there that Donald McKay, perhaps the greatest clipper ship builder of them all, made his reputation before moving on to his famous East Boston yard, where he built the fastest clipper ships the world has known, some of which attained twenty-one knots, and one of which sailed 436 nautical miles in a single day. It was a long time before a steamship did as well, and even when steamships were everywhere, clippers were preferred for long voyages. But by McKay's day everything was moving to Boston, and Newburyport and Salem were falling into decay. Salem was stubborn, however, and it was not until 1893 that the last square-rigger out of that port struck its colors. Both cities turned to manufacturing; both tried cotton. Salem succeeded and Newburyport failed, but managed to do something with silverware. The great cotton centers were elsewhere.

The two cities are most celebrated today for their magnificent Federal architecture, stalwart square, stately mansions fronting the street, their gardens behind them, their captains' walks on their roofs, built by men whose ships bore the Stars and Stripes —Old Glory—into every port in the West Indies and the Far East. These cities were in their palmy days during the most intense period of American nationalism. The men from them and Cape Ann showed the British navy how to sail ships and how to fight them. The *Wasp* was built at Newburyport (the only Navy vessel built there for the War of 1812) and cruised the English Channel, in the very teeth of the enemy, to capture thirteen British merchant ships before mysteriously disappearing with all hands and never a trace of wreckage, thus providing years of gossip for the Newburyport society belles who had danced on her decks at the launching party. As much as the war hurt them (and Jefferson's Embargo before it), the people of Cape Ann and the neighboring communities could still take pride in United States naval victories and the magnificent seamanship of their local heroes. They were proud of their tradition. After all, Cape Ann men had helped man the first ships to serve under General Washington in the Revolutionary War.

Newburyport, through its urban redevelopment plans, is seeking to restore some of its historic water front. When it was threatened with destruction recently, citizens roused themselves and demanded that it be preserved. When one sees what is being done to restore, refurbish and put to attractive use less picturesque properties in newer sections of the country, one gasps at the indifference of the residents and the lack of imagination of the real estate developers along the New England coastline. With its old brick warehouses, Newburyport could build a memorial to its great days that would in turn attract more tourists in a week than the city now sees in a year.

Long ago the city lost its most curious mansion, the home of Lord Timothy Dexter, who made his fortune during and after the Revolution by buying up paper money for a fraction of its cost and then cashing it full value when the United States adopted Alexander Hamilton's banking system. Dexter was a near illiterate with a sharp tongue and a cunning mind, who awarded himself the title "Lord" and built himself a gaudy mansion ringed with polychrome statues of the Founding Fathers.

Dexter brought his city as much notoriety in his day as another eccentric, Andrew J. "Bossy" Gillis, was to bring it 150 years later. "Bossy" was an insensitive, outrageous, redheaded politician, a Republican, and basically—that is, economically—conservative, but determined to break the Yankee grip on the municipal affairs of Newburyport. He was defeated in his first and last campaigns, which spanned the decades from 1921 to 1965, but in between he was elected mayor six times. He was known as the "boy mayor," and through his antics won national attention, even appearing in vaudeville shows. He was jailed for cutting down elm trees that were not his to cut down, sued countless times, jailed again for libel, managing always to make a comfortable living for himself with a gasoline station built in violation of the zoning laws and in violation of any sense of aesthetics. No major economic accomplishments occurred under Gillis, but the class structure that preceded him toppled.

Newburyport was also the home of John P. Marquand, the novelist, whose creation, George Apley, is to many people more real than the man who created him. Marquand chose to live in Newburyport. William Lloyd Garrison chose to move out. He spent some time there editing a newspaper and trying to bring the city to life after its shipping failed, but, not succeeding, took himself to Boston, where, as the saying goes, he made a name for himself.

While Garrison was still in Newburyport, and grieving over the Negro's plight, Frederick Douglass, one of the sterling black heroes of the United States, would come to visit him. At that time the trains of the Boston and Maine had a Jim Crow system which Douglass declined to recognize. He always sat in the sections reserved for whites, and each time would be thrown out by the trainmen. Douglass was a powerful and determined man. He held so tightly to the seat he was in that when the trainmen took him out they had to take the seat with him. The Boston and Maine quit. The Jim Crow system disappeared; Douglass sat where he wished.

Newburyport boasts that it is the birthplace of the United States Coast Guard. To return for a moment to Beverly and its claim, it is the birthplace of the United States navy only if you do not put a capital N on the word. It long stood in the shadow of Salem. Roger Conant came over to Beverly from Salem, and in 1668 it was incorporated as a town, spreading along the shore of the Bass River. As with other North Shore settlements, fishing and trading became the main part of its life. Oil tankers still come to Beverly Harbor. Although crusty old John Endecott, one of the Puritan fathers, scorned it as "Beggarly," it prospered. John Balch, one of the planters who came over with Conant, built his house there in 1638, and it is still standing, second only to the Fairbanks house in Dedham as the oldest frame dwelling in America.

When the Revolution came, Beverly was to win its unique distinction. General Washington needed ships badly to harass British merchant shipping, and Beverly was to supply the first ship and sail it with honor and success. The ship was the *Han-*

nah, a schooner of seventy-eight tons burden, a hair more than 18 feet in the beam, with a deck length of 60 feet and a keel of 46 feet. She was built by Colonel John Glover of Marblehead, one of the great heroes of the Revolution, at his Beverly wharf, and was converted for naval service. She sailed under the pine-tree flag on September 5, 1775. The *Hannah* was the first of eight vessels in Washington's fleet, and six of them were built at Beverly. She mounted four four-pounders, and on her first day at sea had to elude British warships, and on the second day made history.

Of the second day, Captain Nicholas Broughton, her commander, recounted, "I saw a ship under my lee quarter; I perceived her to be a large ship. I tacked and stood back for the land; soon after I put about and stood towards her again and found her a ship of no force. I came up with her, hailed; and asked where she came from; was answered, from Piscataqua, and bound for Boston. I told him he must bear away and go to Cape Ann; but being very loth, I told him if he did not I should fire on her. On that she bore away and I have brought her safe into Cape Ann Harbour." The ship, the *Unity,* was carrying much needed naval stores as well as lumber. Cape Ann Harbour was, of course, Gloucester Harbor. To this day, the office of Harbour Master still carries the old English spelling.

The *Hannah,* however, was not in the service of the Continental navy, but of the Continental army, under the command of General George Washington. The United States Navy would come later, but who is going to cavil over Beverly's brag? Beverly is also proud of the presence of the United Shoe Machinery Corporation; electronic manufacturers; three colleges; and one of the most modern newspaper plants in the nation, as well as the state's most successful summer theater, the North Shore Music Theater, slowly building into a significant cultural center.

A bridge over the Bass River takes us to Salem. The bridge

was built with the proceeds of a lottery, or at least the first one over the river was. When Duc François Alexandre Frédéric de la Rochefoucauld-Liancourt, French philanthropist and indefatigable traveler (not to be confused with the earlier la Rochefoucauld, the epigrammatist), came through Beverly and Salem in the late eighteenth century, he unaccountably put down the length of the bridge as 15 feet, rather than 1,500. The Reverend Timothy Dwight, then president of Yale, who toured the area to correct the erroneous impressions of America given by such foreign travelers, graciously acknowledged that it must have been a typographical error.

Dr. Dwight was a stickler for such detail. He had found Beverly "decently built," the "commerce considerable," and the "fishing extensive." Today the fishing isn't extensive, but the rest is true. "Learning has, however," Dr. Dwight continued, "been an object of no great attention or encouragement in Beverly, although several very intelligent people are numbered among its inhabitants. The last two ministers, Dr. Willard and Dr. McKeen, were elected to the presidency of Harvard and Bowdoin colleges, and were both men of great respectability and worth." With three colleges within its boundaries, the city (such as it has become) can lay claim to having made learning an object of some attention since Dwight's visit.

But over the bridge to Salem. "Salem is a commercial town in the absolute sense," Dr. Dwight declared. "As a commercial town, Salem ranks next to Charleston, South Carolina, being the sixth in the United States. It is also the sixth in population. In wealth, proportioned to the number of its inhabitants, it is the first." It was not yet 1800 when he went through.

He observed that the harbor was ill-suited for such heavy commerce. "All vessels drawing more than twelve feet of water must be unladen at a distance from the town by lighters, and the wharves at low water are left dry. Nor are the encourage-

ments on the land side much greater. The produce of almost all
the interior is engrossed by Boston. The inland trade, therefore,
is of little consequence." Dr. Dwight was prescient; his observations contained within them the discernment of the disadvan-
tages that would doom Salem.

Not long after Dwight went on to Boston and Cambridge, Jefferson imposed his notorious embargo, which, with the War of
1812 that was to follow, prompted a Newburyport poet to cry
out:

> Our ships all in motion once whitened the ocean
> They sailed and returned with a cargo;
> Now doomed to decay, they have fallen a prey
> To Jefferson—worms—and embargo.

Just as Salem today far excels Newburyport in manufacturing,
so did it excel it in the heyday of the China trade and of the
clipper ships. Salem, indeed, reached such prominence that it ri-
valed Boston, New York and Philadelphia as a port. Nathaniel
Bowditch of Salem corrected the errors in the standard navigational guide used by the British navy and gave the world his
immortal book, *The New American Practical Navigator*. Salem
gave the nation its first self-made millionaire, Elias Hasket
"King" Derby, who, like many another New Englander, sent his
ships privateering during the Revolutionary War. They say he
was the only shipowner to make money at it. He made his
packet from the China trade, and his *Grand Turk*, an ex-priva-
teer, was the first Salem ship to come home from the Orient with
a bundle and show other New Englanders the way.

When the rush was on, scarcely a day went by in Salem when
a merchant ship failed to return heavy with cargo, one of them
with the officers sleeping on deck because their quarters were
filled with spices. In one three-week period, among the boats returning were seven from the West Indies, seven from the Iberian
peninsula, and three from Canton. The last three paid $53,000 in

customs duties. It was inevitable that a Salem man, George Crowninshield, in 1816 had built for himself the most luxurious of ships, *Cleopatra's Barge,* with mahogany cabins, gold and silver service, and the bow painted in variegated colors, herringbone stripes on one side, horizontal stripes on the other. When King Liholiho of Hawaii saw it, he could scarcely contain himself and gave in exchange a whole shipload of sandalwood (which sold high in China) to have it for his own. Unfortunately, he cracked it for good on a coral reef.

For Salem people the best was none too good. Samuel F. B. Morse, the portrait painter and inventor of the telegraph, was called upon to paint Crowninshield's picture, which hangs today in the Peabody Museum in Salem. As early as 1799, shipowners and captains had formed the East India Marine Society; and in 1824 they built a gray stone hall as a place to meet and to show off some of their trophies—"natural and artificial curiosities"— collected by their vessels.

In 1867 the museum was named the Peabody in honor of one of its greatest benefactors, George Peabody, the noted philanthropist. In it today one finds one of the nation's most elaborate collections of ship models, marine paintings, nautical instruments, shipping invoices, manuscripts, shipwrights' tools, portraits of merchants and captains, and innumerable exotic articles brought back from the Far East, from Indonesia, from Africa, from South America. To dazzle the imagination are displays from Tibet and Korea, from Melanesia and Micronesia, and paintings of some of the great ships that went to those lands. Ernest Dodge, the curator, has written about it all, and has re-created the trips and the role played by the great New England merchants in those exotic countries.

Almost directly across the street from the Peabody Museum stands the headquarters of the Essex Institute, a museum and a library which preserves and offers to public scrutiny half a

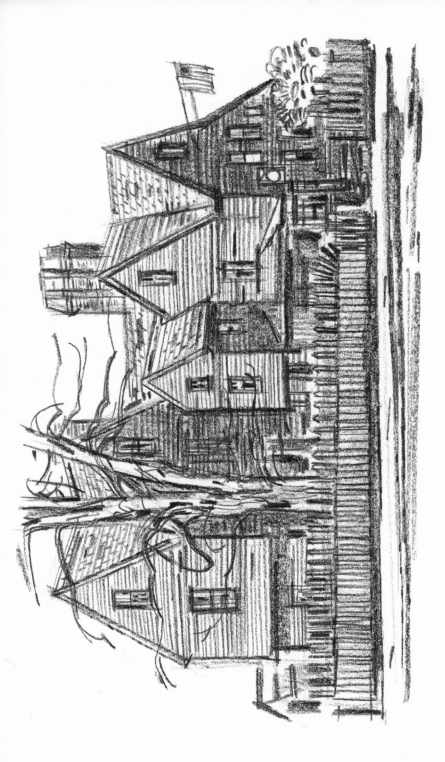

dozen historic buildings, several the work of Samuel McIntire, who was to Salem what Charles Bulfinch was to Boston, and besides that, an exquisite worker in wood, whose wheat-sheaf reliefs, urn finials and intricate moldings give Salem's great Federal mansions an incomparable touch. Both institutions are supported entirely by private endowments and private gifts.

So too is Salem's most famous house, the House of Seven Gables, immortalized by Nathaniel Hawthorne, open year-round to visitors who thrill to climb its secret staircase entered by moving an innocent-looking panel. The House of Seven Gables stands on the harbor's edge, and to its rear are the Hathaway House, built in 1682, and the Retire Becket House, built in 1655, and also Hawthorne's birthplace, moved about ten years ago from its original site on Union Street. The House of Seven Gables was built in 1668 by John Turner, and it does have seven gables. Hawthorne, of course, visited it many times. There are other houses in Salem, a score of them, which are exceptional for their beauty, their history or their age. The Pickering House has been occupied by the Pickering family for ten generations and was the home of Colonel Timothy Pickering, who served as Secretary of State under both George Washington and John Adams after serving as quartermaster general in the Continental army. The Pierce-Nichols House and the Pingree House are both owned by the Essex Institute, and both were designed by McIntire.

One could go on about Salem's historic treasures at inordinate length. Hawthorne, of course, is its most famous author, and a great bronze statue of him stands near the Essex Institute. The famous Peabody sisters, one of whom Hawthorne married, were Salem girls. Then there were Jones Very, sonneteer, eccentric and mystic; Nathaniel Bowditch, the great authority on navigation; and the Reverend William Bentley, diarist extraordinary, and the most brilliant man in the United States in his day.

Salem also had its day of shame. As Dr. Dwight on his memorable journey wrote when he approached Salem: "It would be thought unpardonable in a traveler when giving an account of Danvers if he should pass without notice the convulsion produced here in 1692 by the supposed prevalence of witchcraft." Danvers was then part of Salem.

Before that convulsion was over, fourteen women and five men were hanged, and a sixth man crushed to death with stones heaped upon him. Above that 150 more were jailed, but were freed by the governor the following year. One of the judges was John Hathorne, an ancestor of the author, and it is said that Nathaniel added the "w" to his name not merely for the flowery intimation but to dissociate himself from the worst villain of the whole episode.

The custom house where Hawthorne was employed for a while has been made a historical preserve by the Federal Government. Nearby, Derby wharf thrusts itself 2,000 feet out into the harbor, handsomely restored and preserved. Salem has a sense of its history, and yet, once again, it is almost wholly private citizens who do the caring, while state and city governments remain unimaginative, showing less concern than the Federal Government.

If Beverly boasts the first ships in the service of the Continental army, Salem boasts the first resistance to British redcoats and the first bloodshed. The confrontation occurred on February 26, 1775, at the North Bridge when 250 redcoats under the affable Colonel Thomas Leslie arrived under orders from General Thomas Gage to seize ammunition and cannon belonging to Captain Richard Derby, a wealthy Salem merchant. The townsfolk confronted the British troops, stood between them and the munitions, which indeed had been sequestered elsewhere, and sneered and slanged at the British soldiery. One of the troop lost his temper and wounded Joseph Whicher with his bayonet.

The wound was trivial but historic. Leslie did not get what he came for, and when he returned to Boston, General Gage ordered a court-martial. The stand of the good people of Salem and Beverly at the North Bridge was the first such resistance to British authority.

Colonel Leslie had landed at Marblehead when he came to seize Derby's cannon. There is a sense in which this southern anchor of "Cape Ann-side" is an integral part of this great collection of historic harbors, and a shipping history that considered the whole as one great port would catch a facet of history that is lost in the fragmentation suggested by arbitrary town lines. Marblehead today is a lovely town, constructed on the same irreducible granite that constitutes Cape Ann. Its harbor, which once had a bustling fishing industry, is today the yachting capital of the Eastern seaboard, and daily throughout the summer season sends thousands of white sails out onto the waters of Massachusetts Bay to race and otherwise disport. In winter too, for this is one of the leading frost-biting centers, innumerable dinghies with their two-man crews race over diminished courses in the coldest and foulest of winter weather. To be sure, the courses over which they race are held within the harbor, and the club launch guarantees to get racers out of the water within two minutes in the event they capsize. Two minutes is enough, and the sharp gasp of anyone going into the chilly brine is sufficient to make the most daring skipper move with greater caution for the rest of the race.

Marblehead's beginnings are almost as raffish as those of Sierra Leone. In *Massachusetts,* the WPA guide published in the 1930s, an anonymous author has caught it as well as anyone could: "Reckless, hardbitten fishermen from Cornwall and the Channel Islands settled Marblehead (Marble Harbor) in 1629 as a plantation of Salem. Their rude huts clung to the rocks like seabirds' nests. Said a Marbleheader of a later day—'Our ancestors came not here for religion. Their main end was to catch fish.' As might have been expected from such ungodliness, early Marblehead was a favorite with the powers of darkness. Many a citizen met Satan himself riding in state in a coach and four, or was chased through the streets by a corpse in a coffin. The eerie lament of the 'screeching woman of Marblehead' resounded across the harbor, and Puritan Salem hanged old 'Mammy Red' of Marblehead who knew how to turn enemies' butter to blue wool. Within a decade unruly Marblehead was without regret permitted to become a separate town, 'the greatest Towne for fishing in New England.'"

Ivan Sandrof, urbane essayist, in his book, *More Massachusetts Towns of 1840,* supplying commentary for the wood engravings of J. W. Barber, writes of Marblehead that it "is one of the most appealing of Bay State towns, taken from Salem and incorporated in 1849. Once known as Marmaracia, or Marble Harbor, its narrow, winding ways and ancient houses preserve the past. Fishing and shipping made Marblehead second only to Boston. Horny-handed Marblehead salts led by John Glover stroked muffled oars across the Delaware on the memorable night of December 25, 1776, to help seize 1,400 British and Hessians at Trenton. At war's end, Marblehead had 1,000 orphans, 500 widows, and had become the center of privateering. Marblehead sent 1,000 men to the War of 1812, and gave to history Elbridge Gerry, a signer of the Declaration of Independence and a vice-president of the United States. The most famous painting of the Revolution, 'The Spirit of '76' is here and St. Michael's (1714), one of the oldest Episcopal churches. Turning its back on the sea, Marblehead once began shoe manufacturing and other industries but two disastrous fires ruined it. Today with colorful nylon burgees snapping, Marblehead is the yachting center of the Eastern seaboard."

No community gave more to the American Revolution or suffered more because of it. Moreover, it gave the self-sacrificing hero John Glover, he who built the *Hannah*, and commanded the 21st regiment of the Massachusetts Militia, set up his headquarters in the Craigie mansion in Cambridge (where Longfellow was to do his finest work) and turned it over to Washington when the commander-in-chief came on from Virginia. Washington was to be grateful indeed to Glover during that famous crossing of the Delaware at McKonkey's Ferry. Thirty-foot freight boats bore the Continental troops across, each, as Samuel Eliot Morison points out, "manned by four or five men of Colonel Glover's webfooted Marblehead regiment."

The controversy surrounding the famous painting "The Spirit of '76" is a long story in itself and better told elsewhere. However, there are several versions, and Marblehead has to fight hard to demonstrate that its copy is the original. To stand before it, however, whatever its provenance, is to feel a patriotic twinge. It is a most impressive canvas.

With its winding streets, sudden corners, narrow lanes slipping down to the shore, Marblehead's old quarter is one of the most picturesque settlements north of Boston. If its new sections look like nothing more than suburbia, suburbia can look most attractive. The town is proud of its past and proud of its polish, and harbors a number of distinguished authors and artists, not least among them Harry Kemelman, author of *Friday the Rabbi Slept Late* and *Saturday the Rabbi Went Hungry*, detective stories with distinction, and Samuel Chamberlain, etcher extraordinary, whose photographs of New England are internationally celebrated, and whose book *Etched in Sunlight,* a collection of his etchings showing his architectural training, is perhaps the town's great twentieth-century contribution to art.

But one must always return to Salem. It has too much to offer. We have skimped the Peabody Museum and scanted the Essex Institute. We have forgotten William Driver, an early nine-

teenth-century sea captain from Salem who has the distinction
of having invented the name "Old Glory" for the American flag,
a sobriquet casually given that has stuck. We have also forgotten or neglected Salem's connection with the pine-tree flag
which was carried by the local militia when they marched out
to confront Colonel Leslie at the North Bridge and which was
flown from the mast of the *Hannah* when it sailed. The pine tree
on the flag was, of course, intimately connected with the shipbuilding of Cape Ann, for it was American shipwrights who
taught the British navy the value of pine in boat building, and
His Majesty's agents used to mark off in the forests of New England those trees that were reserved for the crown. The ship-
builders of Salem, Essex and Newburyport, I'm afraid, did not
always respect those markings. But they did respect the pine
tree; and not only did they put it on their flag, they put it on
their shilling.

All literate Americans immediately associate Nathaniel Hawthorne with Salem. Too few know of one of Salem's greatest figures, the Reverend William Bentley, pastor of the East Church
from 1783 to 1819, a twentieth-century man in a parochial age,
an ecumenist before the word was coined, and one of the most
monumental diarists of his age. The four volumes of his diaries
have been lush source material for historians ever since. He was
the outstanding scholar and linguist in the colonies, a Unitarian
before there was a Unitarian church, a Jeffersonian when his fellow clergymen were all Federalists, a true Republican when too
many were still hankering for an aristocracy, a man of broad
sympathies in an age cruelly partisan in its religious views. He
was a scholar when ordination was becoming simply one's own
inspiration.

He refused the presidency of the University of Virginia when
Jefferson offered it to him, saying that he preferred to stay with
his flock. He missed scarcely a ship launching when Salem was

a great port; and he was host to almost every famous man who
visited the city in the days of his pastorate. Best of all, he was
an accurate observer, the prime talent we seek in any diarist.

Let us give some of the flavor of his diary by quoting a passage dated June 29, 1802:

"Having long proposed to visit Cape Ann, I went down in the
Stage driven by Mr. Low. In passing Mingo's Beach we observed the spot where two negroes passed their Chaise back-
wards over a bank 15 feet, without loss of their lives. They were
in the act of opening a new road round the great hill in
Manchester, which is so steep & rough, as to be almost impass-
able. We observed a great plenty of the Kalmia, both Latifolia
& augustifolia, or the American laurel. The Pond lilies were
also in bloom & afford a most pleasing sight in the ponds. I
reached the harbour & Mr. Low kindly conveyed me to the
mills in Uppertown, Roger's Parish, where I found my friend
Capt. John Gibaut, & his Father & Mother, to whom my visit
was directed. We found men blowing rocks in this rough road,
which continually is becoming better from the great labour bestowed upon it. After Tea we visited the Mill, & saw the new
stones drawn from Danvers, which of a less diameter moved
with a much greater velocity than the other stones, the upper
stone being above two tons weight. We visited the new road cut
through the farm which communicates with the road to Gee's
point at which the branches of Squam and Mill rivers seperate
& form, & we returned by saw mill lane. On this road Capt.
Gibaut has bought a small lot of land with a farm house. This
was once a flourishing part of the Town & has a great depth of
water. A Mr. Wheeler lives on the point." Wheeler's Point is a
bright summer colony to this day in Gloucester. Salem can be
proud indeed of the Reverend Mr. Bentley, a benign bachelor,
and man of parts. You can visit the room he occupied for years

in the Crowninshield-Bentley House, now located at Essex Street and Washington Square West. The house is owned by the Essex Institute.

Salem is one city where the Federal Government has shown some interest in preserving historic sites. The Salem Maritime National Historic Site covers nine acres bordering on Salem Harbor, not too far from the haunted settlement of the House of Seven Gables (settlement is the right word, as a matter of fact, since a social service of the settlement variety is connected with the house). The oldest brick house in Salem, Derby House, and the Hawkes House and Rum Shop welcome visitors regularly. The city of Salem contributes the services of one constable to the Essex Institute and that's about it, but, as in Ipswich, the sense of history is sinking into the minds of the residents, and the future should be brighter. In the past, such institutions as the Essex Institute and the Peabody Museum (as well as an old automobile museum which recently burned) were maintained solely by private citizens of extended means who were willing and eager to take on certain enterprises and give them support. Too often a social whirl attended such sustaining membership, and the general public felt itself excluded, if it was not actually so excluded. But the private fortunes are diminishing, and the tax laws out of Washington are becoming less and less imaginative. If the Federal Government does not recognize the social value of permitting private fortunes to devote themselves to such enterprises as the maintenance of historic monuments, the stocking of museums, the editing of manuscript collections and the like, then the Federal Government will have to take on the burden. The results will be less desirable than what we have now in such a city as Salem, because the caprice of human interests is what often gives character to such collections as the Smithsonian in Washington, for example. On a lesser scale but even more worthy, the Peabody Museum and the Essex Institute in Salem, and other comparable institutions on Cape Ann, need dollars.

Ipswich has been fortunate in the foresight of its planners, who have worked out an agreement with the Federal Government for the refurbishing, restoration and repair of the pre-Revolutionary homes of the town. Salem needs similar interest on the part of the Federal Government, the Commonwealth of Massachusetts and the local government. One can conceive with dread a future in which the oil wells of Texas will deplete New England of its antiquities just as the New World bought up art treasures of the Old World, or the West, the riches of the East. New England needs an awareness of itself, and there is no better place for that awareness to begin to burgeon than on history-rich Cape Ann and among its storied neighbors.

⊰ 7 ⊱

Gloucestermen versus Nova Scotia

In the year 1895, the House of Representatives of the Great and General Court of the Commonwealth of Massachusetts was concerned with the "Sacred Cod," "quaintly wrought in wood and painted to life," which for more than one hundred years had hung in the old House Chamber in the Bulfinch State House, as the Bay State capitol is called. The representatives were about to move from their old quarters to their new chamber in the gray stone extension which had been added to the original building. Some time before, the House had appointed a committee to prepare a history of the unique emblem. The representative from Rockport, Loring Woodfall, introduced an order that the Sacred Cod be hung in a suitable place over the Speaker's Chair. Three days later the order was debated and adopted.

The codfish was rehung and still hangs, not painted to the life, but in gold. Once burned, once stolen by Harvard students, it has either been remade or returned. In the Massachusetts Bay Colony's House of Assembly, it hung as early as 1773, for in that year Thomas Crafts, Jr., submitted a bill for fifteen shillings "to painting Codfish." That particular cod replica disappeared, presumably snatched by a retreating English redcoat as a war souvenir. The original is believed to have been carved by John Welch in the mid-eighteenth century. As historians have pointed out, the cod was to Massachusetts what wool was to England or tobacco to Virginia.

"The first product of American industry exported from Massachusetts," wrote the House committee on the history of the Emblem of the Codfish, "was a cargo of fish." The authors then added: "Even the neighboring colony at Plymouth seems at first to have depended upon Cape Ann for a supply of fish."

As early as 1634 a merchant of the New World had eight boats fishing out of Marblehead. All Cape Ann was alive with fishing vessels, and the waters offshore seethed with their wakes. For a long while Marblehead (southwest of Gloucester Harbor) led the way, but on the eve of the Revolution Gloucester had seventy ships in the harbor. It wasn't until the middle of the nineteenth century that Gloucester's pre-eminence made it supremely the queen of ports. Whaling was left to the ports south of Boston—New Bedford and Nantucket taking the lead. A few whalers went out of the North Shore but not successfully, the last of them the *Mt. Wollaston*. Whaling, to which Edmund Burke turned his famous phrases, ran ahead of codfishing for a while, but when whaling was in its death throes, the Gloucester fleet's great days were still before it.

What the Revolutionary War and the War of 1812 did that most hurt Cape Ann fisheries, aside from destroying ships, was to close to them the markets in the West Indies. Before the Revolution, Gloucestermen had unrestricted trade with the British ports. Afterward they found them closed. Even then a certain amount of illicit trade was carried on, as it had been with French and Spanish ports closed to Gloucester ships when Cape Ann was a British colony. Thus in the Revolutionary War and the War of 1812, a great number of Cape Ann fishermen from Newburyport on the north to Marblehead on the south went into the naval forces of the Revolutionary colonies or the newly formed United States Navy, or became, with disputed financial results, privateers, or better, smugglers. We have seen the role that Beverly played in giving George Washington and the Continental army a naval arm.

When the Treaty of Paris, which closed the American Revolution, was being negotiated, the chief issue became the North Atlantic fisheries, the use of the Banquereau and the Grand Banks. John Adams, one of the five negotiators, refused to sign unless the men of Cape Ann and Massachusetts retained their ancient right not only to the high seas (which England would have made only a privilege) but also to traditional uses within the territorial waters of the British possessions in the north. Adams won what has been conceded a prime diplomatic victory. The men of Gloucester were still able to sail to the Grand Banks, fish within Canadian territorial waters, and land in uninhabited sections of Nova Scotia and Labrador to cut and cure the fish they had caught. They were not granted the same privilege in Newfoundland; that was reserved for British subjects. It is not fair to say that the United States never lost a war or won a treaty, because John Adams won that one.

From the end of the Revolution until the War of 1812, the men of Cape Ann enjoyed relative freedom on the fishing banks, although not much prosperity. The Revolution had annihilated not only the Gloucester fishing fleet but its merchant ships, and the rebuilding was slow. But another British abuse was growing.

The men of Cape Ann did their part on the gundecks in both wars. We have seen Cape Ann men manning Washington's first ships, and we should remember that the men of Marblehead rowed his army across the Delaware River. Gloucester men were aboard the *Constitution*, which so distinguished itself in battle as to leave English faces red for two generations. But Cape Ann fishermen were, generally speaking, not officers. They were too independent a breed of cat to welcome the cat-o'-nine-tails or the brutal discipline of the quarterdeck in the early nineteenth century. If they did not relish service in the United States Navy, they resented even more impressment into British service. Bad as conditions aboard any naval vessel may have been in those years, conditions aboard a British man-of-war were worst of all. The British officer was a gentleman (and a brute), and the able seaman—the man before the mast—was nothing. The British courts offered felons jail or service in His Majesty's navy, and the wise ones chose jail. The kangaroo courts in a British jail were probably more humane than justice before the mast on a British man-of-war. Thus when ten thousand men were impressed into the British navy from American ships (more than six thousand specific cases were submitted by the American government to the British), the American temper was raw. In brief, the average American seaman, kidnaped from his own ship to a British warship, or, indeed, a deserter from the British navy seized from a fishing vessel or a merchant ship out of Cape Ann, promptly declared, to bring a modern advertising slogan to bear, "I'd rather fight than switch." The United States of America declared war on June 18, 1812. Fight they did.

America won that war, but, so far as Cape Ann fishermen were concerned, lost the peace. John Quincy Adams, who, by the way, had been trained in the law in Newburyport, determined as he was, could not secure the confirmation of rights to the fisheries as had his father. The best he could do was sign a treaty that did not overtly abandon them. The result for Cape Ann fishermen was almost a century of conflict with authorities in Canada.

The salience of the North Atlantic fisheries was demonstrated by the Treaty of Ghent. The British were insistent on taking back from the United States of America what John Adams had won at the Treaty of Paris. In the Treaty of Paris, however, the Americans, having won rights and privileges to the territorial waters of Canada, had granted the British navigational rights in the Mississippi River. Those rights were inestimably more important in 1814 (because of the Louisiana Purchase) than they had been in 1783. That was the issue on which the fishery rights stumbled. Henry Clay was determined that the Treaty signed at Ghent should not confirm those river rights for the British. John Quincy Adams (whose father's genius had meant so much at the Treaty of Paris) was determined that the Treaty of Ghent should not abandon the fisheries. They finally finessed the subject; they didn't mention it at all, and Britain lost her rights in the Mississippi. The result for Cape Ann fishermen meant tribulations until early in the twentieth century the Permanent Court of Arbitration at The Hague settled the matter, it is hoped, forever.

In the meantime, Gloucester men were frequently being fined by Newfoundland authorities, or having their ships impounded. Chasing a school of mackerel, on the Grand Banks or nearby, a Gloucester schooner might well run over, or drift over, the three-mile limit. Where is the three-mile limit? Three miles out from that promontory or that shore? If the Gloucestermen were indifferent as to where it was, so were Newfoundland policing agents eager for fees. Cape Ann men had their ships impounded when they had been guilty of no crime, and the Canadian courts were all too ready to accept the word of their agents. The conflicts were innumerable and interminable.

In 1818 England and her former colonies got together to try to straighten out the matter of the fisheries. The men of Cape Ann were forbidden to go within the three-mile limit excepting in certain parts of Labrador, the Magdalen Islands, and designated areas of Newfoundland. The new situation was not what had existed from time immemorial. Cape Ann men had always fished where they pleased when they were British subjects and the broad North Atlantic had seemed entirely British waters. Ghent had been outrageous; and 1818's convocation little better.

The Gloucestermen suffered what they deemed a definite diminution of their rights. It cannot be said that they were determined to honor the new covenant. They fished where they had fished before and be damned to whoever tried to stop them. They fished wherever they thought they could get away with it. One thing was certain: They were not going to stop seining a school of mackerel they had discovered 5 miles out because the mackerel in their finny passion spun closer to the shore.

The altercations that resulted have nowhere better been set forth than in the book *That Great Pattillo* by Joseph Garland, one of the few distinguished literary men who have put, and are still putting, Gloucester history on the record. Pattillo was a born competitor, of Scottish descent despite the sound of the name, and a massive man. His escapades in defying and outwitting the Canadian authorities have a splendid rogue quality.

The desire to excel is native to the heart of man and lies at the heart of every fish story. The fishermen of Cape Ann not only competed in the size of their catches but invariably raced their ships one against the other in all sorts of weather and in all sorts of circumstances. They raced from the Grand Banks to the Boston market or to the home port of Gloucester in the determination to get the highest price for their catch, and the first to market got it.

The optimum moment to cut out from the sail-dotted bank and run for market could be a matter of delicate decision. Should one wait until every barrel was full? Or strike for home with a substantial catch, since the market price might vary so as to become a major factor in that algebraic decision? Coming home from the northern banks could be a difficult sail, since usually the ship was tacking against the wind. The expressions "down Maine" and "down East" were coined not because the men of Gloucester thought of north as down and south as up but because the prevailing wind in New England is from the west, and when one sailed to Maine the ship was going "down" wind. To sail back against the wind, to head up into it, to tack zigzagging against its knife edge, offered the best test of seamanship, especially if the wind was close to gale force. But most of all the men of Gloucester raced from masculine exuberance, what Robert Frost called "sheer morning gladness at the brim." They loved to race, and Gloucester skippers liked to be called "sail carriers" and delighted to "drive" a ship. So they raced against each other; and if no other ship was around, they raced against the clock or against the sun. Schooners were designed for speed; getting to and from the banks fast was important.

In his *Marine Dictionary*, as early as 1769, William Falconer defined a schooner as a "small vessel with two masts, whose main and fore sails were suspended by gaffs reaching from the mast toward the stern; and stretched out below by booms, whose foremast ends were hooked to an iron which clasped the mast so as to turn therein as upon an axis, when the after ends were swung from one side of the vessel to the other. This vessel was generally a fast sailer, and principally employed in trade by those who made speculations where dispatch was requisite." "Where dispatch was requisite . . ." tells the story. The schooner was meant to get there fustest with the mostest. Racing was basic to each trip out and back, and for Cape Ann men above all others. For the Nova Scotian speed was not the same imperative.

The best races, of course, were never recorded in history or log. The formal International Fishermen's Races of the 1920s and 1930s, which were arranged between the men of Gloucester and the men of Nova Scotia, were never really satisfactory, and to this day the dispute runs as to which were the better men and which had the better ships. Those races were artificial, the work of sportsmen, not fishermen—colorful, exciting, to be sure, but calculated. The boats were built to race, not to fish, and were not the working champions of either fleet.

On reflection, one finds there was only one suite of races that was *au naturel,* so to speak. That was the 1920 race when the *Esperanto* out of Gloucester, built at the well-known Tarr and James yards in Essex, met the pride of the Canadian fleet, the *Delawanna.* Like many such competitions, the race was promoted by the newspapers. The daily journals in Halifax, duly proud of their schooners, mostly out of Lunenburg, challenged the men of Gloucester to a race. The race proved to be what the later races also became, not a race of one port against the other, but a race of one country against one city, Gloucester. But Gloucester had about it, even in the twenties, something of the character of the cities of ancient Greece, the quality and spirit of a city-state.

In Canadian waters, the *Delawanna* had bested her compatriots. The trial races there pitted fishing boat against fishing boat; the work horses of the sea, fancied up a bit for speed, but fishing boats designed as fishing boats, working schooners, rigged the same as if they were putting to sea for a spell of halibuting. When the *Delawanna* had proved herself the champion of the Canadian fleet, the challenge was flung to Gloucester, and the old port fermented with excitement.

Gloucester had known competitive sailing for a long time. As early as 1907 Sir Thomas Lipton, that patron and patron saint of sail racing, had offered a cup for a competition among American schooners. Schooners had competed by class, and the people of Cape Ann had lined the shore, crowding every eminence, to watch as best they could, or had put to sea themselves in a variety of craft to see the fun.

In 1920 what was being offered was an international competition. Nova Scotian and Cape Anner had been competing informally for years. There was a friendly rivalry there, and also a

touch of bitterness. The men from the Cape had not forgotten how the Canadian government agents had harassed them in the coastal waters. Putting the rivalry into a formal competition was an excellent way of letting off steam or voiding bad blood, like two high school enemies put into the ring with sixteen-ounce gloves.

The rivalry was more than international. What had prompted the Canadian pride in its fleet was a reluctance to relinquish sail. The auxiliary engine had two decades earlier demonstrated its ability to get to a school of fish while the all-sail schooners sat with drooping sails waiting for a breath of air. The Canadians had been slower to go to power than the Gloucestermen, and in the race they thought they could prove something about sail, if only because the men of Cape Ann had turned to engines and perhaps forgotten how to haul a halyard fast, trim a jib precisely, or bring a schooner about smartly.

The Canadians set down the terms for the races, which were aimed at giving them an advantage. Gloucester was given ten days to get a boat to Halifax, all ready to race. That was not so easy as it appeared. The Gloucester fleet was out to sea, and there was no radio at the time, although this was the harbor where remote radio control would be invented. At length one of the fleet appeared, the *Esperanto,* named for an artificial international language, and strangely for a Gloucester ship, but it was a portent. The *Esperanto* was going to say things on the high seas that every mariner understood.

She had been launched at the Tarr and James yard in Essex on June 27, 1906, and had made her maiden fishing voyage ten days later under Captain Charles Harty. She was fourteen years old in 1920, and had served her masters well, mackereling, haddocking, halibuting, shacking, seining, codfishing. The *Esperanto* was a working ship, no doubt about that. She was a lucky ship. In her fourteen years, she had lost only one hand. Only recently she had been bought by the Gorton Pew Company and sent dory hand-lining, and she was coming home with a quarter of a million pounds of salted fish when she was commandeered for the race. No time was left for a new suit of sails, or indeed, for anything more than a scraping and some paint, before she left Eastern Point in the most celebrated departure ceremony in the history of the port.

On the way "down east" the *Esperanto* did not make remarkable time, but James B. Connolly, the Boswell of the fleet and its skippers, testifies that she proved she could fly if the wind was hard. She was given an exuberant welcome by the people of Halifax. Captain Martin Welch, who had been selected to race her, was a Nova Scotian by birth, and it was something of a homecoming. He was a small, dark-haired man, rosy-cheeked, daring, cool and accomplished. He proved it. Captain Thomas Himmelman of the *Delawanna* knew his ship and what it could do. Welch had never sailed the *Esperanto* until he brought it from Gloucester to Halifax—400 miles—in thirty-eight hours. But he knew the Nova Scotian waters as well as Himmelman, and he knew his crew. The *Esperanto* with Captain Welch at the wheel won two races hands down, and took off with the trophy and a cash prize. During the two races, Marty Welch never left the wheel.

The first was held on October 30, 1920, over a 40-mile triangular course. The *Esperanto* crossed the finish line eighteen minutes and twenty-eight seconds ahead of the *Delawanna*. It was evident that the Lunenburg schooner had no chance against the Gloucester schooner in a heavy wind.

The night before the second race, November 1, the Nova Scotians lightened their ballast in hopes of a light breeze. They got it. But it didn't help much. The Nova Scotian champion got away first and held its lead for three-quarters of the course, but on the final leg, the daring—near folly—of the Gloucester skipper made the difference. Devil's Island is well named; it has a nasty shore line. On that crucial leg, having just about overtaken the flying *Delawanna*, Captain Welch cut to windward of the Nova Scotian, between it and the shore. It was a perilous passage, and could have whitened the hair of the owner's representative. But R. Russell Smith, the Gorton Pew man aboard the *Esperanto* and speaking for the owners, was caught up in the drama. "To hell with the kelp and the rocks, Marty," he cried; "keep her to it." Welch held the course, passed the *Delawanna*, and won the second race by seven minutes and twenty-five seconds.

When the word reached Gloucester, the city exploded with delight. The custom among Gloucester's racing schooners was for the winner to brandish a broom aloft, as sure a sign of victory as a laurel wreath at an Olympiad. The *Esperanto* came home with a broom at her foretopmast head. That told the story for anyone who hadn't heard. The cup offered by the Halifax daily and the $4,000 in prize money were safe in a lazarette below. No crew ever returned to more banquets, fetes, parties, free drinks, cheers and congratulations than the happy men of the *Esperanto*.

The races after that degenerated into competitions bugged by red tape, bad sportsmanship, whining, false claims, false starts and embittered denunciations. The humiliated Nova Scotians had built a schooner designed for speed first, fishing second, the *Bluenose*. She was 143 feet overall, where the *Esperanto* had been less than 108 feet, and carried 10,000 square feet of canvas. She was launched in 1921 and promptly challenged the city of Gloucester. But the champion of the Atlantic schooners was not able to compete. Seven months after her great victory over the *Delawanna*, the *Esperanto* suffered the fate of many a fishing schooner, for in May of 1921 she struck a submerged wreck off Sable Island and went down.

The schooner *Elsie,* thirteen years old, not the fastest in the Gloucester fleet, but one of the few without an auxiliary engine, was named to defend the cup the *Esperanto* had won. The *Elsie,* under Captain Welch, lost both races. Running with the wind she led all the way, but fighting to windward she was not so subtle as the *Esperanto,* and the *Bluenose*'s prodigious spread of sail won the day.

Gloucester never built a schooner as big as the *Bluenose,* but after the *Elsie* was defeated Captain Clayton Morrissey built the *Henry Ford* and challenged for the trophy. Ballyhoo and hoopla had taken over now. The trial races were attended by newspaper coverage to match that given the America's Cup races today. Representatives of both governments were on hand, formally and informally. A Canadian destroyer was even assigned to accompany the *Bluenose.* But the captain of the *Bluenose,* Angus Walters (who sailed her in every race), having retrieved the cup, was now chary about exposing it. A Boston schooner called the *Mayflower* had been showing her wake to everything on the Grand Banks, but when she put in a challenge, Walters declined, contending that the *Mayflower* was a yacht in disguise, even though the *Bluenose* was designed to race.

Captain Jeff Thomas, one of Gloucester's celebrated skippers, had put every dollar he had into the schooner *Puritan,* designed to beat the *Bluenose* or the *Mayflower,* but before she could race she was wrecked, as so many before her, on Sable Island.

Although the *Henry Ford* was the biggest schooner built for Gloucester, it was still smaller than the *Bluenose.* Clayt Morrissey promptly beat the *Bluenose* in two races in 1922, only to find himself disqualified both times, once because the two skippers (by mutual agreement called from deck to deck) ignored a whistle signifying a false start, and again because a racing committee said that the *Henry Ford* was carrying too much sail. This last ruling sounded like absolute nonsense to Morrissey and his crew, who had been raised in the tradition that the proudest designation that could be given a Gloucester skipper was a "sail carrier"; that is, a man who refused to trim, let alone lower, his sails when reaching across a gale-swept stretch of water. You carried as much sail as you dared; the more skilled the skipper (and the better the ship) the more sail you carried, let the elements do their worst. Loaded with haddock or halibut, weight that all but eliminated freeboard, the sprightly schooner would be driven—or "druv," as the fishermen said— through churning, foaming waters until it seemed as if the helmsman himself was submerged. After one such voyage, an old salt reported, "I've crossed the Bay o' Fundy a hundred times before, but never till then did I cross it under water." The schooner was the famous *Nannie Bohlen*. Her skipper, Tommy Bohlen, said, "I druv her, and I druv her, and I druv her. But could I make her quit? The man never lived who could make the *Nannie Bohlen* quit." Gloucester skippers never blamed their ships; they blamed only themselves.

To be told that they had to remove sail from the *Henry Ford* became too much for Morrissey and his crew. They quit. But the world was watching. Not only had race committees taken over with yacht club rules, but the races had become international events. The crew of the *Henry Ford* was having a mug-up of rum when an appeal to them to race again was made by no less a person than the Secretary of the Navy, Edwin Denby, who was among the spectators. Morrissey at length agreed. Denied her full suit of sails, the *Henry Ford* could not match the *Bluenose*. The cup stayed in Nova Scotia.

The dispute over the race between the *Henry Ford* and the *Bluenose*, and those over the later races between the *Columbia* and the *Bluenose* and the *Gertrude L. Thebaud* and the *Bluenose*, not only ended in recriminations and even vilification, but were marked by one unusual issue: Both parties made absolutely contradictory claims. The pride of a schooner captain was the ability of his ship to sail in rough weather. They yearned for heavy weather on a race day; they detested drifting matches. Captain Angus Walters always contended that the *Bluenose* was at her best in heavy weather; the late Captain Ben Pine, who sailed many of the International Fishermen's Cup Races for Gloucester, always maintained that the *Bluenose* could win only in light airs. Author Connolly makes the same claim, and his animadversions on the races were extremely derogatory not only to the seamanship of the Nova Scotians and the seaworthiness of their vessels, but of their sportsmanship. The Nova Scotians responded with exactly the same derogations. Three facts stand out: The *Bluenose* ultimately retained possession of the trophy; the *Gertrude L. Thebaud* wrenched it from her once; and Captain Angus Walters ran away to the fishing banks rather than race the speedy *Columbia* out of Gloucester with Ben Pine at the wheel.

The *Columbia*, according to historian Gordon W. Thomas, whose book, *Fast and Able,* is an indispensable guide to the careers of two score of Cape Ann's famous schooners, was a beautiful ship, but a hard-luck ship. It was the name they gave her, some said. Fishermen considered it unlucky to give a ship too "high-falutin' " a name. *Esperanto* might have been some Italian girl's name, so they didn't condemn that. But Columbia, the Gem of the Ocean! It left a superstitious mariner uneasy. She was built at the Story shipyard in Essex, towed by tug to Gloucester, and rigged there in record time. On April 26, 1923, she made her maiden trip. Connolly says of her that she looked like a swordfish in the water with her beautiful sheer running back from a pert bowsprit. She is even today popularly deemed the fastest schooner ever out of Gloucester, and she logged seventeen knots at one time. They didn't ever go faster than that. The *Thebaud* is said to have matched that speed, but not for long, perhaps for a moment in a gale. The *Columbia's* jinx set in on her second voyage in July of the same year. The French steam trawler *La Champlain* rammed her on the port side in a fog off Sable Island, smashing bowsprit and rail and carrying away her forerigging. The *Columbia's* crew took to their dories, but seeing that the ship would not founder, Captain Alden Geele called out, "Let's go back aboard and see if we can save her for the race." They brought her home.

That fall the Gloucester elimination race was held in air too light for any of the three competitors to finish within the five-and-a-half-hour limit set for the 40-mile course. At the third buoy, however, the *Columbia* was so far ahead that the judges designated her to represent the Gloucester fleet. Her rivals that day had been the *Henry Ford* and the *Elizabeth Howard*. She would race the *Henry Ford* again and beat her fair and square, but her most stirring and controversial adventure would come before that.

On October 22, 1923, the *Columbia* sailed for Halifax, but suffered some slight damage and had to return. Three days later Ben Pine took her down to Halifax in thirty-eight hours. On October 29 the first race was held, and the *Bluenose* won by one minute and twenty seconds, but only after damaging the *Columbia* with her boom when Walters turned the big ship against the Gloucester schooner for fear of hitting a reef. The crew of the *Columbia* felt that their ship had been fouled; Walters felt that he had been, that Pine had tried to run him on the rocks. The second race was also won by the *Bluenose* but only by cutting on the wrong side of one of the markers. The committee awarded the race to the *Columbia,* and Walters, in high dudgeon, refused to sail again. The Cape Ann men were certain that Walters knew the *Columbia* was the better ship and didn't dare race. The authorities offered the cup to Pine, who declined it, asking only that the *Bluenose* be made to race. Walters, however, had taken the big ship out to sea, safe from summons. Pine left the cup in Canada and came home disgusted.

The *Columbia's* hard luck was not yet paid out. One good year of fishing lay ahead of her, and in the fall of 1924 she came in with $18,573 worth of salt cod, a share of $360 per man. In 1926 the jinx struck again. The *Columbia* ran aground in Nova Scotian waters and had to be towed into Halifax for mending. She made a comeback. In October of the same year she was matched again with the *Henry Ford.* Clayton Morrissey was confident his ship could win. The *Columbia* won on two successive days, the latter being appropriately October 12, Columbus Day. She took the first race by one minute and a half and the second by four minutes and fifty-five seconds. Almost one year later, the *Gloucester Daily Times* read: "No Hope Now For *Columbia*—Lost with All Hands in the Gale of Aug. 24 off Sable Island." Captain Lew Wharton, who had taken her dory hand-lining, had perished with her and her twenty-one-man crew. That was the most lives lost with any one ship out of Gloucester. Four Canadian fishing vessels were lost in the same storm. As it so happens, most of the men aboard the *Columbia* when she went down were Nova Scotians, and the captain himself, although a Gloucester resident for years, was a native of Liverpool, Nova Scotia. The *Columbia's* first skipper, Alden Geele, like Jeff Thomas on the *Puritan,* died aboard ship, but not the *Columbia.* He was found dead in the cabin of the *Thomas S. Gorton* the year before the *Columbia* foundered. He never had to shake his head over her worst disaster.

The *Gertrude L. Thebaud* was the last of the Gloucester schooners to challenge for the international trophy. She was launched on Saint Patrick's Day, 1930, and like the *Bluenose* was designed first for racing, secondly for fishing. In honor of Saint Patrick the invitations to the launching at the Story yard were green and gold. It was a gala day in Essex. The *Gerty* was towed to Gloucester to be rigged, was fitted with an auxiliary engine, and sent fishing. When the time came for the race, the engine was, of course, removed. There was no question about the *Gerty's* class. She took the *Bluenose* in three straight races. On one leg she averaged fifteen-and-a-half knots. They raced twice after that, and each time the *Bluenose* won three out of five races. Film actor Sterling Hayden, one of the crew aboard the *Thebaud* in the last match, still recalls the thrill of those races. Hayden was an unknown at the time, not even an aspiring actor, but a skilled all-sail sailor. Boston newspapermen made his movie career a certainty by their stories of his prowess, and the photographs of him that showed his Viking features to the country. Tom Horgan, Associated Press feature writer, himself a sound skipper, used to claim that the *Thebaud* would have won if Sterling Hayden had been the skipper. Whatever the answer to that question may be, it is certain that Ben Pine was no Marty Welch.

The claim that these schooners attained seventeen knots is doubtful, but such speed was possible in short spurts. The *Thebaud* established an all-time record for schooners when she sailed from Gloucester to Halifax, a distance of 400 miles, in thirty hours. The *Esperanto* and the *Columbia* had each taken thirty-eight hours. The late Roy Parsons, who, as editor of the *Gloucester Daily Times,* made that famous run aboard her, would recount that the wind never slackened, nor would Captain John Matheson trim a square inch of sail all the way, come gust, squall or gale. No schooner before or since made that run in that time. Men who love ships for what they are and what they are meant to be are never happy discussing any of the International Fishermen's Races excepting the first, when the *Esperanto,* after fourteen years of service, spruced up her spars, took on a new coat of paint and went up and licked the best that Canada had to offer. The later racing schooners were a different breed. Of them, Philip Bolger, noted Gloucester marine architect, puts it succinctly when he says, "Remember, none of those ships would have been built if it hadn't been for the races." He was referring to the *Bluenose* and the subsequent challengers. Fish they did, but fishermen they weren't; they were designed for another purpose.

The greatest races were those that pitted the men of Gloucester, one against the other, before international chauvinism and the aspirations of outsiders soured the situation. Perhaps the greatest of these was that among the best of the Gloucester fleet in 1892, the 250th anniversary of Gloucester's incorporation as a town, referred to as the Great Anniversary Race. It was sailed in winds better than 50 miles an hour—deemed proper weather for a Gloucester fisherman. That day the water surged over scuppers, gunwale, rail and deck, and churned around the man at the wheel. Maurice Whalen, Irish-born and one of the great Gloucester skippers, brought the *Harry Belden* home the winner. In his book *The Port of Gloucester,* James B. Connolly, who often wrote fiction when he thought he was writing history, can readily be trusted in this instance:

"The competing schooners put out that morning with all sail set, and the word of their skippers that no sail would come off that day except what the Lord took off. Timid men had been known to cut halyards at the pin-rail on a desperate passage to let a mainsail run down, and so save a vessel from being capsized. To prevent any happening of that kind this day, three skippers sailed out that day with their main halyards lashed aloft. . . . Even the sail-carrying captains admitted that it was rough going. Vessels were rolling down to their swifters—four to five feet above the quarter-rail and men at the wheel were going up to their necks in water."

These races between members of the fleet, without the eyes of the world upon them, with no patriotic passion lashing them to

seek mean advantages, were the true measure of man and ship.
The International Fishermen's Cup Races, with thousands of
pleasure boats cluttering up the harbor, with bitter feeling on
both sides, with officials with slide rules redesigning the boats
before they could sail, leave the true expert yawning. These
were hybrid racers and not the real McCoy.

The Canadians, nevertheless, are justly proud of the *Bluenose*.
They have put her replica on the back of their ten-cent piece,
and they have put her picture on a commemorative stamp. The
Canadian government sent the ship to the Chicago World's Fair
in 1933 as an exhibit. In 1935 she was invited to England to participate in the Silver Jubilee of King George V, and the King
gave her a sail from his own yacht. Captain Walters became
something of a national hero for Canada, which lacks in national heroes, and even after the *Bluenose* was lost, he had, in
his advanced years, the marvelous experience of having an exact
replica built and of sailing aboard her. This is the sort of tribute
the city of Gloucester and the fishing industry, if it had a sense
of history or public service, might well do for the *Thebaud* or
the *Columbia*.

Schooner racing isn't dead and gone, but the competing vessels now are the property of sportsmen. In 1969 and in 1970 a
fleet of them gathered to race the old course where the wraiths
of Maurice Whalen and Marty Welch and Clayton Morrissey
can be heard calling across the fog-scarved waters. In 1969 the
air was too light to drive the schooners, but they did move
across the waters with their gaff rigs and topsails, magnificent
beings from an age that is past, lovely in their lines, gracious in
their movement, splendid in rigging and sails, more than enough
to tell everyone on shore, or those sailing as spectators, that
something wonderful went out of the world when the gasoline
engine came in, and the wind, mistress of a million ships, was
left alone.

Something of that sadness I tried to catch in a poem of my own:

> The wind is alone in the streets of the city,
> Sobs, sobs in the pits of dispassionate stone,
> Finds no flesh in the smoke from the chimneys,
> Ranges the waterfront all alone.
>
> Feeling for sails that are there no longer
> Puffed, puffed like the breasts of giant swans.
> The wind is a drag on the sleek, steel warships,
> A jerk at the airship's ailerons.
>
> The windmills moved to the constant waters
> But the warm, willful wind still fed the world,
> While the sails were stars and the seas were heavens.
> The heavens went black; the sails were furled.
>
> Coal, oil, coal oil are slaves not lovers
> With mechanical lust that can never atone
> For the tease, freeze, fire and the bursting passion;
> But time has grown tired and the wind is alone.

The Fishermen of Gloucester

The glorious period in the history of Cape Ann was the era of the fishing schooners, the era of sail, before steam, gasoline and diesel oil powered the boats. By a pathetic irony of misplaced values, the cowboy, who was for the most part an illiterate, semi-skilled laborer on horseback, has become a heroic figure in our folklore (thanks to television and the unhistorical, falsified depiction of revolver duels) while the fisherman, a figure truly heroic, who risked his life constantly in a titanic battle with the elements and whose antecedents run back past the beginnings of history, is ignored. The fisherman, even if he could not read type (although most of them could) had to be able to read the face of the sea, the moods of the sky, the strain in a line or a sail, because his companions' lives and his own depended on his individual skill and the collaborative efforts of him and his fellows. Neither purblind, vulgar Hollywood nor the faceless, unimaginative masters of television have been able to bring that heroic figure to the screen. Hollywood, with its genius for vulgarizing everything, botched the filming of *Captains Courageous*, Rudyard Kipling's classic story about life on a Gloucester schooner out on the Grand Banks, and television has not even tried to come to grips with the drama.

James Brendan Connolly, a Harvard College dropout (he ran

off to win the hop, skip and jump in the first modern Olympic games) became the chief chronicler of the Gloucester fishing fleet, and none of his stories were ever taken up by motion picture producers to be filmed for immortality. Here were true drama, high adventure, incomparable scenery, incredible courage, comedy, tragedy, exceeding all the tawdry low life of the West, and Hollywood overlooked it all in the days when it was still possible to film it. Today one would have to build the schooner, the wharves, the dories, the trawls—the whole bit.

We have lost too much. We cannot even understand that age, which ended about the turn of the century with the acceptance of auxiliary power. We have moved into decades that have lost the sense of affection a man might have for a ship such as marked the age of sail. The clipper ships were gigantic, but not impersonal; the schooners were intensely personal. It has been said over and over that the men who sailed ships thought of them as women. A ship was always "she" even when she bore a man's name. It is no accident of nomenclature, but something that runs deep in the nature of man. Man and vessel were locked in a partnership straining for fulfillment and sometimes survival. Rivers and seas are feminine; favorable winds are feminine. The wind, the sea, the ship, all feminine; and man, the lesser physical force, knew an intercourse with nature in the nineteenth century and before which was lost when steam and gasoline and the diesel destroyed a relationship that was always mystical and sometimes magical.

Despite Rudyard Kipling's paean to steam in "M'Andrew's Hymn," with its vivid expression of a Scottish engineer's affection for the engines below deck which he tends like a mother hen her chicks, the idea of affection for an engine is forced. We are at our most natural, our most human when we are in command of the elements or in close communion with them and with nature. The men who sailed without engines, with only line, canvas and wood, knew a height of actual living, an excitement of existence which we have lost. First of all, they pulsed with something handed down to them by their troglodyte ancestors moving across some smoking marsh in a primordial and unrecorded eon. They had total perception, not the apperception that bugs so many of us today—a sickly self-consciousness—but a constant, acute awareness of everything around them, of the wind, its intensity and its direction, its capriciousness or its insistence, of the color of the sea and the impassiveness of its face or the indications in the wrinkles on its surface, of the very imperceptible in it, if you will, the ominous containment beneath its reflections which warned of danger to come. They were students of the sky, its tints, the manner in which the sun, worn by the abrasiveness of the hours, melted at last across the west; of the clouds, the thunderheads, the fleece, the heightening coloration of their shifting shapes. Beyond that they had something else, something it would be embarrassing to call ESP, but surely a sixth sense, a sailor sense, that has been lost to the Western world or reduced to a triviality of sports in yacht races, where once it meant the difference between financial success or failure, between life and death not merely for the man on watch but for the whole crew, his brothers, sleeping below. He had to have strength to handle a 10-foot oar in a rough sea, and a delicacy of touch with a needle and thread, fingers sensitive enough to learn from the feel of wood, or cloth or hemp, ears keen enough to evaluate the creaks in the joints of a surging vessel or the thousand voices of the wind. He had to be sensitive enough in his temperament to live for months in close quarters with his fellow man, and stand ready to die with him and perhaps for him.

Not since Greek warriors fought back to back when Athens was supreme, when the life of each depended on the courage and physical condition of the others, has there been such a brotherhood as manned the schooners out of Cape Ann. For all the deaths it occasioned, for all the meanness and human viciousness that no doubt attended many a voyage outward bound and many a voyage home, there were an exhilaration and an excitement to working and racing under sail that no workaday job today can offer, and a dignity in the chores that American labor everywhere has lost.

Fishermen were not paid by the week but always by a share of the catch, a profit-sharing system that American industry might well re-examine. The best of them, when the going was good, made a comfortable living, and the captains banked money. To be a "highliner"—a captain who brought home the biggest catches—was the goal of every ambitious young man in the fleet; to be an able-bodied fisherman with a "site"—a job aboard a schooner—was the ambition of every lad in town. It was a satisfactory life—a career with pride—and the absence of a college degree or a high school diploma was of no consideration. Courage, industry, ability and the knack of getting along with one's fellows were what counted.

Ethnic rivalry and religious prejudice were not unknown on Cape Ann, but from the earliest days in Gloucester, Irish, English, Portuguese, native-born Americans, Nova Scotians, Prince Edward Islanders, Newfoundlanders, Italians, and various Scandinavian breeds sailed together, worked together, died together and sometimes gave their lives for one another. The rivalry between the crews of various schooners would be strenuous and even bitter, but a vessel in trouble could count on the assistance of the first schooner to sight her.

This was a far cry from the early seventeenth century when Breton or Basque fishermen, at the sight of an English or Dutch ship, would fly into waters too shallow for the larger ship to follow. Captains of merchant ships in turn learned to fear the criminal elements among the far-flung fishing fleets that sailed regularly from Europe to the Grand Banks to catch cod to feed the

Old World. Given a chance, a clutch of those fishermen would board a merchant vessel, cut throats, rob, loot and steal. The Spanish galleons that were bringing home the plunder of the continents they had discovered and claimed for their Most Catholic Majesties were careful to keep a sharp eye on the raffish fishermen who combed the banks of the North Atlantic. The Gloucestermen, a century later, were of a different breed; they were the American workman at his best.

During Prohibition, to be sure, they did their share of rumrunning, and the traffic between Cape Ann and the islands of Saint Pierre and Miquelon ran high. One of the largest schooners ever, the *Patara,* was built as a Canadian rumrunner in 1921, and plied that trade until 1931 when she was bought by the Central Wharf and Vessels Company of Gloucester and sadly reduced to carrying herring from Newfoundland to Gloucester. By that time Franklin Delano Roosevelt had been elected President and repeal was in sight. The *Patara* tragically was lost the following year with all hands, for even freighting in New England waters was hazardous.

The trade of fishing was particularly perilous, and not merely in the fall and winter when prodigious storms raked the Atlantic and massive waves shook the shores. From 1830 to 1892, 576 vessels were lost with 3,224 lives. The winter fishing for halibut and haddock on the banks off New England, Nova Scotia and Newfoundland was the most dangerous game of all.

The horrors the men faced, the drama they lived, the experiences they went through, the tortures they endured have been recorded and recounted a thousand times, and fill volumes. Yet they were, among strangers, the most reticent of men, and on shipboard, with one or two exceptions, kept no logs. True, when foul weather held them to the fo'c'sle, or when a layoff stranded them and they gathered around a cracker barrel or beside a bar, enjoying smoked fish and hard liquor, they relived some of their adventures or debated the comparative worth of a schooner or a skipper. On those occasions there was no exaggeration—beyond a happy distortion, perhaps, to heighten the effect—but woe to the man who went too far off the course, for all his listeners had been through as much or, if not the same, something very like. For the stranger, the landlubber, they might on occasion spin a yarn, and then the gift of imagination and puckishness shone through. They bore their honors lightly, and their tragedies stoically.

Take the story of William T. Lee and Jack Devine, dorymates, sent out from the schooner *Deep Water,* a halibut catcher, in November, 1880, a cold time of year any place on the North Atlantic, and icy cold with the wind squalling and the waves breaking. Their job was to haul in the trawl, along with such halibut as might have been hooked. They had taken part of the mile-long trawl into the boat when a wave hit them with exceptional violence and threw both of them into the water. Devine grabbed the gunwale almost immediately and hauled himself back into the dory. Lee had been pitched too far away for that and, encumbered with heavy clothing and rubber boots, could not keep afloat. Devine meanwhile was bailing as fast as he could to keep the dory from foundering. Lee was going down for what, to him, must have seemed the last time when his hands touched the trawl line leading to the boat. He was now perhaps 12 feet under water. Promptly he began to pull himself hand over hand toward the surface and the dory, but fate had more torment in store for him. Still under water, he caught one finger on a hook and pierced the flesh. With the other hand he tore the hook away and part of the finger with it; and, at the instant when his endurance was almost exhausted, he broke the surface of the sea and grabbed the gunwale of the boat. At that moment another hook caught his trousers, and he had to free himself of that. When at last he clambered into the dory (Devine unable to help him except to keep the boat from capsizing again), he fell senseless in the bottom. Surely a sufficient day's work. When he recovered, Lee declined to return to the schooner until he and Devine had bailed their boat, hauled their trawl and settled the halibut. They then rowed back to the *Deep Water,* where the mutilated and mangled finger was treated at last.

The major hazard for dorymen was to get separated from their ship in a fog or a blizzard, to be caught downwind and lost on the North Atlantic with no food and no water. In June, 1879, on St. Peter's Bank Michael Coleman was lost with his dorymate N. Choate Allen. They subsisted on raw halibut for four days, rowed 160 miles and were finally picked up by a Nova Scotia schooner. But in March of the next year, Coleman's luck was not that good. He was lost with his dorymate James McGrath, having left the schooner *Procter Brothers* to attend to their trawl when a gale carried them away from the vessel. The month of March is one of the windiest and coldest on the North Atlantic, and for five days the two men, without water or food, except again raw fish, were driven by the winds until they reached Sable Island, well named "the Graveyard of the Atlantic." Both men were unable to walk when they reached shore, and had to be carried by rescuers, professionals maintained on Sable Island to assist wrecked ships and lost men.

So many Gloucester and Cape Ann ships have been wrecked on Sable Island that that drear and dreadful place is almost part of the Cape Ann story. In French, "sable" means "sand," and that is all it is—a 50-mile-long shifting sand bar piled up through the centuries by the confluence of the Gulf Stream and the Labrador Current. The island itself, exposed portion of the sand bar, is the 20-mile-long, mile-wide strip of dunes, some rising to 100 feet. Around it stretch miles of shoals, and beyond those, particularly toward Nova Scotia, is the Sable Island bank.

The whole is about 100 miles southeast of Nova Scotia. Marram grass gives color to the crest of the island, and wild horses roam its fields. There are no trees. Until 1873 there was no lighthouse. Because of the meeting of the cold and warm waters, fog is common, and in the fog the island is imperceptible until one is upon it. In stormy weather, one never gets close enough to see it, except for the whitecaps on the miles of shoals. The island itself is moving like a predatory thing as the ocean erodes it on the west bar and the currents pile up sands on the other side. In its time it has consumed six of its own lighthouses. Five hundred ships, they say, have been wrecked there, and the best authorities state that more than two hundred have been counted. One of them was the *Maskonomet,* to give us still another spelling of that worthy's name. The professional lifesavers who were maintained there by the Canadian government are needed no longer because of modern warning systems. Five thousand seamen are said to have drowned there. As late as 1947, sailors were warned if their ship was grounded not to attempt to go ashore but to wait for the lifesaving crews maintained on the island. Such were the men who rescued James McGrath and his dorymate Michael Coleman. Although both men had to be carried along the shore, they were soon back at work.

The Fishermen's Own Book, published by the Procter Brothers of Gloucester in 1882, is filled with such stories. Among the stories, the statistics, the verses, the anecdotes and the advertisements in the book is the following minatory paragraph:

A CAUTION WHICH SHOULD BE HEEDED

If the fishermen would only take the precaution to place a jug of water and some hard bread in their dories, it would oftentimes save much suffering and perhaps life. It is full time that masters and owners of fishing vessels interested themselves in this matter and insisted that it should be done. The expense and trouble is but trifling compared with the benefits which might follow, and it should be among the duties required of fishermen each trip to see that every dory was provided with the wherewithal to sustain life when lost in the fog or driven out of sight of their vessel, as is frequently the case. There is no excuse for the fishermen if they fail to comply with this simple duty, and we trust that they will heed this advice and provide a remedy for one cause of danger and suffering attending the business.

The words sound more than a bit like the admonitions given to motorists today to fasten their seat belts. To be lost in winter weather on the banks without food and water was terrible indeed, but it was the cold that was worst of all. What good was a jug of water if it froze and broke? Even aboard the schooners, the cold was a torment, and one of the worst of chores was pounding the ice that accumulated as the schooner, heading for home, bucked through icy seas, loaded with fish, and threatening momentarily to founder under the weight of the catch plus the multiplying weight of the ice that thickened on the bow, the gunwales, the lines, the deck, gripping the entire ship in an iron shroud.

The torments that such men went through, their heroism, their fortitude, their sheer physical endurance, pale beside the story of one man, Howard Blackburn, and his adventure, told and retold a thousand times—nay, ten thousand times—in Gloucester saloons and taverns, fo'c'sles and deckhouses, schoolrooms and kitchens. A bust of the man stands in the Sawyer Free Library in Gloucester, a mustached iron man, his indestructibility under outrageous fortune, his persistence through suffering, caught by the noted Gloucester sculptor, Leonard Craske. Craske's "Man at the Wheel" (also known as "Fisherman at the Wheel," "Gloucester Fisherman," the "Fisherman's Statue," and other similar names), the famous bronze of a fisherman in his sou'wester, standing on Western Avenue—the mall, the causeway or the boulevard, as it is variously called—

looking out to sea, must rank with Michelangelo's *David*, Daniel Chester French's *Lincoln* and Bartholdi's *Liberty* among the most photographed statues in the world. His bust of Blackburn is less well known, but as a portrait of a man it is superb. When Craske did the statue, Blackburn was a local hero, but internationally celebrated as well, particularly among men who knew the sea and how wicked it can be.

The story of Howard Blackburn's ordeal has been definitively recounted by Joseph Garland in his book on the man, *Lone Voyager*. Although it had been told a thousand times before, whenever it is told again the teller must acknowledge a debt to Garland.

Blackburn was an experienced hand when at the age of twenty-three, standing 6 feet 3 inches tall, and weighing more than two hundred pounds, he signed aboard the schooner *Grace L. Fears* under substitute skipper Alec Griffin at Liverpool, Nova Scotia. The *Grace L. Fears* was out of Gloucester, and so, for that matter, was Blackburn. He was home on a visit to his native place when he signed. They sailed north to Burgeo Bank, directly south of the west end of Newfoundland, looking for halibut. Blackburn was given Thomas Welch as his dorymate, an experienced man, and the two went out, set their trawl, more than a mile in length, and returned to their ship. Threatening weather sent them back out to recover the trawl, even though the catch would be light. In a short time they were caught in a squall. They had been working so that the mounting wind would help in getting them back to their ship. The squall surprised them and came from the opposite quarter. They found themselves desperately rowing against it, at length in a blizzard that obscured everything 10 feet from the dory. Their efforts with their 10-foot oars were getting them nowhere. At length they threw out the anchor.

The gale was now at full fury, and the anchor, when it caught

in the raging sea, kept bobbing the boat so severely that it constantly filled with water. They kicked in the head of one of the
barrels or kegs used as a buoy on the trawl and used that to
bail. They were barely able to keep ahead of the water, and all
the time the air was getting colder. With the darkness, the spray
froze on them and the dory. They jettisoned everything except
one codfish. If the worse came to worst, they could eat it raw.
During the night they were able occasionally in the rising and
falling sea to catch the dull glare of the torch atop the *Grace L.
Fears.*

When dawn came, there was nothing to see but the storm, a
demented fury of mountainous waves, wind that bit, and snow
that stung. They couldn't row against it without danger of capsizing. They tried to hold the bow of the dory into the wind.
Blackburn lost his mittens while making a sea anchor with one
of the kegs. He still took his turn bailing. When he saw his
hands freezing solid, he curled them around the oars and let
them freeze that way, cupped like claws. Ice began to cover the
dory and, taking their halibut-killer sticks they used to club the
fish before dragging them aboard, the men alternated bailing
with the keg and smashing the ice. His frozen hands senseless,
Blackburn clubbed the ice with them without realizing it. He
took off a sock to save his fingers, and lost the sock. Occasionally the two of them would crouch in the bow of the dory to get
shelter from the sadistic wind. By the second night Welch was
unable to get up from the bow to take his turn bailing. Blackburn kept at it. During the night Welch died.

Blackburn tried to put on Welch's mittens, but they wouldn't
fit his curved, immobile fingers. At dawn on the third day the
storm abated and the sea grew calm, moving in long swells. His
hands hooked on the oars chaffed away like dry ice. All day he
rowed, and into the night. When it fell he threw over the
drogue, or sea anchor, and although the wind lashed again, the

boat mercifully shipped no water. At dawn on the fourth day he pulled in his sea anchor and began to row again, his dead dorymate a statue of ice in the bow. He passed an island which he thought was deserted and rowed on, seeking humankind. At twilight on the fourth day, tortured by thirst, he found a river inlet, a wharf and a hut. When he climbed onto the wharf, he knew his feet were frozen. In the broken hut, its roof partly gone, he found a bed and collapsed. But he didn't dare sleep. He shivered until morning. His teeth chattered so, he later said, that he was afraid they would break.

In the morning he found his dory grievously damaged. Waves had pounded it against the wharf in the night. He had to recover a thwart from the water. The plug had been knocked out of the drain hole. He dragged the boat to the shore. In lifting the frozen body of Welch from the boat, he ruptured himself and had to pause to push his intestines back through the broken stomach wall. At length he cleared the dory of water, replaced the thwart, and set himself to rowing again, leaving the body beside the wharf.

On the fifth night, fighting the current and ice cakes in the river, he made his way to civilization. He had reached Little River, an impoverished fishing village. The people led him over the ice of a cove to the home of Frank Lishman, whose wife was familiar with frostbite and had her own methods of treating it. His hands were held in a bucket of brine for an hour of intolerable agony. For five weeks she nursed him. In the end he had only his left thumb remaining and part of the thumb on his right hand, but the flesh had healed. It was the fourth of June when he returned home to Gloucester. The Atlantic Halibut Company gave him his share of the trip he hadn't completed. It was eighty-six dollars.

He had, however, become a legend. At the end of the American Revolution the British navy was at a strength it had never before enjoyed. It had 478 ships. When Blackburn came home in June, 1883, there were 259 ships sailing out of Gloucester Harbor, and the number was increasing. What Nelson had meant to the British fleet, Blackburn came to mean to the 3,000 men of the Gloucester fleet. Artists depicted his ordeal, and he made money selling the reproductions in his little tobacco store. Captain Joseph W. Collins, a highliner with a flair for the written word, told the world the story in a booklet entitled *Fearful Experience of a Gloucester Halibut Fisherman, Astray in a Dory in a Gale, off the Newfoundland Coast in Midwinter.* Blackburn was a celebrity, and fellow celebrities came from around the world to see him and shake his stump, or watch him pick up a dime from the glass top of a counter with the highly developed muscles at the base of his half-thumb.

Further adventures were ahead of him—he was to sail to Europe alone in his sloops, the *Great Western* and the *Great Republic,* not once but twice. Having become a legend in his youth, and lived to seventy-three, he was not merely fifty years a hero, but the figure of a man whose endurance under implacable impositions showed clearly that human will has that affinity to godliness that makes man supremely man.

⊰ 9 ⊱
The Lone Voyagers

In recent years a number of adventurers have sought to cross the Atlantic Ocean or sail around the world in difficult circumstances, either by sailing alone in a very small boat, or sailing alone in a boat that one man would not ordinarily handle, or by rowing across with a companion. All England turned out when Sir Francis Chichester, to prove there will always be an England, brought his *Gipsy Moth* into Plymouth after circumnavigating the globe. Robert Manry, after years of that most sedentary of labors—copy editing on a Cleveland newspaper—took the 13½-foot *Tinkerbelle* out of Falmouth on Cape Cod and sailed alone to Falmouth, England.

Both Manry and Chichester recounted their voyages in books that make fascinating reading for the seagoing and interesting reading even for someone who cannot tell a halyard from a grommet. Manry's account is entitled *Tinkerbelle: The Story of the Atlantic Crossing*. The title of Chichester's book also features the name of his boat: *Gipsy Moth Circles the World*.

Somehow it would seem appropriate that the first man to sail the Atlantic alone from West to East should have been a Gloucester man with the blood of Vikings in his veins. As it so happens, it was. He was Captain Alfred Johnson, immortally known as Centennial Johnson. The sobriquet "Centennial" was

hung on him by the people of Gloucester after his trip and bears
on the date of his sailing. He left Gloucester on June 15, 1876,
and he considered his adventure a contribution to the celebration of the 100th anniversary of the establishment of his adopted
land, the United States of America. He called his 20-foot boat
the *Centennial,* and when he returned home after his historic
voyage, he found he had won the name for himself. Centennial
Johnson he became, and Centennial Johnson he is spoken of
today by hundreds of Cape Ann people who more than likely
could not tell you his first name. What they do remember is that
he was the first man, so far as is known, to sail the Atlantic
Ocean alone from America to Europe or vice versa, and that he
set a fashion which for a short while was a rage and still inspires others.

The trip took him forty-seven days from Nova Scotia, and,
like other solitary mariners since, bent on such a goal, he very
nearly lost his life in rough weather. Salt water got into his food
supply and he had a bout with a shark, nor were those his worst
trials. He arrived in England unscathed, never apparently having suffered any of the hallucinatory effects which sometimes
come with such loneliness amid perils and extended strain, or
from illness or fatigue (pep pills being then unknown). He had
sailed as a boy in his native Denmark, and he had been sailing
seven years with the Cape Ann fishing fleets when he undertook
his famous voyage. It was not the best year, from the point of
view of weather, to make such a trip. The record books show
that in 1876 the Gloucester fishing fleet lost twenty-seven vessels
and 212 men. As we shall see, an Atlantic gale almost destroyed
the *Centennial* and its twenty-nine-year-old skipper, which
would have made the macabre score twenty-eight Gloucester
vessels and 213 Gloucester men.

Johnson was well prepared for his trip. It is part of the folklore of the town to say that he crossed the Atlantic in a dory

and to leave it at that. His boat, however, was a very special dory.

The first dory was created in Amesbury on the periphery of Cape Ann for Cape Ann men, and one still occasionally hears it called a Cape Ann dory. It is an extraordinary vessel, with high sloping or flared sides, an overhanging bow, and a stern quite similar, although often with a notch or pink in it for sculling. The word "sculling" today conjures up a vision of college men on the Thames or the Charles River in sleek shells, rowing in competition. To scull a boat, a man puts a single oar over the stern's transom, and by moving it from side to side and reversing the blade each time, propels the boat forward. The method has the advantage of enabling him to see where he is going without craning his neck, since he is standing facing the bow. You can also step a mast in a dory quite easily, using one thwart for the partners, and, with a rudder or tiller or even an oar over the notch in the stern, sail it like a catboat. Customarily a dory was rowed by a man sitting on a thwart with the oars held to fulcrum by tholepins (oarlocks came later). When the dory was in its heyday during the great years of trawling, two men crewed one dory (as we have seen in the Blackburn story), and to say "He's a good dorymate" was the finest compliment a Gloucester man could pay another, unless he was to call him a damn good dorymate. There were, of course, even more profane extrapolations of the salute. Dories were usually 12 to 18 feet in length, and, sturdy vessels that they were, they could hold two tons of fish. They had distinctive lines, a functional perfection which has caught the eye of thousands of artists from Winslow Homer to Andrew Wyeth.

Fishermen will tell you that under some circumstances dories can have their devilish side. They are heavy to row, and their sides flare so high that broadside to the wind—their bottoms being flat—they will move in a direction the oarsman does not want them to go. Worse still, there are circumstances which can turn a dory bottom up. That done, however, they are not too difficult to right. This is what one storm did to the *Centennial* and to Johnson.

As we have pointed out, Johnson's boat was a very special dory. First, it was 20 feet in length, and it was made of oak strong enough to smash concrete, or, in any event, to "smash ice," and was given additional timber to make it even tougher than that. It was decked over (which, of course, dories are not) and had a cockpit from which Johnson could sail her, and a hatchway to take him below into a cabin or a hold. He also gave her a centerboard in order to move across the wind; a mast which could be readily stepped and quickly shipped and lashed; four sails, with fore-and-aft rigging—a mainsail, two jibs, and a square sail—and a bowsprit to spread the jibs. He had been designing the boat in his mind and on scraps of paper for two years. He was careful to include three watertight compartments. Whatever happened to the *Centennial*, it was not going to sink.

To build the boat, he called upon Higgins and Gifford, a well-known Gloucester shipbuilding yard, dealers who described themselves as manufacturers of yachts, and advertised that they built sailboats, rowboats, yawl boats, quarter boats, seine boats, pilot canoes, launches, dinkeys (sic) and DORIES. They put the word DORIES in full-face sans-serif capitals to make it clear that dories were a specialty with them. In their advertisements of the day under references, they added laconically the one line, "Most any fitter in Gloucester or New England." They had never built a boat like the *Centennial*, but the plans amused them and they did a proficient job. Johnson, his eye on the anniversary, had them paint her red, white and blue.

Into the hold he put a supply of food—condensed milk, canned meats, hardtack, tea and coffee, molasses—and sixty gallons of water, calculated to last him ninety days. To conserve the water, he had a tarpaulin in which to catch and hold rain. On top of his supplies undercover, he placed a mattress. He planned to sleep days and sail nights. In that way he was less likely to be run down.

He had trouble with his compass from the start. Feeling that it was being interfered with by the ballast he had thrust under his stores, he decided to shift the ballast and put in at Barrington, Nova Scotia, to do so. In three days, he was away again, plowing across the banks he knew so well, and heading for the broad deep. He took the shipping lanes, and more than a dozen vessels were to sight and hail him. Most of them hove to and offered assistance, assuming that his small craft was in distress, being that far from the mainland. One captain proposed taking Johnson and his craft aboard and depositing them offshore England to spare him the difficulties of sailing the ocean alone. He declined. He accepted a bottle of brandy from a German sea captain and nearly fell overboard taking it from the water. Newspaper reports of his progress were meager, but some of the ships that sighted him passed along news of the stages of his trip. He was able to check his compass against theirs, and this was a big help. A ship, the *Maggie Gander*, reported that it had given him bread and porter. He could stand such assistance because water had got into his food supplies during one storm.

It was in August that he capsized. The *Maggie Gander* had just given him assistance when the storm struck. He unstepped the mast, made it fast, tied a lifeline around his waist, and then threw out the drogue, a tough canvas sea anchor. Despite this, the *Centennial* broached, was smashed by a heavy sea, and capsized. Johnson managed to clamber onto the bottom of the overturned boat and was thus exposed to the raging Atlantic for twenty minutes, a very perilous perch. Then another wall of water struck him and spun the *Centennial*, enabling him to right her. The sloop had half filled with water, his food supplies were damaged, and the kerosene stove went overboard. But the dory was right side up; the iron ballast and the watertight compartments had done their work.

Even from that day on, it was not clear sailing. On August 8 his sounding line touched bottom off Ireland, although the fog hid the shore. The next day a passing ship gave him a bearing on Wexford Head, Ireland, and on August 10 he sighted Wales and put in. It was his forty-seventh day out of Nova Scotia. Rested and provisioned, on August 21 he sailed up the Mersey River to Liverpool. By then all England knew of his whereabouts, and the cruise up the river was triumphal.

Johnson returned to Gloucester, high praise and feting. After the feting he quietly returned to fishing. He lived to be eighty, hale and hearty and happiest when he was playing cards at the Master Mariners' Association quarters in Gloucester with his fellow captains who, like the rest of the world, had taken to calling him Centennial.

The year after Johnson made his historic voyage, Captain Thomas Crapo of New Bedford sailed the Atlantic in a 19.55-foot boat with a six-foot beam, a shorter but larger craft than the *Centennial*, and he took his wife with him. She became the first woman to make the trip in a small boat. It took them forty-nine days. People were now bent on beating the *Centennial's* time. In 1878 Andrew and Asa Andrews of Beverly sailed a 19-foot dory to England. The precursors of Madison Avenue were now getting into the act, and Andrews tried to sail alone under the sponsorship of the *New York World*. He had to be rescued. But he didn't quit easily. In 1892 he sailed a 14½-foot boat to Portugal from New Jersey. It was called the *Sapolio*, to advertise the soap of that name. In 1880 George S. Thomas and Fred Noman took a 16-foot 7-inch Higgins and Gifford boat from Gloucester to Cowes on the Isle of Wight in forty-six days and then back again.

All that finally prompted Howard Blackburn, the "fingerless navigator," as the newspaper called him, to try his hand at it. A demon drove the man. He had abandoned a Klondike expedition after sailing to San Francisco around Cape Horn, and was at loose ends. It was 1899 when he took his sloop the *Great Western* alone to England, and 1901 when he took the *Great Republic* alone to Portugal. It must be remembered that he was fingerless, having only his thumbs. Although he had devised numerous ingenuities to enable him to get things done, he had the most exasperating difficulties with knots, lines, fittings and the like. To haul a mainsail, he had to wrap the halyard around his body and lean away, and then make another hitch and lean away again. His two trips took the edge off the challenge, for how was a man to match Blackburn's feat unless he crossed with one hand behind his back?

At the height of all this, another Nova Scotian transplanted to America decided quietly to make navigational history. He was Joshua Slocum, the first man to circumnavigate the globe alone in a sailing vessel. Moved by a sense of history, and the appropriateness of things, in 1895 he chose Gloucester as the port of departure. He sailed from Boston to Gloucester, where he spent two weeks fitting out and provisioning the *Spray,* an old wreck he had completely rebuilt himself. He had constructed her in Fairhaven, near New Bedford.

When he sailed into Gloucester, as he recounts, he was apprehensive and put forth his best seamanship, for he knew the country's most expert sailors were watching. His arrival was dramatic. It was the first time in a career of seagoing and adventure (he had run away to sea when he was twelve, and he was now fifty-one) that he had sailed into any port alone, and his "heart was in his mouth." The weather was rough, the sea white, the wind strong. For a moment or two, as he approached his berth, it appeared as if the *Spray* might crash against the

pier, but Slocum brought her in so "quietly, after all, that she would not have broken an egg." The crowd on the wharf cheered. The esteem of such a mariner as Slocum for Gloucester and its traditions was praise indeed.

The late John Hays Hammond of Gloucester, a multimillionaire in his day acclaimed as the country's most famous civil engineer, tells an amusing story out of his Africa days of Slocum and his trip around the world. The famous navigator stopped at South Africa and was presented to the great Boer leader Oom Paul Kruger, a strict fundamentalist in matters Biblical. Kruger was convinced that the world was flat.

"In what direction, captain," Kruger said to Slocum, "do you intend to continue your voyage?"

"I'm going right around the world, Mr. President," replied Slocum.

"Don't lie," warned Kruger in all seriousness, "you mean across the world."

From Gloucester also sailed another famous ship on a historic voyage, one that was to shake the world with the claims and counterclaims of raging controversy. Dr. Frederick A. Cook (whose father's name was Koch), president of the Explorers Club of New York and one of its founding members, sailed from Gloucester on his way to the North Pole, or, in any event, closer to it than any man ever got by foot and sled. Not sentiment or a sense of history brought Cook to Gloucester to prepare for his famous voyage, but sheer practicality. He wanted as sturdy a ship as he could get, and a Gloucester schooner filled that bill.

Under Cook's watchful eye, one was refitted for Arctic sailing and renamed the *John R. Bradley* for Cook's financial backer. The *Bradley* sailed out of Gloucester on July 3, 1907, heading north. Cook took the hardy vessel up the west coast of Greenland, and far in Grant Land set up his furthermost base. From there, with Eskimos, he made his sprint for the pole. On April

21, 1908, he reached it. On September 1, 1909, Cook telegraphed
that he had reached the pole. Five days later Peary telegraphed
that he had. He gave the date of his achievement as April 6,
1909. When he heard that Cook had beaten him, he was enraged; he simply denied that Cook had made it and set out to
discredit him. He wasn't able to do that, but he besmirched
Cook's name and ruined his life. He had behind him the influence of the United States Navy and other powerful friends in
Washington. The United States Senate, however, cautiously re-
frained from honoring Peary for "discovering" the pole, and
merely commended him for his Arctic exploration. The Royal
Danish Geographical Society gave Dr. Cook its gold medal in
recognition of his discovery, and that award still stands. While
Peary had the Navy and the Establishment on his side, there
was one thing he did not have, and that was history. Polar history has now demonstrated that it was Peary's claim that was
false and his so-called discoveries such as Crocker Land and
Peary Channel and Peary Land were false claims. The distinguished Canadian historian, Farley Mowat, has exposed the
whole sorry story in his book *The Polar Passion*. The record
should be set straight, and there could be no better beginning
than a bronze plaque on a Gloucester pier noting that thence
Dr. Cook set out in a Gloucester schooner on the voyage that
was to take him to the North Pole. Donald MacMillan, another
great Arctic explorer, like Cook recognized the worth of
Gloucester schooners.

Cape Ann men have gone to the Arctic and the Antarctic,
have sailed around the world, and still plot such romantic voyages. The sea is in the blood of these men. The late William
Robertson of Ipswich was with Admiral Richard E. Byrd on his
Antarctic adventures and painted convincing pictures of be-
furred men busy in the polar regions. He is not to be confused
with William A. Robinson, also of Ipswich, a textile engineer

who at the age of twenty-five decided to sail around the world. He did it, but not alone. He had friends accompany him to Bermuda, and a Bermudan sail with him to Tahiti. The Bermudan, Willoughby Wright, found Tahiti too alluring and stayed there, and a native of Tahiti then became Robinson's sole crew. He was Etera, who stayed aboard until the end of the voyage. Robinson put it all down in his book, *10,000 Leagues Over the Sea*.

He set sail on June 23, 1928, in a 32-foot sloop, the *Svaap* (meaning "dream" in Sanskrit), and sailed more than 30,000 miles, returning to America in late fall of 1931. He had been gone three years and five and a half months. He left at a time when the world was caught up in such adventures, the prosperous twenties which Westbrook Pegler called the "Era of Wonderful Nonsense." He came back to a world in financial depression. The entire trip, including the price of the boat and the wages of the crew, had cost him $5,000. His book appeared the following year, and he was the toast of Cape Ann, a handsome, dashing figure.

No wonder that he won the heart of Miss Florence Crane, daughter of Richard T. Crane, whose Castle Hill mansion we visited in the chapter on the town of Ipswich. Their wedding was a major social event in Chicago and was reported in detail by society news reporters even to the detail that Miss Crane wore a veil that was once the property of an Austrian empress. But the big news was that the couple would honeymoon on the *Svaap* on a round-the-world cruise, with Daniel West, a cousin of Robinson's, aboard both as cook and as an artist who was to collaborate with Robinson on his next book. The cruise was interrupted when Robinson was stricken with appendicitis in the Galapagos Islands and was saved when his bride managed to radio a message to the outside world. She then nursed him until a United States Navy plane flew in to take him to Panama for surgery. The Chicago heiress evidently had enough of the sea-faring life, because she later divorced Robinson and married a Russian prince, Serge Belliselsky, while Robinson sailed off to the far Pacific islands to seek the life that Willoughby Wright had found some years before. One thing Robinson did for Ipswich before he left, however, was to restore shipbuilding there for a short while during World War II when he built landing craft there, and before that a schooner or two.

Joshua Slocum died at sea. Had he followed the seagoing practices of Centennial Johnson, he might have lived longer than he did. He disappeared with his boat on his way to the West Indies, and his son believed that he was cut down by some steamship while crossing the shipping lanes. Had he sailed by night and slept by day, as *Centennial* had, who knows but he might have escaped? And whatever became of the fisherman's light he was given by his friends in Gloucester which he said would make running him down at night the equivalent of running down a lightship?

≽ 10 ≼
Gloucester Castles,
Museums, and Houses

Cape Ann and its neighbors have more than their share of seventeenth-century houses (each town has at least one) and elegant nineteenth-century mansions, but it also has more than its
share of historical societies with their spate of relics and treasures, and substantial museums, some first-rate, others of a most
curious nature. Rockport has the Sandy Bay Historical Society,
which features, not unexpectedly, the granite industry, and is
fortunate in having as curator Dr. William D. Hoyt, whom we
have mentioned before, a scholar, historian and collector.
Manchester's Historical Society has as its headquarters the loveliest old white mansion in the center of town, directly across
from the library. We have seen what Ipswich has done and is
doing to preserve its antiquities, and have remarked on the little
museum of documents dealing with our constitutional freedom
which is to be found at Castle Hill.

In Salem we found the Peabody Museum and the Essex Institute, institutions so rich in their possessions and their histories
that each could be in itself a book. In fact, if, as we have remarked, New England is the authentic version of America, and

Cape Ann is the authentic version of New England, there are some statistics here to support the case. Twenty-three cities and towns in Essex County have local historical societies which are members of the Bay State Historical League. Of the cities and towns that have concerned us, Beverly, Essex, Newburyport, Gloucester, Ipswich, Manchester, Marblehead, Rockport, Rowley and Wenham all have historical societies belonging to the League. Newbury also has such a society, although it is not associated with the League.

Once again it is necessary to remember that all the work involved in the formation, maintenance and pursuit of the virtues of such historical societies and museums is borne by private citizens and supported by private funds. Cities and towns, boards of aldermen and school committees, all concerned with support of education, and with budgets bursting for that purpose, somehow do not often see such institutions as supplemental aids to learning. It is a New England failing, for New England is a section of the country too used to having private citizens carry public burdens. In Manchester a citizen built the library; in Gloucester one built the reservoir, another gave the library, a third built the new museum, others fought and saved the Fitz Hugh Lane House—a unique piece of architecture intimately associated with one of the city's most historic figures. Elsewhere we shall see the lack of social conscience on the part of the fishing industry. For example, the city of Gloucester does not even have a schooner as a museum to assist citizen and scholar in the re-creation of the past.

Motoring into the city of Gloucester from Manchester on the south, one crosses Blynman Bridge over the famous cut at the entrance to the Annisquam River, moves along Western Avenue past the "Man at the Wheel," and, confronted by the Tavern, a popular dining and drinking spa, turns left. The traffic signs soon indicate a right turn, and one realizes one is in an old town that took its character before the automobile dictated the pattern of growth. The motorist is once again pointed at water, turns left, and sees on his right a three-story gray stone building, boasting seven gables, which might be a small asylum and, indeed, was once a jail. For that reason it is, or was, popularly known as "the Old Stone Jug." It dominates a knoll whose sides slope gently to it. There are at the moment no trees, no shrubbery. A sign designates it as the home of Fitz Hugh Lane, and it can serve us here as a symbol.

First, it was a building well worth saving, but was labeled for razing under the urban redevelopment plans of the city of Gloucester. Representations of private citizens saved it, and the city is now faced with what to do with it, just as the nation on all fronts is faced with the problem of what to do with the arts, which cannot survive without subsidization that private fortunes can no longer provide. Every city and town is now charged, as European cities and towns have been for a long time, with preserving its monuments. Just as it must be evident to the city of Gloucester that it should have a schooner on public display to memorialize its days of greatness, and that the fishing industry will never have the wit, conscience or imagination to establish such a public museum, so it is becoming evident that the city as a corporation must move to guard its historic treasures. In the preservation of the Fitz Hugh Lane House, Gloucester has taken that first step. The ridiculous idea of turning it into a barroom was seriously advanced. Fortunately, the house stands, a striking landmark, with a bright future before it as a tourist attraction, particularly as the fame of Lane grows.

Leaving Gloucester to work out its problem, let us look at the museums that private citizens have given the city. There are four: a Bible museum; Beauport, a curio of architecture and decoration sometimes called "the most fascinating house in America": John Hays Hammond's medieval castle that is a hodgepodge of periods and centuries, an eclectic pudding of a piece but a whopping tourist attraction; and the Cape Ann Historical Association's museum, which is autochthonous, harmonious and exquisite. All four are worth visiting; the last is worth extended contemplation in our purpose to deepen our knowledge of the nature and history of Cape Ann.

The least of the museums is the Bible Museum at 58 Middle Street, which is associated with the Open Church Foundation, another endowment of Congregationalist Roger W. Babson. The land on which it stands was purchased by one of his ancestors, Isabel Babson, in 1663, and here he was born in 1875. The museum benefits today from gifts from the members of the Open Church Foundation, drawn from many denominations. Not only are various Bibles exhibited, but various curiosities of Biblical history, including a brick from the wall of the palace of Nebuchadnezzar, who laid waste Jerusalem six hundred years before Christ and carried Jews into their Babylonian captivity.

Among the Bibles on display is the Treacle Bible of 1568, so named because the twenty-second verse of the eighth chapter of the Book of Jeremiah asks is there no "treacle in Gilead" rather than "balm." Another is the so-called Breeches Bible, which reports that Adam and Eve, on their expulsion from Eden, covered their nakedness with breeches rather than leaves. Still another rare volume is the Reverend John Eliot's Algonquin Bible which he translated into the tongue of the tribe.

A second edition of Martin Luther's translation of the Bible into German is displayed, dated 1535. There are a Latin translation of the Psalms dating back to 1472, a 1378 translation of the New Testament, and fragments of the Gospels dating back to the first and second centuries. The walls are decorated with a large colored map of the Holy Land and similar appropriate pictures.

The museum called "Beauport" is certainly one of the most

extraordinary in the United States of America, and is the creation of the late Henry Davis Sleeper, a man of independent means who came to be known as the leading interior decorator in the country.

As William B. Blanford and his wife, Elizabeth Clay Blanford, who are curator and chief guide to the museum, explain: "Beauport is not a house of period rooms, but of rooms decorated with thousands of objects of early Americana and European pieces brought to this country by settlers or imported by them and used in their homes." What gives the house its style are its infinite variety, the striking contrast between the various rooms, and Sleeper's dramatic gift of selection.

The museum was in one way almost an accident. Sleeper, in 1904, built a small summer cottage on the shore of Gloucester Harbor on what is now Eastern Point Road, but the idea of making it into a museum did not come until three years later. In that year he discovered the William Cogswell House in Essex, in a state of decay and about to be razed. He took from it some beautiful wood paneling and began to expand his cottage, one room after another, until the count today stands near thirty. The Cogswell paneling helped create the center of the house.

The idea then formed in his mind to present "an interpretation of Early America through the medium of interior decoration." Paul Hollister and Samuel Chamberlain in their book *Beauport at Gloucester* quote Sleeper as saying, "Mightn't it be fun to have a house in which each room could recapture some of the spirit of a specific mood or phase or 'period' of our American life from the time of Plymouth down through the Revolution and the early Republic?" In a curious way the building does that, although it almost seems more a post-factum imposition than a theme running through the beautiful sequence of rooms.

Sleeper lived in the house as it grew, and entertained lavishly. The list of artists, writers, singers, sculptors, playwrights, and

musicians who were guests there would fill pages. From Lady
Gregory to Noel Coward, from Henry James to Elsie Janis, thus
ran his list of guests. Sleeper was an intimate of A. Piatt Andrew, who was for many years Gloucester's distinguished Con-
gressman, a man of taste and cultivation and, like Sleeper, a patron of the arts. Their inclinations and sympathies were similar,
and with the outbreak of World War I in Europe both felt an
obligation. With a third friend, they organized, staffed and supplied the American Field Service in France before the entry of
the United States into the conflict. Sleeper returned to complete
Beauport and to establish his reputation as one of the most
tasteful interior decorators in the country.

One of his proudest influences was responsible for the unparalleled Winterthur Museum. In his foreword to a book on American furniture, Henry Francis du Pont wrote: "Seeing Harry
Sleeper's house in Gloucester, Massachusetts, made me decide to
build an American house at Southampton." In the creation of
the American Wing of the Metropolitan Museum in New York,
experts studied Beauport. On Sleeper's death, there was a danger that dealers might plunder the collection, but Mrs. Helena
W. McCann, a Woolworth heiress, bought it intact, and lived in
it as a summer home. Her children, as a memorial to her,
deeded it to the Society for the Preservation of New England
Antiquities, a private organization that owns and manages more
than half a hundred properties. Of all their properties, Beauport
is the most visited, as it is the most visited of the Gloucester museums.

One enters the museum by Cogswell Hall through a massive
front door, onto some of the sixty hooked rugs in the Sleeper
collection, many of them designed by Edward Sands Frost, the
first commercial designer of hooked rugs. In the hall are some
China Trade porcelain, and examples of early American Fraktur
work, a sort of primitive method of manuscript or document il-

lumination. From Cogswell Hall we pass to Central Hall, which
is dedicated to George Washington. Two features catch the eye
here, despite Sleeper's dictum that no one thing may dominate a
room. One is a magnificent collection of amber glass, beautifully
back-lighted. The other is a dumb stove, which was one designed to receive heat by pipe from a fire on a floor below; but
this is designed in the form of George Washington, standing majestically with a toga over his uniform, looking for all the world
as if his right arm were in a sling. No matter, he is impressive,
and equally so, the entire hall.

After that we wander from one room to another: the Jacobean
Room, the Paul Revere Room, the Byron Room, the Strawberry
Hill Room, the Little Lady Room, the Passage, the Pine
Kitchen, the French Foyer, the Franklin Game Room, the Nel-
son Room, the Stairway, the Belfry Bedroom, and the Upstairs
Sitting Room, the Indian and Mariner's Rooms, the North Gal-
lery, the China Passage, the Cloister, the Octagon Room, the
Golden Step Room, the Green Dining Room, the South Gallery,
and the Chinese Room.

An inventory of the rooms and their contents would fill an encyclopedia. Porcelain, china, woodenware, pewter, wedding
rugs, coffin rugs, a burl bucket, hutch tables, a soldier's canteen
made of wood, a Franklin stove, amber glass, Sandwich glass,
Waterford chandelier, primitive paintings, Chinese wallpaper
made for the New Jersey Revolutionary statesman Robert Morris, an original pine-tree flag, red tole Argand lamps, demijohns, ancient figurines, tinsel pictures, Sheraton furniture, a "tall
man, short man" mirror with two looking glasses at right angles
so the short man might look up and the tall man down, redware,
Toby jugs, Hepplewhite, copper luster pieces, scrimshaw, an ob-
long piano, a jade-colored Bristol glass vase, a pencil post bed,
and on and on and on and on run the innumerable items. They
have been brought together by Sleeper's gift of arrangement,

and every room has its cult of worshipers who avow it to be the finest. Without doubt, Beauport is unique, and its claim to be "the most fascinating house in America" is not far from the truth.

The contrast with Hammond Castle is extreme. They have much in common. Both are examples of architecture that is European and foreign to the Gloucester shore, with no local tradition behind either of them. Each was the home of a brilliant eccentric with his own views on collecting and decorating and the money to do it. Each of these manor lords loved to entertain, and each preferred to choose his guests from the world of the arts. Josef Hofmann, Leopold Stokowski, Igor Stravinsky, Albert Spalding, Henry Hadley, George Chadwick, Madame Antoinette Szumowska and Timothée Adamowski, George Gershwin, Lily Pons, Mary Garden (who spurned Essex clams) were among the musicians who came. From the theater Hammond had as dinner companions Laurette Taylor, Nazimova, Clifton Webb, Ramon Novarro, Mrs. Patrick Campbell, Burgess Meredith, Billy Rose, and more. Statesmen and prelates, the Vincent Astors, local painters and poets, Mrs. William Howard Taft—a list, in brief, to top even Harry Sleeper's. The meals were so memorable at the Castle that Mrs. Corinne B. Witham, curator of the Hammond Museum, has prepared a cookbook of some of the inventor's favorite recipes.

During his last years Hammond opened his home to the public at stipulated times as a museum, beating the tax system, and on his death he bequeathed the museum to the Cardinal-Archbishop of Boston, the late Richard J. Cushing, who was also a dinner guest at the Castle. Hammond had offered the estate to the city of Gloucester, but the city fathers had declined the gift. Hammond had high admiration for the Cardinal, and the medieval quality of the museum with, indeed, many sections of the structure itself and many pieces standing in it, were of a religious motif or ecclesiastical origin. It was Hammond's home, and he ordered the pieces for his own convenience rather than in any chronological order. Aside from the days when it was open to the public, it was guarded by formidable dogs.

The Castle, which raises massive twin stone towers beside the sea and sports flying buttresses, Gothic windows, and a drawbridge, has within an eclectic collection eclectically arranged, as we have indicated. Hammond began his collecting of medieval materials about 1910 and pursued it, with diminishing vigor, until his death. In Europe Gothic and Renaissance architecture occasionally occur in the same building, and they meet in Hammond Castle. The main chamber—indeed, the dominant center of the Castle—is the Great Hall, an enormous stone room 100 feet long, 25 feet wide and 58 feet high. Its proportions, it is said, are similar to those of the old Cathedral of Saint Nazaire in Carcassonne, France. A bishop's chair, fifteenth-century Spanish, at the head of the room is flanked by two Italian chairs from the eighteenth century. To one side is a giant fireplace. The whole has a monastic effect.

In this hall is the magnificent pipe organ which inventor Hammond spent twenty years assembling. Some say he designed the hall to house the organ, and he meant it as the perfect instrument.

Upstairs is a bedchamber called the Cardinal's bedroom, with floor tiles taken from the palace of Diego Columbus, son of Christopher, in Hispaniola, and a fourteenth-century bed from Italy made of wrought iron raising a crimson canopy with gold-embroidered fleurs-de-lis.

The family dining room where Hammond entertained his celebrated guests is paneled with wood taken from a provincial house in central France, and centered in it is a twelfth-century table. The windows of the room came from the ruined palace of the Knights Templar at Avignon. So it goes. There are a rose

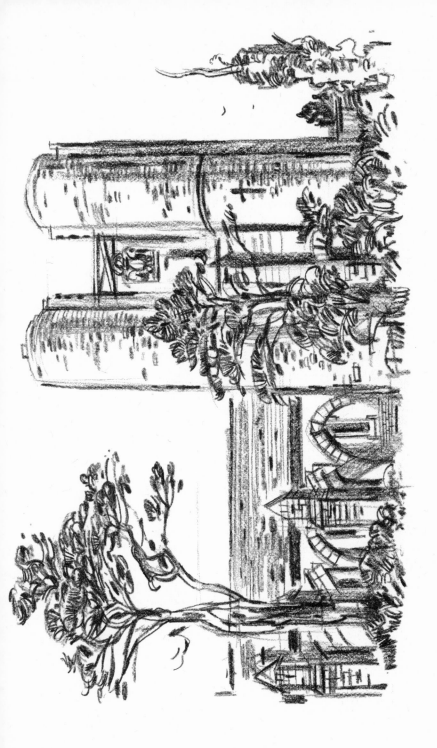

window, (a copy of that in Reims Cathedral), a Sicilian room with clay jars dug up from an ancient Roman apothecary shop, a conservatory atrium with four Renaissance columns at the edge of a pool, and endless curiosities. The whole is worked, of course, into an arrangement which, despite its diversity, does not jar. Choral groups as well as organists use the Castle, and lectures on antiques are given. The whole is an exotic growth on the Cape Ann shore, and if lacking in interest to scholars, is a stunning tourist attraction.

The quarters and contents of the Cape Ann Historical Association, formerly called the Cape Ann Scientific, Literary and Historical Association, stand in remarkable contrast to the other more publicized museums in Gloucester. It is, however, an *organic* growth, native to the soil, clinging tight to its purpose. Despite its name, it confines itself pretty much to the city of Gloucester and its immediate environs. From a historical view, it houses the most important collection on the Cape north of Essex Institute and Peabody Museum in Salem. The heart of its worth is the collection of Fitz Hugh Lane paintings.

Unlike Hammond Castle or Beauport, the "Scientific," as the natives call it, is not the work of one man, but the ongoing achievement of an association. Beauport and the Castle reached a state of completion, more or less, with the deaths of their creators and, like the Gardner Palace in Boston, are unlikely to suffer either addition or diminution. The "Scientific" is vital—altering and growing—with local directors, and continuing concern for history and the intellectual life of the area. Local poets have read there, and lecturers are brought down from Boston. Additions are made to the collection, evaluated and displayed in proportion to the space at hand. While Hammond Castle and Beauport need only such moneys as will sustain them (Beauport is aided by a foundation), the "Scientific" depends on the dues of its members, the half-dollars collected at its doors, a small en-

dowment, and the generosity of its benefactors. Growth is always more of a challenge than preservation of a status quo.

While, as we have said, the "Scientific" is not the conception
or the creation of one man, there are two men who deserve special recognition for the state of the museum and its collection as
they stand today. They are the late Alfred Mansfield Brooks,
and the present curator-president, Hyde Cox, whose home is in
Manchester, but whose interests have chiefly centered in the city
of Gloucester.

Under Brooks the Fitz Hugh Lane collection was, for the
most part, assembled, and the unparalleled collection of the
local artist's drawings collated. Under Cox, a second, and spec-
tacular, addition to the museum has been built, and the association's treasures arranged with impeccable taste. The original
Pleasant Street quarters of the association were in the white
clapboarded Captain Elias Davis House, an early nineteenth-
century (c. 1804) dwelling not too distinguished architecturally.
In 1936 an addition was constructed to accommodate the growing heap of materials contributed by members and friends.
There was a danger of its becoming like "grandma's attic," to
use the phrase of Walter Muir Whitehill, author of *Independent
Historical Societies,* who had high praise for the Gloucester
collection. That danger was averted by Curator Brooks. He
brought to the organization, on his retirement from teaching, a
peerless sense of discrimination, an ever-acquisitive mind, a
Gloucester background rooting down through centuries, far-
flung blood relationships, wit, and a charm of manner that in-
spired confidence. He also had scholarship. Under him the Lane
collection grew.

The task of displaying that collection fell to his successor,
who shared many of his enthusiasms. What has resulted has
been a tidy ordering of the Association's business, increased donations, and a major anonymous gift which permitted the con-

struction of the finest building in the city of Gloucester in decades. Donald Monell, whose presence has given Cape Ann an architect to match its painters and poets, was chosen to design the addition to house the Lane paintings and the marine collection of the association.

In what can be called sympathetic contemporary design, a four-story building (one of them below the level of Pleasant Street), 50 by 70 feet, has been attached to the earlier addition to the Captain Davis house. Of brick and precast concrete, painted white to blend with the clapboarding of the original building, the new structure is set back from the street by a garden courtyard, where a great black anchor stands as sculpture against the wall. Four towering arched windows give style to the façade and light to the two display floors.

Within are the gentle rooms of the Davis house, with their authentic furnishings, display cases with overseas treasures brought to Gloucester homes by ranging mariners, or native handmade comforts and luxuries of early American homes. A silver bowl by Paul Revere tells of the Revolutionary period, and elsewhere hangs an original "red coat" taken from one of the British soldiers.

The Fitz Hugh Lane collection is hung and lighted chastely, and one is immediately aware of an absolute lack of any sense of clutter. What makes the Lane collection brilliant in display is not merely the sequence of the years but the juxtaposition of the paintings and the pencil sketches the fastidious artist made in preparation for his oils. We can sit here for hours and walk with Lane off into space, whether it be his *View of Gloucester Harbor,* an oil painting about a yard in length that re-creates a century, or his view of Riverdale, of similar size, that shows what can only be called the sanctity of a countryside in haying time.

In all, the museum has 33 paintings by Lane and 105 drawings. Most are on the first display floor of the new building, and despite the museum's provincial status, the serenity and peace remind one of the Frick Museum in New York. With the new building, and diligent financial management, the directors are now able to keep the museum open year-round from 11:00 A.M. to 4:00 P.M. The Castle and Beauport are open to the public only in the summer months.

What the Cape Ann Historical Association is most in need of are financial assistance, some of which could come from the city in view of the institution's collaboration with the schools, and additional donations of paintings, not merely of Fitz Hugh Lane but of some of the great figures who have painted on the Cape, from William Morris Hunt to Stuart Davis. It needs also additional admission receipts from the people of Cape Ann, too many of whom live in ignorance of the contents (one city councilor walked by its doors daily for a year without even looking in on the newest piece of construction in the city). The building of the new air-conditioned wing, and the tasteful display of the Lane collection, have already increased annual attendance from two hundred persons a year to three thousand.

Every Cape Ann community has its historical society, and each is a little museum. Wenham boasts an extraordinary collection of dolls. All have ship-minded exhibits of one sort or another, although in this regard also the Gloucester historical museum excels, with its second display floor given over to a marine collection featuring some exquisite scale models of brigantines, schooners and other vessels. Then, too, one must remember the various art galleries on the Cape, of which dozens flourish, and the art associations whose ever-changing hangings are museums in themselves wherein the visitor is curator and critic, discoverer and damner. No section of the country offers such variety of exhibitions in so small a geographical compass.

❧ 11 ❦

Flora, Fauna, and Folklore

In an age when man is more and more conscious of his alien-
ation from nature, the essential wholesomeness of Cape Ann be-
comes more and more evident. There is no resident of the Cape
who cannot, by a five-minute walk, reach either woodland, an
expanse of marsh, or the sea. Any one of those, or the still extensive acreage of pasture and meadow, can give him a source from
which he can draw the psychic replenishment nature has always
provided. To live on Cape Ann is to become a naturist, if you
will (a word I take to mean an amateur naturalist), unless one is
completely lacking in the sensitivity that abounded here in the
nineteenth century.

Not only does Cape Ann lie in one of the major flyways
through which myriad flocks of birds migrate in spring and fall,
but it thrusts itself 12 miles into the sea, and consequently be-
comes more than ever a welcome landfall for weary birds pursuing their instinctive flights from one land to another or from one
end of the world to another.

More than that, Cape Ann, in itself, offers innumerable nesting places for a variety of shore birds as well as other species
common to the East Coast. The result is that bird watchers
abound, of varying intensity and knowledge, from John Kieran
to the humblest housewife who supplies sunflower seed or bread

crumbs to the feeder in her back yard to keep the bird population alive during the exhausting winters.

The variety of natural conditions on Cape Ann—rivers, swamps, salt water marshes, deciduous woods, conifer groves, open fields, brush, scrub, sea cliffs, offshore islands, miles of sandy beaches, dunes and rocks—all have their appeal to different species. Add to the natural advantages a population which, well above the national average, builds birdhouses, stocks bird-feeding apparatus, and reads the ever-growing literature of ornithology, and you have created a syndrome that generates interest in nature even among the normally unconcerned.

Fortunately, too, interested citizens are seeing to it that more and more land is held by conservation trusts of one sort or another. Plum Island is a 6-mile-long peninsula of beach, with dunes rising to 100 feet in some places, swamp, piny woodland and salt-water marsh with great dikes and impoundments constructed to ensure suitable conditions for waterfowl. Most of it is under the control of the Federal Government and makes one of the great wildlife sanctuaries of the East Coast, a refuge not for birds and beasts only, but for man and woman weary of the cacophony of the highways and the tensions of the town.

Persons living in the city are fortunate in the course of their day to see a robin. Pigeons, starlings, and English house sparrows are the customary birds one finds in the city. The whole spectrum of bird life is thus denied the urban population, a panoply that comes to life vividly on Cape Ann whether one chooses to scan the shore for sandpipers, the coastal waters for ducks, or the woodlands for thrushes, warblers, and other songbirds.

To scrutinize the range of shore line which contributes to Cape Ann's unique character, let us start at the northernmost reaches, on the south shore of the Merrimack River where Plum Island drops 6 miles almost due south, flanked by the Atlantic

Ocean on the east and Plum Island River on the west. In the mouth of the Merrimack River—thanks in part to a sewer outlet —there is a constant congregation of gulls and other sea birds. Crossing over from Newburyport to the island, we soon enter the Parker River National Wildlife Refuge, as it is called, taking its name from a large stream that runs through a broad salt marsh from the west to join Plum Island River. Those marshes themselves provide impenetrable bird refuges, often alive with black-bellied plover, shy ducks, and numerous other waterfowl. On the island, one can watch the warblers at Hellcat Swamp or take to the prodigious stretch of beach to catch sight of pelagic wanderers, perhaps a jaeger brought close to shore by a recent storm or the pursuit of prey. In the impoundments on the west side of the island, geese, brant and ducks feed unmolested, knowing themselves safe from hunters.

Farther down, coot paddle in flocks, indifferent to the yellowlegs and herons feeding along the shore. To this refuge the purple martin has returned after years of mysterious absence from Massachusetts. Here, when the lemmings are scarce in Labrador, the fierce snowy owl descends to survey a bleak winter scene before fleeing north again to his arctic hideaways.

Across from the tip of Plum Island lie Great Neck and Little Neck in Ipswich, and southeast of them, Castle Hill and Crane's Beach, in much of its topography the match of Plum Island. The 4-mile stretch of beach is backed up by sand dunes that creep like predatory primordial monsters, all but animated, with here and there a treetop sticking out of the crest of one where the woods have been devoured. As on Plum Island, wildlife abounds. The dunes prey on the plants, and in turn minor vegetations thrust their roots into the sand to stop its relentless march under the whip of the wind. Hudsonia spreads its graygreen tiny leaves in one place; and in another, beach grass sends down questing roots to anchor in the sand.

There are woods behind Crane's Beach sufficient for an owl to hide from besetting crows, and growths of pine that sustain the siskins through the winter. You will be lucky—if very circumspect—to see the red fox, but he is here. Chipmunks and woodchucks are almost as common as squirrels; and in the marshes, muskrats reign, slinking through the waters, half-submerged, noiseless until they dive and disappear. The animals most readily noticed—and loveliest of all—are the deer that forage on the lawns and in the woods.

Shore birds are the basic treasure of this great spit of sand. The least tern and the piping plover nest here, or will until picnickers in power squadrons at length overrun too often the farthest reaches of the sands.

A keen and patient observer over a span of four seasons might find one hundred species of bird on these reservations, although he will have to go farther inland for others, certain birds of the forest, such as the hermit thrush, or of rocky streams, such as the Louisiana water thrush. Don't mistake the bats for birds. They, too, are here in limited variety.

Continuing southeast along the coastal waters, we come to Coffin's Beach and Wingaersheek Beach, two more magnificent sandy strands on the north side of the Annisquam River. We have seen that waterway at its southern end where it runs the narrow cut at Blynman Bridge and enters Gloucester Harbor. At Wingaersheek Beach, it enters Ipswich Bay; and if you like your fish large, there are tuna here, or if you like your mammals very large, you can occasionally observe whales spouting.

The marshes along the Annisquam River and the mud flats exposed at low tide also provide ideal feeding grounds for various shore birds. The great blue heron stalks the remote inlets of the marsh majestically, indifferent to the scavenger gulls overhead. He is the great hunter, and his long beak, like an *épée*, is swift and sure.

Crossing the Annisquam River where it enters Ipswich Bay, we come back to the cap of the Cape, for this is the island, and moving along the waters of Ipswich Bay, past Annisquam Light, we come to Folly Point and Folly Cove, and then to the most seaward thrust of Cape Ann, Halibut Point.

Beyond Halibut Point is Andrews Point, and the two rank among New England's finest vantage points for observing the oceanic birds. Off the shore, in turbulent seas, the common eider keeps his harem, and even the king eider has been seen. In the coldest weather, purple sandpipers can be seen shuffling back and forth on the gleaming rocks. Guillemots, dovekies and kitti-wakes are birds a man might travel a good many hundred miles to observe, but they can be caught here by sharp binoculars, without putting out to sea. At times, the gannet dives close to this shore, dropping from 50 feet in the air to kill its prey.

Turning south, one drives past Pigeon Cove, one of the Cape's most historic regions, and so into the town of Rockport. Off the coast are the Dry Salvages—Yankee slurring of Champlain's "Les Trois Sauvages"—Straitsmouth Island, Thacher's Island and Milk Island, called by John Smith the Three Turks' Heads in happy remembrance of three combatants he decapitated. These islands make crowded nesting sites for herring gulls and the great blackbacks. Our journey has brought us to Gloucester's eastern shore, rugged, rocky coastline where tumbling, racing, exploding surf cannonades snowy spray high into the air, to the perpetual fascination of tourist and artist alike. Along here ducks flock: buffleheads and goldeneyes, browns and mallards, scoter and merganser.

Not all the fishing done off these shores, of course, is commercial. Yachts rigged for tuna move in and out of the harbors. Charter boats take fishing parties wherever they want to go, and regular fishing trips leave the Gloucester wharves, and some-times hover not too far from the sewer outlet to make sure some fish are caught. Here and there, anglers stand in the surf to catch bass. Along the boulevard with the famous Leonard Craske statue of the "Man at the Wheel" looking down on them, dozens of fishermen—male and female, young and old—lean against the iron railing at high tide day or night to drop their hooks in the harbor waters.

Beside them, a group of bird watchers led by an Audubon expert will have mounted their telescopes to catch a glimpse of the singular, furtive Barrow's goldeneye, so different from its gregarious fellows. In the harbor lies Ten Pound Island, where Winslow Homer boarded and painted—deserted now, and the subject of council debate as to its future and happiest potential use. Looking beyond the island and across the harbor, we see Eastern Point Light and the breakwater over which storms break their white rage trying to reach the moored ships.

Near Eastern Point, along the rocky shore we pursued from Rockport south, lies Mother Ann, the figure of a reclining woman espied in the rocks, familiar for centuries and for centuries unchanged. Near her too is a take-off point where the monarch butterflies muster in legions before they rise in a golden cloud to challenge the ineffable distances.

Not all Cape Ann fauna are natural or palpable. Standing on that breakwater and looking out on the ocean, on Massachusetts Bay, one might think he saw Old Triton rise and sound his horn, or a sea serpent raise its scaly visage. That is indeed what did happen. Triton did not surface, but the sea serpent did, and no sighting is more authenticated, despite the claims of the good people of Nantucket. The monster was reported in Gloucester Harbor in 1817, 1818, and 1819. Those might be described as the bonanza years for sea serpent sightings, at least on the North Shore of Boston and Cape Ann. Numerous persons saw the visitor, men and women standing on the shore, sailors from their ships, knowledgeable men through their spyglasses. As early as 1638 the serpent had been seen on Cape Ann, and on that occasion coiled like a cable on a rock. Indians dissuaded English colonists from shooting it, saying that the monster might attack if not killed instantly.

On the nineteenth-century sea serpent, there is no more articulate witness than the Reverend Cheever Felch, who saw it from a longboat of the U.S.S. *Independence* at the same time as the crew of a government ship surveying the harbor saw it.

"The animal," wrote Felch to a Boston newspaper, "was then between 30 and 40 yards distance from us. He soon sunk, but not so deep but we could trace his course. He rose again within 20 yards distance of us, and lay some time on the water. He then turned, and steered for Ten Pound Island; we pulled after him, but finding he was not pleased with the noise of our oars, they were laid in, and the boat sculled. We again approached very near him. . . . From my knowledge of aquatic animals, and habits of intimacy with marine appearances, I could not be deceived. We had a good view of him . . . for half an hour. . . . His color is a dark brown, with white under the throat. His size we could not accurately ascertain, but his head is about three feet in circumference, flat, and much smaller than his body. We did not see his tail; but from the end of his head to the farthest protuberance was not far from 100 feet. I speak with a degree of certainty, from being much accustomed to measure and estimate distances and length. I counted fourteen bunches on his back, the first one say, ten or twelve feet from his head and the others about seven feet apart. They decreased in size toward the tail. His motion was sometimes very rapid, and at other times he lay nearly still. . . ." No line of dolphins that; and the description coincides with the testimony of other witnesses who did not have the same vantage point.

Gloucester folk were not above strange tales. There was a witch who turned into a crow and harassed soldiers hundreds of miles from home. When the soldiers shot the crow with a silver button, the witch fell with a broken leg back in Gloucester. Our sea serpent story is of a different order from that yarn, and the testimony of the Reverend Mr. Felch is hard to discount. Experts sent down to Gloucester from Boston were not convinced, however, and the sea serpent, no doubt in pique over such skepticism, has not reappeared. Fifty years after the fact, Louis Agassiz, the naturalist, was not ready to discount the story.

Witches and mystery also attend Dogtown Common in Gloucester, a ghost town of sunken, overgrown cellar holes, an upland that was once common land for pasturing cattle and cutting timber in the late seventeenth century. In the early eighteenth century a village grew. Because one rich man built a house there in fear of pirate raids along the coast, the legend rose that such was the provenance of the whole village. Historians dismiss the thought. Once a hundred families lived in Dogtown; in 1830 the last inhabitant was taken to the poorhouse. The isolated moors were just not attractive territory. Not for homesteading, let us say, because they have become most attractive for picnickers, mycologists, lovers, family outings, hikers, naturists, naturalists, wild-flower clubs, and bird watchers. The uplands also provide some of the finest blueberry picking on Cape Ann.

The name "Dogtown" was given to the area in its days of decay when only half a dozen homes were left there, most of them occupied by crochety old women each of whom seemed to have a watchdog. Besides those, other wild dogs roamed the area, and hence the name. It is no surprise that some of the women were regarded as witches by the less compassionate citizens. What also gives Dogtown distinction is the landscape, grassland interspersed with growths of red cedars, the whole with large boulders—erratics from the glacier—scattered over it. One of these—a great gaping thing—is called the Whale's

Jaw. Stranger still, and yet not so strange, knowing what we do of the character of Roger W. Babson, are the inscriptions carved on some of the larger rocks.

They read, "Never Try, Never Win," "Help Mother," "Keep out of Debt," "Get a Job," and similar wholesome bits of counsel. Babson had them carved not merely for the edification of the public, since he who runs may read, but to give employment to Finnish stoneworkers during the depths of the depression, the onset of which he had so correctly predicted. Not long ago Melvin T. Copeland, George Fisher Baker Professor of Administration, Emeritus, of the Harvard Business School, organized a committee to save Dogtown Common from the threat of real estate developers. The battle seesawed, with the city council unable to come to grips with the matter, but was finally resolved by the need for a new reservoir for the city, which is always troubled by a lack of potable fresh water. A good portion of Dogtown was already a watershed for the Babson Reservoir. Now the remaining acres are the watershed for the new Goose Cove Reservoir, and the development predators seem to be thwarted. Knowing their indestructibility, however, Copeland's group, now disbanded, feeling the battle won, are nevertheless standing by to guard for the people of Gloucester one of the most unusual public parks in New England. For the pleasure of antiquarians just about every cellar hole in Dogtown has been identified as the site of the home of various residents long deceased.

The upland is also the site of one of the city's more poignant stories, "James Merry and the Bull." Merry was a seaman who brought back from Spain memories of bullfighting. A big powerful man, 6 feet 7 inches and better than 250 pounds, he decided to fight his bull calf by wrestling with it. He had little trouble putting the calf to the ground, and performed the feat several times for friends. In the bull's third year, it was more than a match for him, and friends had to rescue him. Later he was found dead in the pasture, the victim of the bull's brute strength and innocent rage. He had tested himself against the animal once too often.

Some interesting excavating has been done at Dogtown by Frederick H. Norton, professor of ceramics at the Massachusetts Institute of Technology. Roger W. Babson, again, had a hand in preparing a Cape Ann Tourist's Guide, in which he reports that Norton found "a great many fragments of native redware, imported English and Italian red, yellow and brown earthen-ware, Chinese porcelain, stoneware from Staffordshire, 1720–1780," and other specimens, now on exhibition at the Sandy Bay Historical Society in Rockport.

History and topography have given Dogtown an air of mystery, an aura of romance. Marsden Hartley, who loved to paint there, and had a poet's gift with words, said this of its remote reaches:

"Dogtown looks like a cross between Easter Island and Stonehenge—essentially druidic in its appearance. It gives the feeling that an ancient race might turn up at any moment and review an ageless rite there . . . sea gulls fly over it on their way from the marshes to the sea; otherwise the place is forsaken and majestically lovely as if nature had at last formed one spot where she can live for herself alone." Such legacies in our day are rare; and worth the cherishing. Any smack of commerce in Dogtown would be a blasphemous intrusion.

In delightful contrast to the open upland of Dogtown Common are the deep woods of Ravenswood Park on Western Avenue, miles to the southwest in the Magnolia section of the city. Ravenswood Park is the acreage given to the city by Samuel Sawyer, and since enlarged through the energy of the trustees. This woodland has broad dirt roads circling within it, and mossy, winding paths twisting in and out among the oaks, alders, pines and hemlocks and other trees that crowd each other today as they have for centuries. One of the paths leads to a granite peak which affords to the persistent a magnificent view of the harbor below.

In the park grows the magnolia glauca, and the spot marks its northernmost attainment. From this flowering plant, so far here from the warm, companionable climes where it makes a sturdy tree, the section takes its name. In Ravenswood—and this is the only place on Cape Ann where it is found—the magnolia seeks the swamp and, overshadowed by hemlock, beech and maple, still manages to put forth its creamy petals. Wilson Flagg, a noted Cape Ann naturalist, tells of it in his *The Woods and By-Ways of New England:*

"The only [magnolia] that grows wild in New England is of small stature, sometimes called the Beaver-tree. It inhabits a swamp near Gloucester about 20 miles from Boston. This place is its northern boundary. The flowers are dull white. without any beauty, but possessed of a very agreeable fragrance, causing them to be in demand. The Magnolia wood is annually stripped of flowers and branches and the trees will probably be extirpated before many years by this sort of vandalism." That was 1872; the magnolia survives, but barely; and again, only through the careful nurture of public-spirited citizens. Something splendid shines in the plant struggling to maintain itself in such chilly isolation so far from its usual habitat.

Wild flowers lend charm not only to Ravenswood and Dogtown but all the Cape. There is a lily pond of unusual size, more than a half-mile stretch. All the customary wild flowers abound, and rarities such as the pitcher plant and the sundew, two of America's three insect-eating plants, are here. Here too is spice-bush, sweet pepper bush, laurel, hobblebush and partridgeberry with its twin flowers, columbine and bluets, asters and sweet-brier, skunk cabbage and Dutchman's-breeches—there is no end

to them. Elliott Rogers, one of the best authorities, estimates that 5,000 varieties of plants grow on Cape Ann, but warns that to see some of the most attractive of wild flowers, the explorer may have to go deep into the swamps. Near Ravenswood Park, by the way, is a spring that gushes forth the sweetest water on Cape Ann.

On the shore east of Ravenswood is Rafe's Chasm, a deep gash in the granite where the tide rushes in as into a thunder hole, rumbles, roars, and fires spray in the air as from a cannon. Not too far from the chasm is the Reef of Norman's Woe, made famous by Longfellow in "The Wreck of the Hesperus," although the *Hesperus* was never wrecked there, but off Portland, Maine, where Longfellow spent his childhood. However, dozens of other ships have been wrecked on the ugly excrescence of rocks lying on the top of the water and surrounded by black evil boulders which leave no escape for the derelict ship in a thundering sea. But the people of Gloucester who gave the name "Magnolia" to their southernmost village have given the name "Hesperus" to its main street. One of Cape Ann's most popular writers on nature, Nancy Larter, makes her home in Magnolia. Her late artist-husband Robert Larter, carved unique wood sculpture, and his murals still make history live on the walls of Salem State College.

Magnolia is blessed with a heron-haunted pond lying very near the beach, and another farther inland. At both, migrating birds find respite from the elements, to the delight of birders, before pushing on to their breeding grounds.

If the magnolia glauca has given its name to the village of Magnolia, and Cape Ann has given its name to a dory, the town of Ipswich has given its name to a bird. The Ipswich sparrow is considered by some experts to be a subspecies of the savanna sparrow, but others consider it a distinct species. It is, in any event, quite discernible, and is so named because it was the first identified by naturalists on Crane's Beach in Ipswich, where indeed it can still be seen. It nests on Sable Island. The bird is about 6 inches long, a good-sized sparrow, and sandy in its coloration, which makes it difficult to see as it moves along the beach and about the dunes and in and out of the coarse beach grass. Some fear that it may be lost to us, particularly if Sable Island, instead of merely shifting location, disappears before the onslaughts of the sea.

Man, however, more than alterations of nature, threatens our wildlife. The passenger pigeons that once darkened the skies (and from which Pigeon Cove in Rockport may take its name) are now gone. Two stragglers were shot in Magnolia in the late nineteenth century. The great auk has been wiped out, and the Labrador duck. These species have fallen before the great polluter and the great destroyer—man.

Cape Ann people have been bellwethers in recent years in the conservation fight, and now the whole nation seems to be rallying. A "Window on the Marsh" campaign saved a beautiful stretch of marshland along Route 128 from extension of hideous commercial construction which has already soiled in part what could be a beautiful entrance to historic Gloucester.

≥ 12 ≤

The Islands

If a woman's crowning glory is her hair, the same epithet might be given to the islands attending any such headland as Cape Ann. Cape Ann's islands range from a craggy reef to one of the most extraordinary summer resorts on the Atlantic seaboard, and have been used to hang pirates, sequester a professional killer from the gang he betrayed, make motion pictures, provide bird sanctuaries, house a hotel or two, support farms, inspire artists and welcome summer residents and countless picnickers.

"The only man who wants to own an island," said Dr. Samuel Johnson, "is the man who never has." The soundness of his judgment is confirmed by the history of Cape Ann's islands. Most of them are uninhabited, and those that are occupied, with one or two exceptions, have changed ownership many times over the years. Pearce Island, or Merchant's Island, in the Annisquam River is one that has remained more or less in one family, the Merchants, for several generations. Once upon a time there was a farm on Pearce Island, and the cows had to be led across the flats at low tide to Rust Island, which isn't an island at all, and so to the mainland to be covered, as the euphemism goes, because that's where the nearest bull was. Today the summer residents of Pearce Island gather rain water in barrels and store it in cisterns because there is no other supply. None of the Cape's islands are farmed today.

If we consider the Dry Salvages as an island, although it is more reef than island, crags above water, we are back to the beginnings of European exploration of Cape Ann, for it was these ghastly rocks that Samuel de Champlain called "Les Trois Sauvages," a name the Yankee tongue corrupted to its present meaninglessness, for they are rarely dry and could salvage nothing. They have won international fame and literary immortality (although they are likely to outlive all poems and perhaps the English tongue) from T. S. Eliot in his *Four Quartets*. They remain a menace to shipping and a romantic name on the charts.

The most famous wreck in the history of Rockport, and perhaps of Cape Ann, certainly the first desperate shipwreck there of which we have an account, occurred not at the Dry Salvages or at some dreadful "flats" nearby, but on Thatcher Island (almost everyone except the chart says, "Thacher's"), which thereby received its name.

Our vision of the amount of shipping along the New England coast in the early seventeenth century is so diminished that it is difficult for us to believe that as early as 1635 Isaac Allerton was providing regular sailings between the Piscataqua River in New Hampshire and Boston. But he had a pinnace that provided this service, and in August, 1635, it put in at Ipswich to pick up the Reverend John Avery, his wife and their six children. Boarding the pinnace with him was his cousin, Anthony Thacher, a London tailor, only newly come to New England, his wife, and their four children, and another relative. Counting the crew, there were aboard the boat twenty-three persons.

That August was the month when New England was ravaged by one of the worst storms in its history. William Bradford gives an account of it in his famous book. For the whole second week of August, the wind blew with incredible force and tides roared in higher than any the Indians could remember. The Reverend Mr. Avery was on his way to become minister for the unregenerate fishermen of Marblehead. He went with reluctance, and would have preferred to remain at Newbury. But at the insistence of the Reverend John Cotton and others, he agreed to go to Marblehead and battle the Devil at close quarters.

The pinnace set out in the middle of the second week, and found the weather so bad it was unable to get around Cape Ann. It put in at Sandy Bay for anchorage, but it could not escape the fury of the Great Storm, as it was known. The anchor dragged, and the pinnace and its doomed passengers were blown toward the granite grinders of the rocks and reefs of Rockport's shore. The charts show Avery's Rock north of Thacher Island and for many years it was thought the pinnace broached there. The site of the disaster was Crackwood's Ledge, a submerged reef about 300 feet from Thacher Island. Thacher was saved and the General Court gave him the island, but the account he wrote to his brother in England some time afterward is such a vivid document, and so rarely reverted to, that it is worth quoting at some length. If only all tailors, or department store owners, wrote as well today:

"I must turn my drowned pen and shaking hand," he wrote, "to indite the story of such sad news as never before this happened in New England. There was a league of perpetual friendship between my cousin Avery and myself never to forsake each other to the death but to be partakers of each other's misery or welfare, as also of habitation in the same place. Now upon our arrival in New England there was an offer made unto us. My cousin Avery was invited to Marblehead to be their pastor in due time, there being no church planted there as yet, but a town appointed to set up the trade of fishing, because many there (the most being fishermen) were something loose and remiss in their behavior. My cousin Avery was unwilling to go there; and so refusing, we went to Newbury intending there to sit down.

"But being solicited so often both by the men of the place and

by the magistrates and by Mr. Cotton and the most of the ministers, who alleged what a benefit we might be to the people there
and also to the Country and Commonwealth, at length we em-
braced it and there consented to go. They of Marblehead
forthwith sent a pinnace for us and our goods. We embarked at
Ipswich, Aug. 11, 1635, with our families and substance bound
for Marblehead we being in all twenty-three souls, namely:
eleven in my cousin's family, seven in mine, and one Mr. William Elliot, sometimes of New Sarum, and four mariners. The
next morning, having commended ourselves to God, with cheer-
ful hearts we hoisted sail.

"But the Lord suddenly turned our cheerfulness into mourn-
ing and lamentations for on the 14th day of Aug. 1635, about ten
at night, having a fresh gale of wind, our sails being old and
done were split. The mariners, because that it was night, would
not put to new sails but resolved to cast anchor till the morning.
But before light it pleased the Lord to send so mighty a storm as
the like was never known in New England since the English
came, nor in the memory of any of the Indians.

"It was so furious that our anchors came home. Whereupon
the mariners let out more cable which at last slipped away.
Then our sailors knew not what to do, but we were driven before the wind and waves.

"My cousin and I perceived our danger and solemnly recom-
mended ourselves to God the Lord both of earth and seas, ex-
pecting with every wave to be swallowed up and drenched in
the deep. And as my cousin, his wife, and my tender babes sat
comforting and cheering each other in the Lord against ghastly
death which every moment stared us in the face and sat
triumphing on each one's forehead, we were by the violence and
fury of the winds, by the Lord's permission, lifted upon a rock
between two high rocks, yet all was one rock. But it raged with
the stroke which came into the pinnace so as we were presently

up to our middles in water as we sat. The waves came furiously and violently over us and against us, but by reason of the rock's proportion could not lift us off but beat her all to pieces. Now look with me upon our distress and consider of my misery who beheld the ship broken, the water in her and violently overwhelming us, my goods and provisions swimming in the seas, my friends almost drowned, and mine own poor children so untimely (if I may so term it without offence) before mine eyes drowned and ready to be swallowed up and dashed to pieces against the rocks by the merciless waves, and myself ready to accompany them. In the same room whereas he sat, the master of the pinnace, not knowing what to do, our foremast was cut down, our mainmast broken in three pieces, the forepart of the pinnace beat away, our goods swimming about the seas, my children bewailing me, as not pitying themselves, and myself bemoaning them, poor souls, whom I had occasioned to such an end in their tender years, when as they could scarce be sensible of death, and so likewise my cousin, his wife and his children; and both of us bewailing each other in Our Lord and only Savior, Jesus Christ, in whom only we had comfort and cheerfulness, insomuch that from the greatest to the least of us there was not one screech or outcry made, but all as silent as sheep were contentedly resolved to die together lovingly, as since our acquaintance we had lived together friendly.

"Now I was sitting in the cabin room door with my body in the room, when lo! one of the sailors by a wave being washed out of the pinnace was gotten in again and coming into the cabin room over my back, cried out, 'We are cast away! The Lord have mercy upon us! I have been washed over-board into the sea and am gotten in again.' His screeches made me look forth; and looking toward the sea and seeing how we were, I turned myself to my cousin and the rest and spake these words: 'O Cousin, it hath pleased God to cast us here between two rocks, the shore not far from us for I saw the tops of trees when I looked forth!'

"Whereupon the master of the pinnace looking up at the scuttle hole of the quarter-deck, went out at it; but I never saw him afterwards. Then he that had been in the sea went out again by me and leaped over-board towards the rocks, whom afterwards also I could not see. Now none were left in the barque, that I knew or saw, but my cousin, his wife and children, myself and mine and his maid servant. But my cousin thought I would have fled from him, and said unto me: 'O cousin leave us not, let us die together,' and reached forth his hand unto me.

"Then I, letting go my son Peter's hand, took him by the hand and said, 'Cousin, I purpose not. Whither shall I go? I am willing and ready here to die with you and my poor children. God be merciful unto us, and receive us unto Himself,' adding these words, 'The Lord is able to help and deliver.'

"He replied, saying; 'Truth, cousin, but what His pleasure is we know not. I fear we have been too unthankful for former deliverances, but He hath promised to deliver us from sin and condemnation and to bring us safe to Heaven for all the sufficient satisfaction of Jesus Christ. This therefore we may challenge of Him.'

"To which I replying said: 'That is all the deliverance I now desire and expect.' which words I had no sooner spoken but by a mighty wave I was with the piece of the barque washed out upon part of the rock, where the waves left me almost drowned. But recovering my feet I saw above me on the rock my daughter Mary, to whom I had no sooner gotten but my cousin Avery and his eldest son came to us, being all four of us washed out by one and the same wave. We went all into a small hole on the top of the rock, whence we called to those in the pinnace to come unto us, supposing we had been in more safety than they were in. My wife, seeing us there, crept up into the scuttle of the quarter-deck to come unto us. But presently came another wave and dashing the pinnace all to pieces carried my wife away in the scuttle as she was, with the greater part of the quarter-deck unto the shore, where she was cast safely but her legs were something bruised, and much timber of the vessel was there also cast. She was sometime before she could get away being washed by the waves. All the rest that were in the barque were drowned in the merciless sea. We four by that wave were clean swept away from off the rock, also into the sea, the Lord in one instant of time disposing of 15 souls of us according to His good pleasure and will. This pleasure and wonderful great mercy to me was thus: standing on the rock as before you heard, with my eldest daughter, my cousin and eldest son, looking upon and talking to them in the barque, whereas we were by that merciless wave washed off the rock as before you heard, God in His mercy caused me to fall by the stroke of the waves flat on my face, for my face was towards the sea. Insomuch that I was sliding off the rock into the sea, the Lord directed my toes into a joint in the rock's side as also the tops of some of my fingers with my right hand, by the means whereof, the wave leaving me, I remained so hanging on the rock only my head above the water, when on the left hand I espied a board or plank of the pinnace, and as I was reaching out my left hand to lay hold on it, by another wave coming over the top of the rock I was washed away from the rock and by the violence of the wave was driven hither and thither in the sea a great while, and had many dashes against the rock. At length, past hope of life and wearied in body and spirit I even gave over to nature and being ready to receive in the waters of death, I lifted up both my heart and hands to the God of Heaven (for note, I had my senses remaining perfect with me all the time that I was under and in the water) who at that instant lifted my head above the top of the water, that so I might breathe without any hindrance by the waters.

"I stood bolt upright as if I had stood upon my feet but I felt no bottom nor had any footing to stand upon but the waters. While I was thus above the water I saw by me a piece of the mast as I suppose about three feet long, which I labored to catch in my arms, but suddenly I was overwhelmed with water and driven to and fro again, and at last I felt the ground with my right foot, when immediately whilst I was thus groveling on my face I presently recovering my feet was in the water up to my breast and through God's great mercy had my face unto the shore and not the sea. I made haste to get out, but was thrown down on my hands with the waves and so with safety crept to the dry shore, where blessing God, I turned about to look for my children and friends but saw neither nor any part of the pinnace, where I left them as I supposed, but I saw my wife about a butt length from me, getting herself forth from amongst the timbers of the broken barque; but before I could get unto her she was gotten to the shore. I was in the water after I was washed from the rock, before I came to the shore, a quarter of an hour at least.

"When we were come each to the other we went and sat under the bank, but fear of the seas roaring and our coldness would not suffer us there to remain. But we went up into the land and sat us down under a cedar tree which the wind had thrown down, where we sat about an hour, almost dead with cold. But now the storm was broken up and the wind was calm. But the sea remained rough and fearful to us.

"My legs were much bruised and so was my head, other hurts I had none, neither had I taken in much quantity of water, but my heart would not let me sit still any longer but I would go to see if any more were gotten to the land in safety, especially hoping to have met some of my poor children, but I could find none, neither dead nor yet living. You condole with me my miseries, who now begun to consider of my losses.

"Now came to my remembrance the time and manner, how and when, I last saw and left my children and friends. One was severed from me sitting on the rock at my feet, the other three in the pinnace, my little babe (Ah, poor Peter!) sitting in his sister Edith's arms, who to the uttermost of her power sheltered him from the waters, my poor William standing close unto them, all three of them looking ruefully on me on the rock, their very countenances calling unto me to help them, whom I could neither go unto neither could they come at me, neither would the merciless waves afford me space or time to use any means at all either to help them or myself. Oh I yet see their cheeks, poor silent lambs pleading pity and help at my hands. Then on the other side to consider the loss of my dear friends, with the spoiling and loss of all our goods and provisions, myself cast upon an unknown land, in a wilderness, I know not where, nor how to get thence. Then it came to my mind how I had occasioned the death of my children, who caused them to leave their native land, who might have left them there, yea and might have sent some of them back again and cost me nothing. Those and such like thoughts do press down my heavy heart very much. But I must let this pass, and will proceed on in the relation of God's goodness unto me in that desolate island on which I was cast. I and my wife were almost naked, both of us, and wet and cold even unto death. I found a knapsack cast upon the shore, in which I had a steel and flint and powder horn; going further I found a drowned goat; then I found a hat and my son William's coat, both of which I put on. I found also two cheeses and some butter driven ashore. Thus the Lord sent us some clothes to put on and food to sustain our new lives which we had lately given unto us, and means also to make a fire, for in a horn I had some gunpowder which, to my own and since to other men's admiration, was dry. So taking a piece of my Wife's sackcloth which I dried in the sun, I struck fire and so dried and warmed our wet bodies; and then skinned the goat and having found a small brass pot we boiled some of her. Our drink was brackish water. Bread we had none. There we remained till the Monday following; when about three of the clock in the afternoon, in a boat that came that way, we went off that desolate island, which I named after my name—Thacher's Woe—and the rock Avery his fall, to the end that their fall and loss and mine own might be had in perpetual remembrance. In the isle lieth buried the body of my cousin's eldest daughter, whom I found dead on the shore. On the Tuesday following, in the afternoon, we arrived at Marblehead."

In 1771 the colonial government bought Thacher's Island and built twin lighthouses on it. They still stand, but only one light flashes, tended by the Coast Guard. A mile north of Thacher's is Straitsmouth Island, standing at the southeast edge of Sandy Bay, which also bears a lighthouse familar to navigators. Like Thacher's, Straitsmouth, slightly smaller, is in charge of the Coast Guard. A few years back, the United States Attorney Paul Markham, wishing to sequester Joe Barboza, an admitted racketeer, lest he be bumped off by the gangsters he had turned state's evidence against, put him under guard on Thacher's Island, in the caretaker's house. Lobstermen were immediately curious about the comings and goings of strangers to the island, and Barboza was removed to Dolliver's Neck in Gloucester to an unoccupied estate, isolated and fenced, which had been for sale with no takers. He remained there for the duration of the trial of his former confederates, found guilty through his testimony.

Moving south from Straitsmouth and Thacher, we come to Milk Island and Salt Island. The first is nothing but a bird sanctuary today. Salt Island once bore fishermen's shacks, and can be walked to at low tide. Milk, slightly larger, was once owned by Hollywood executives and used as a hunting preserve, but it is almost too small for that. Hollywood has long had its eye on Cape Ann, and Salt Island was the scene of the making of *The Thirteenth Bride*, half a century ago. Gloucester memories still recall the papier-mâché castle mounted on the island for the filming.

Larger than Milk Island and smaller than Thacher's is Kettle Island off the Magnolia shore, today a breeding place for herring gulls, great black-backed gulls, cormorants and black-crowned night herons. Poison ivy makes most picnickers and amateur explorers stay on the rocky beach and the granite shore and avoid the center. Nearby is Egg Rock, without vegetation, and quivering with birds. Several other small islands off the Manchester coast are without interest except to local residents and small boat enthusiasts, and it is not until we come to Misery Island and Little Misery that we get back into the stream of history. As early as 1630, the 1,800 acres of Misery Island bore the name that has stuck to it since. Early records refer to it as "Morton's Misery," or "Moulton's Misery," but which Morton or Moulton and what the nature of his "misery" is not told. Like other islands of the Eastern seaboard and particularly ship-minded New England, it was soon stripped of timber. As might be suspected, when the trees were coming down, a staging went up to dry fish. Once again the name of the Sagamore appears in the records, this time spelled Massaconomet, when his son sold the island to Bartholomew Gale of Salem. In the early eighteenth century there was at least one house on Misery, and for a while it was used to quarantine victims of smallpox. The island changed hands several times, and visitors reported—and the records show—livestock pastured there decade after decade.

Not until the middle of the nineteenth century did any sense of continuity come. Daniel Nevil, an Irish immigrant, bought the island to quarry the stone for ballast, to raise cattle and to bring up his large family. For half a century the Nevils, also

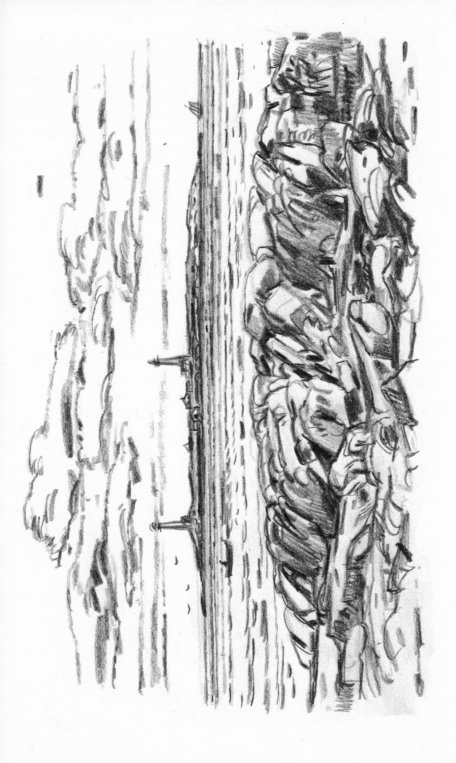

spelled Neville, lived on Misery and made it flower. In the first two decades of the twentieth century, efforts were made to turn it into a summer colony. Several families summered there for a number of years, and a clubhouse and a golf links were established. All withered away. Industrial vultures tried to turn it into an oil farm, but the wrath of the residents on the facing shores blocked that. Fires reduced the remaining buildings, and the whole became, in effect, deserted. About thirty years ago it came into the possession of the Trustees of Reservations, who also control Castle Hill and the Crane estate, and has been left wild and desolate, but not unspoiled, for poison ivy and the casual rubbish of picnickers leave it unattractive. What is needed is an *ad hoc* committee of nature lovers to turn it into an island garden.

The island stands at the entrance to Manchester Harbor and less than a mile from Bakers Island, the nearest of the Cape Ann islands. If Misery Island acquired its name in 1630, Bakers Island was Bakers Island before that. It was Bakers Island when John Winthrop arrived and perhaps when John Smith went by, but who Baker was, or may have been, is lost in the veils of history.

Bakers Island is part of the city of Salem and has been since 1660. It lies, however, 3 miles from Salem and only 1½ miles from the town of Manchester, and the telephone on the island rings through the Manchester exchange. About fifty-five cottages stand on its sixty acres, all of which are privately owned except for the Coast Guard reservation where the lighthouse stands. Like Thacher's Island, Bakers Island once had two lighthouses, not truly twins, for one was somewhat smaller than the other. They were known for years as Pa and Ma Baker, but Ma was doused in 1926 and the tower razed.

You get to Bakers Island by a ferry from Salem, climb a ladder to the high pier, and walk to a summer colony without streets; that is, without paved streets, or without detectable streets. At the Essex County Registry of Deeds in Salem, the deeds show streets—South Shore Avenue, Sunset Avenue, Cliff Street, Winne-Egan Avenue—but on the island they are all overgrown. You walk from one lawn to another. It is one of the charms of the island; everyone is a neighbor.

In the past, Bakers Island had a hotel, as well as a farm the cows of which provided milk for the guests. That's in the past. So is cutting ice on the pond that provides some of the drinking water, pumped by electric power. Electricity came to the island in 1938 by way of a generator mounted by the association. The association consists of the residents of the island banded together to deal with common problems, chief among which are the pier, the generator, the ferry, and the store which somehow manages to provide the necessaries of life when the islanders find themselves out of butter and too late for the ferry. The camaraderie among the islanders is extraordinary even for an isolated summer colony, and sparks minstrel shows, art shows and other community projects. Once in a great while a new cottage is built, but it is expensive to transport the workmen and the materials, and there isn't too much room left. The islanders don't want any more. Nothing snobbish, for cottages do change hands, and newcomers are always welcomed. Bakers Island has not changed too much from the days when the paddle-wheeler brought people to the island. Chances are, it will change less slowly than any other section of Cape Ann. Somehow there is something consoling in that.

≥ 13 ⩽
Inventors and Other Characters

In Manchester there were three sisters named Curtis—Isabelle, Harriot and Margaret—who were of impeccable family background, spinsters all, and, like many eminent Bostonians, for so they considered themselves, devoted to public charities. One now remains, Harriot, who for five years was dean of women at Hampton Institute, an industrial school for Negroes in Virginia. Margaret was national women's open golf champion in 1906, 1911 and 1912. But after World War I Margaret trained in social work and spent a good deal of her time and money aiding refugees throughout the world. Harriot also, by the way, shared her sister's passion for golf and won the national championship herself in 1908. They were magnificent types of the Boston spinster, listed themselves in the Manchester directory as the Misses Curtis, dressed dowdily in their old age, and ignored the world and fashion. They lived frugally in a Chas. Addams house on the Gloucester shore, and can be regarded as ideal specimens of the twentieth-century New England Brahmin.

One day a young matron on the golf course of the Essex County Club was alarmed to see a woman rolling around in the rough, as if in an epileptic seizure. She stood by a minute in dismay, and then called, "Are you all right?"

Maggie Curtis stopped rolling on the ground and raised her

head. "Quite all right," she replied, "I'm just looking for stray golf balls. This is the best way, you know, to find them." Miss Curtis had a Cape Ann spirit that was there from the start and is there today. Their brother-in-law was Charles Hopkinson, the portrait painter, a member of the National Institute of Arts and Letters, and also a resident of the Manchester shore line. A concern for the arts (some of their best pieces went to Boston's Museum of Fine Arts), a sense of responsibility for one's fellows, an utter indifference to vogue, and a concern for form only when it meant good manners—such together they were.

To be sure, their public benefactions were not always, or indeed, often conferred on the town or city in which they lived, but Cape Ann and its neighbors have benefited more from the gifts and legacies and interest of private citizens in public causes than most communities, and very little from the industrial concerns or business establishments that have made their profits from the area. As we have pointed out, the public libraries in these communities were established chiefly by private citizens with private means, as were the historical societies. This, of course, is no surprise in New England, where even the Museum of Fine Arts in Boston is supported entirely by private funds and receives not a penny from the city or the state.

One of Gloucester's greatest benefactors was Samuel E. Sawyer, who gave the city the nineteenth-century white clapboarded mansion in which the public library is still housed. It is named the Sawyer Free Library in his honor. In his will he left the library $120,000 to carry on, and disposed in all of half a million dollars. The Sawyer Medal awarded annually to a grammar school graduate for excellence in studies is named for him. Throughout his life he sporadically made gifts to the city— fences for schoolhouses, a clock for the town hall, and then a clock and bell for the new city hall.

Sawyer was born in Gloucester on November 25, 1815, and

died in December, 1889. He began his business career with a dry goods firm on the Main Street, but made his fortune in Boston. He died a widower and childless and it is said that he often felt his benefactions were not appreciated, and was hurt because of that. It is no doubt true.

One of his finest gifts to the city was a vast acreage of woodland called Ravenswood Park, which stands on Route 127 going from Gloucester toward Magnolia and Manchester, with an endowment for its preservation. Careful management by the trustees has enlarged the area, arranged the construction of a chapel which Sawyer had hoped for, and given Gloucester a place of solitude and refuge where, on foot, without fear of motor traffic and in unspoiled sylvan surroundings, men, women and children can walk peacefully in surroundings that show them, a little, how the shores of Gloucester must have looked when the white man first came in. In an overcrowding suburbia, Ravenswood Park has grown in value as a public recreation spot beyond Sawyer's wildest dreams, through it is still too little used by the public.

Gordon Abbott, Jr., of Manchester, executive director of that peculiarly New Englandish body, the Trustees of Reservations, among whose charges are Castle Hill and Crane's Beach as well as other estates, was for several years editor of the *Gloucester Daily Times,* one of the finest small city daily newspapers in the East. Abbott believes that Cape Ann is a natural magnet, a haven and a refuge for individualistic people—or eccentrics, if you will. He is a competent observer, but even to the casual observer it must seem so.

Art colonies often have a touch of Bohemia which other communities lack. Such colonies generate even on their peripheries a tolerance for the oddball, the offbeat, the kook and the hippie that those communities without the tincture of aestheticism seem to lack. The artist, of course, traditionally went bearded

when others were clean shaven, preferred a beret where other
workmen wore a cap, was barefoot when shoes were *de rigueur,*
and held to casual clothes when black tie formality was expected. This was often caused as much by poverty as by a contempt for convention. But the result is that Cape Ann has its
share of what might be called the infrequent people.

In Ravenswood Park is a bronze plaque honoring a hermit
who lived for eighteen years in solitude and in a comity with
nature that makes Henry David Thoreau seem like a city
slicker. He was Mason A. Walton, and he put it all down in a
small volume, *A Hermit's Wild Friends,* which, while it lacks the
style of *Walden,* is nevertheless an engrossing document. Walton came to Ravenswood Park in the last quarter of the nineteenth century, enervated by a variety of ailments, weak in the
chest, his lungs sore from coughing, and his stomach evidently
raw from gastritis. When no skipper would hire him because of
his pathetic physical appearance, he took to the woods. In two
months' time, living in a tent, he was well. He stayed on, built
himself a hut, meditated on life, wrote a bit, made friends with
the animals—a raccoon named Satan was his most familiar
companion—and welcomed occasional curious visitors.

Long after he was gone, a bearded vendor of herbs, known as
Catnip Bill, wandered the streets of Gloucester, and became the
subject of a children's book, *The Catnip Man.*

Such characters lend color to the Cape, but not the type of
benison we were discussing. Let us look at some of the other
men of Gloucester, fulcrum city of Cape Ann. Here are four:
John Hays Hammond, Jr., inventor extraordinary, whose early
exploits with remote control helped set the stage for the exploration of space; Clarence Birdseye, whose creative perceptiveness
and business acumen gave the frozen fish fillet to the modern
world and, we regret to say, the frozen TV dinner as well;
Roger Babson, financier, churchman and ideational gadfly, who

not only made millions but spent them with idiosyncratic persistence for what he deemed the public good; and Alfred Mansfield Brooks, a professor of the history of art, a connoisseur, author and critic, and moving spirit behind the exquisite collection in the Cape Ann Scientific, Literary and Historical Association.

We cannot discuss John Hays Hammond, Jr., without first discussing his father, a mining engineer for the Guggenheim interests, who led a life of such adventure that even today his two-volume autobiography makes gripping reading, and indeed at times is hair-raising. He saw a great deal of the world, and made a fortune (which his son put to scientific use) after having narrowly escaped hanging in South Africa for his revolutionary activities cheek by jowl with the great Cecil Rhodes.

He was born in San Francisco (like Robert Frost) on March 31, 1855, but after a life of incredible adventure he spent the best part of the last thirty years of his life in Gloucester, entranced by the stories of the fishermen and their adventures on the Grand Banks and in stormy seas. He was educated at the Sheffield Scientific School at Yale, and continued his studies in Europe. After prospecting days in the Far West and Mexico, he took off for Cape Town, South Africa, to work for Barney Barnato, the brilliant, self-educated son of a London Jewish shopkeeper who, with Cecil Rhodes, founded the great DeBeers Consolidated Mines, Inc., which, since the two giants got together, has controlled the diamond markets of the world. John Hays Hammond, Sr., took with him his wife, Natalie Harris Hammond, and his two sons, Jack, Jr., and Harris. Within six months' time he left Barnato and was hired by Cecil Rhodes to take charge of all Rhodes's mining interests. With Rhodes's brother, Frank, Hammond was to become a coconspirator in an attempted revolution in the Transvaal, where the Uitlanders felt they were being unjustly treated by Oom Paul Kruger and his burghers.

Johannesburg was the overwhelmingly English city in the Transvaal, and there Hammond and three others amassed smuggled guns to mount an attack on the arsenal at Pretoria. At the same time, Dr. Leander Starr Jameson, Rhodes's henchman, was poised with mercenaries in a section of Bechuanaland leased to Rhodes, ready to invade the Transvaal when Hammond and his colleagues gave the signal. Jameson jumped the gun, was ambushed, his men killed or wounded, and he himself forced to surrender. This was promptly followed by the arrest of Hammond and his fellow revolutionaries in Johannesburg. They were tried and condemned to be hanged. After some months in an abhorrent prison, they had their sentences reduced to life, to fifteen years, and after payment of a $125,000 fine, commuted, but not before their imprisonment became a *cause célèbre* in the United States. Even Mark Twain visited them in jail. At length freed, Hammond went to England, where Richard, his third son, was born. From England he returned to the United States, where he became the mining expert for the wealthy Guggenheim family, bought his famous summer home in Gloucester, Lookout Hill, and became the intimate of United States presidents.

When Colonel E. M. House, adviser to Thomas Woodrow Wilson, was summering on Coolidge Point in Manchester, Hammond was a frequent visitor at House's retreat, urging upon him and the President more preparedness in the face of Germany's patent intentions in Europe. He was unsuccessful, and blamed our entry into the war on our failure to show more preparedness, which, he believed, would have restrained the Germans.

Some time before this, Hammond had built a laboratory in Gloucester for his son Jack, who had turned inventor with startling success. Years earlier, Jack, Jr., as a boy had visited the laboratories of Thomas Alva Edison, and had been encouraged by that genius, who, however, had warned him to cultivate his business sense; otherwise, as an inventor without commercial acumen, he could end up in the poor house. The elder Hammond took interest and pride in the accomplishments of his son and recounts in his autobiography how the young man moved ships around Gloucester Harbor by remote controls of his own devising, much to the consternation of the Gloucester fishermen, who, like everyone else at that time, felt uneasy in the presence of a crewless ship moving, somewhat erratically, about the harbor.

The father loved to recount one story about his inventive son, and tells it thus in his autobiography:

"There was in the cove an old fisherman called Joe Adams, who had been more or less adopted by the boys. In his declining years, he used to place lobster pots a few yards from shore. Usually, before starting out he took a few drinks. From the terrace the boys would watch him make his uncertain rounds during which he sometimes pulled up the same pot several times within the hour.

"Jack and Harris one day laid a homemade mine about 100 yards off shore, which Jack was going to try to explode by wireless. They didn't know much about explosives then, and put in far too big a charge. Harris was to be stationed at the door of the laboratory to sound a warning should any boat approach too near the mine. After pulling the switch a dozen times without anything happening, Jack buried himself in the complicated wiring and called Harris inside to help. Finally Jack said: 'I have all the connections made. This time the infernal thing is sure to go off. I'll pull the switch when you get outside, and then I'll run to see the fun.'

"When Harris returned to his post, he saw Old Joe calmly pulling up a lobster pot directly over the mine. Just as Harris yelled to Jack, 'Hold everything,' there was a terrific detonation.

Joe and his boat rose fifty feet on a trumpet of water, capsized and came down in a shower of lobster pots, boulders, seaweed, rocks and fish.

"In three jumps Harris reached a rowboat at the foot of the little cliff and battled his way out among the waves to rescue Joe who was splashing about half-drowned. Harris hauled him in, thankful that he was not hurt.

"When Joe had partially caught his breath, he gasped, 'Goda-mighty, did you see what happened to me? I went up right top of a big wave.'

"'Nonsense, Joe,' Harris said, 'we've been watching you for the last quarter of an hour. I saw you lean over to pull in that lobster pot and you fell in.'

"'But I felt it,' Joe insisted, 'My boat's all broke up! As I went up, I could see right over the top of the house.'

"'You're crazy,' Harris insisted, this time with some show of justice, since the top of the house was 100 feet above the water line. 'You must have kicked the boat as you fell. I think you've had a few too many drinks.'

"The people of Gloucester heard the noise of the explosion but thought it was probably blasting in the nearby Rockport quarries. The boys comforted Joe and bought him a new boat.

"To his dying day Joe thought he was the victim of a halluci-nation. But once in a while he would mutter to himself, 'I know damn well the ocean blew up.'"

The father made Gloucester his legal residence in 1903 and was proud of saying that he was better than a native, since he, in his maturity, had chosen it as the best place on earth to live. Much of his time was spent in Washington conferring with Pres-idents Roosevelt, Taft and Coolidge, but Gloucester was to him home. For Jack, Jr., it was home and the site of his significant accomplishments. Harris went on to New York to become a financier; Jack remained in his Gloucester laboratory. If his father was the world's most famous mining engineer, son Jack became known as the "inventor's inventor."

Cape Ann had two fairly tenuous claims on the famous flight of Charles Lindbergh from New York to Paris. Parts of his airplane, *The Spirit of St. Louis,* were made in the Cape Ann Tool Company's Rockport plant, and John Hays Hammond, Sr., was in charge of the official reception in Washington when the Lone Eagle returned a conquering hero. Through John Hays Hammond, Jr., Cape Ann has an even stronger claim on interplanetary travel, for his remote control inventions underlie much of what has since been done to put man out among the stars.

The laboratory that his father built for him on Lookout Hill John, Jr., turned over to his sister, Natalie Hammond, and he built himself a medieval castle on the harbor shore, which we examined when we discussed the museums of the Cape.

Like his father, he was born in San Francisco. Before he was out of his thirties he put on a demonstration of remote control of a motorboat in Gloucester Harbor for the United States Government. He was able to control the boat from a distance of three miles, spin it across Gloucester Harbor, around Eastern Point Light and the breakwater and back. Later he ran the battleship *Iowa* for the Navy in a similar manner. He was then able to control a ship by radio at a distance of 30 miles. But these were not his sole concerns. His work in frequency modulation in radio reception gave great impetus to modern electronic techniques.

Jack's visits as a boy to the laboratories of Edison were a memory that never left him. Among his father's other friends also was Nikola Tesla, the famous Yugoslav, a genius with regard to electric power transmission. Tesla's work influenced Hammond more than Edison's did. Like his father he attended

Sheffield Scientific School at Yale. He went from there to the Patent Office in Washington, an ideal post to observe what was being done in the field that interested him most.

It was in 1911 that he set up his famous laboratory in Gloucester, and it has been reported that the initial outlay for equipment topped a quarter of a million dollars. His father had a gift for betting on the right man, and he made no mistake in backing his son.

His remote control of ships by radio (he finally sent one on a 60-mile trip to Boston and back) was aimed ultimately at dispatching torpedoes. The war was on in Europe, and the German submarine fleet was threatening. Hammond signed an agreement with the United States Government and was able, finally, to control a torpedo under water as well as on the surface. By the year 1916, it is estimated that he held one hundred patents of military value, and the War Department asked Congress to give him $750,000 for their use. The Senate failed to comply, and it was not until 1932 that he was paid.

In turn he became the center of a spy plot. Among his one hundred patents was an incendiary bomb which he had tried unsuccessfully to sell to the British or the United States Government. When the Germans began to drop incendiary bombs on England in World War II, Hammond was under suspicion until it was discovered that one of his employees had stolen the plans.

Throughout the years he was selling patents to the Radio Corporation of America, patents involving improved radio dialing, powerful radio tubes and refinements of frequency modulation. The American Telephone and Telegraph Company was also the beneficiary of his genius. RCA alone was reputed to have paid him half a million dollars on one occasion.

Electronics, broadcasting, fidelity recording, frequency modulation (essential to television), radio-controlled torpedoes which were the basis of intercontinental ballistic missiles, an electronic teaching machine, a propellor of variable pitch to drive better the ships of the world, all owe something to his genius. Not to be forgotten is the magnetic bottle-cap remover which retains the cap in its grip rather than letting it jump onto the table or floor.

In 1926 he built the medieval castle, a hodgepodge of centuries but a mecca for tourists, and not least among its attractions the magnificent organ. Hammond had an early and persistent interest in music and sought the company of poets, painters and musicians the way his father had sought statesmen and fishermen. His inventions in "audio" systems are as numerous as his inventions in remote control, and among his musical friends and advisers were Leopold Stokowski, Serge Koussevitzky, and Igor Stravinsky. One of his inventions was an accentor to improve the tonal quality of his organ pipes, and his enthusiasm led him to assemble a 10,000-pipe organ in his home. This instrument is as eclectic as his castle, but it is musically a triumph, with four manuals and a gross of stops. Today, long after his death, organ recitals at the castle are musical events on Cape Ann and bring musicians and aficionados motoring down from Boston. Richard Ellsasser, E. Power Biggs, Virgil Fox, and Kenneth Wilson are among the well-known musicians who have played the organ and pronounced it a triumph.

In his last years he loved to recall his sailing days on Gloucester waters. During World War I, when it was learned that German submarines were refueling off Gloucester one way or another, Jack Hammond and his brothers were assigned to a ship to patrol the waters off the coast. Several times they, with overearnestness, brought innocent ships to Boston for examination by higher authorities because the ships did not give them a satisfactory account of themselves. He also liked to recall that the first time he was able to propel a motorboat by radio from a distance, he became so excited that he ran from his laboratory without shutting off the equipment. The motorboat was wrecked on the rocks.

One of the sorrows of his life was that he had no children. He married Irene Fenton, an artist, who preceded him in death. Having no direct heirs, he turned the castle over to the Cardinal. The name of the museum and castle is "Abbadia Mare," but not one Cape Ann resident in a thousand could give it to you. To them, it is Hammond's Castle.

Clarence Birdseye was a native of Brooklyn and after graduation from Amherst College became a field naturalist for the United States Biological Survey, 1908–1912. In the latter year he went to Laborador to engage in fur trading under Sir Wilfred T. Grenfell, and stayed with it for five years. During that time, to preserve a barrel of cabbages, he dipped them in salt water and exposed them to subzero winds. He soon learned to freeze rabbits, ducks and caribou meat to ensure a ready food supply. In 1919 he became an investigator for the United States Fisheries Association and began to experiment with frozen fish. That had been done before; it was quick freezing that was new, that preserved flavor. Birdseye developed a method of doing it between refrigerated metal plates; thus was an industry born. In 1925 he began to turn out packages of frozen haddock in Gloucester.

Like so many such inventions, working out the technical problems was not so difficult as arranging for the marketing and public acceptance. It came at last, but only after endless difficulties which Birdseye, who had brought his family to Gloucester, met with endless patience.

His discoveries were not confined to quick-freezing methods only. He experimented with dehydration and packaging of various sorts. His processes for food preservation greatly benefited Gloucester, for they came at a time when the rising standard of living in the United States left Gloucester ships unable to com-

pete with those from Iceland, Newfoundland, and Denmark—
not to forget Russia, whose great factory fishing vessels work
night and day off the New England coast. In 1929 the Postum
Company, along with the Goldman Sachs Trading Corporation,
acquired Birdseye's patents and trademarks for $22,000,000, the
largest sum ever paid up to that time for a single process. His
invention came at the right time for Gloucester, at the beginning
of the depression, and it helped pull the city through, putting
workers to packaging fish.

The factory where he produced his first packages of frozen
fish is closed today, the business moved to Boston. Like Hammond, Birdseye was an inventor. When he died—in Peru, tink-
ering with food processing there—he had more than three
hundred patents to his name, including one on a gun for firing
identification markers into whales to study their migrations. His
mind could not leave problems alone. Coming to Cape Ann, like
many another immigrant, he became interested in wild flowers,
and collaborated with his wife in writing *Growing Woodland
Plants.*

Another Gloucester giant who was to make a national im-
pact was Roger W. Babson, statistician extraordinary. Trained
as an engineer at the Massachusetts Institute of Technology, he
turned securities analyst while recovering from a bout with tu-
berculosis. In 1929 he made a national reputation when, seven
weeks before the crash, he warned that it would be severe and
that his customers should stop buying on margin.

It was September 5, 1929, when he wrote in his newsletter:
"I repeat what I said at this time last year and the year before
that sooner or later a crack is coming which will take in the
leading stocks and cause a decline of from 60 to 80 points in the
Dow Jones barometer.

"More are borrowing and speculating today than ever in our
history. Sooner or later a crack is coming and it may be terrific.

Wise are those investors who now get out of debt and reef their sails. This does not mean selling all you have but it does mean paying up your loans and avoiding margin speculation." He was not so prescient a year later, for he kept predicting prosperity. It was a long time coming, but calling the turn on the crash made his reputation and his fortune. Two principles, he claimed, guided his business thinking. The first was that every business, no matter how local, is dependent upon conditions throughout the world. The second is an adaptation of Sir Isaac Newton's law that every action must have a reaction. Babson believed that every business boom must be followed by a period of recession or depression.

His interests were as fantastic as they were broad. He saved postage stamps and founded three colleges, the most famous being the Babson Institute in Wellesley Hills. Besides the Bible museum in Gloucester, he established a scientific center for the study of gravity in New Hampshire. He built a massive shelter from atomic bombs in Kansas to preserve his records, and gave the city of Gloucester a reservoir. Because of a disagreement with hospital authorities, he refused them money and set up instead a program in Gloucester which will give any pregnant woman fifteen dollars if she will read a book during her pregnancy and write a review of it. He believed it helped them to a normal and happy pregnancy. His Open Church Foundation sought to have Protestant churches remain open at all hours to permit persons to enter for prayer or meditation, and once over a forgotten issue he disrupted a convention of the Congregational Church and marched a group of the delegates out of the hall for a rump session. Studies into the losses to industry caused by insects led him to an interest in conservation and wildlife. All successful men, he said, show one talent: They manage to do what they want to do. He died at ninety-one and left an estate of $9,000,000, $1,000,000 of it in public bequests. One writer said of him, "The phrase 'no comment' never passed his lips. He gave interviews at the drop of a hat; made annual predictions at a great rate; and for a good while wrote a newspaper column which he distributed free to any newspaper that would take it." It is no surprise that it made good reading more often than not. He also found time to write half a dozen books.

His interest in Newton set him and his wife to collecting memorabilia of the great man and indeed was responsible for his founding the Gravity Research Foundation at New Boston, New Hampshire, where he hoped an insulation against gravity might be found. When he heard that Newton's London home had been torn down but the rooms preserved in storage, he bought one of them and had it transported to the Wellesley Hills campus of his college. Then he planted an apple tree on the campus, said to be a "grandson" of the tree that dropped an apple on the Newtonian head. He paid more than $100,000 for a collection of Newton's works and set them up for use by scholars.

Alfred Mansfield Brooks, who must be rated among Gloucester's greatest benefactors, was born in Saginaw, Michigan, but of an old Gloucester family. He was educated in the Gloucester schools, Harvard College and the Massachusetts Institute of Technology, taking degrees in both institutions. After a brilliant teaching career that took him to the University of Indiana, where hundreds jammed his lectures, and Swarthmore College, as well as to the Universities of Wisconsin and Minnesota and to Dartmouth College, he retired to Gloucester, and became curator of the Cape Ann Scientific, Literary and Historical Association.

Like Babson, he lived into his nineties and retained a great devotion to the city of his forebears. His numerous literary

works attest to his wide range of interests: two novels, *The
Newell Fortune* and *Somes House;* books on art and architecture, among them *A Short History of Architecture, Readings in
Art Appreciation, Architecture* in the series "Our Debt to
Greece and Rome," *From Holbein to Whittier: Notes on Drawing and Engraving,* and *Dante: How to Know Him;* and innumerable articles in encyclopedias, magazines and newspapers.

What he brought to the city were impeccable taste and a
determination to make the collection at the Cape Ann Scientific,
Literary and Historical Association not a random accumulation
of antiques but an organic construction indicative of the city's
history and growth and its creativity. From Samuel Mansfield
he secured a magnificent collection of the drawings of Fitz
Hugh Lane; from other friends and relatives—however distant
—he won other gifts of merit. His authority in the field of architecture brought to the society several edifices, including the
Hadley-Parson House.

He was conscious, to put it in his own words, that it was "a
regrettable fact . . . that Gloucester boasts fewer evidences of
her long and eminent past than many a place not half so old or
a tenth as large." Through his efforts, securing the cooperation
of state and city authorities, with funds he raised himself from
public-spirited citizens and friends, he saved from destruction
the White-Ellery House, a seventeenth-century salt-box, once
the home of Gloucester's first town clerk, and of the third minister of the First Church of Gloucester. He then supervised its
scrupulous restoration, and lived to see it opened to the public,
suitably furnished, a handsome monument of the past, on a new
site at the traffic circle where Route 128, having spanned the
Annisquam River, arrives at one of the city's main streets.

The ominous aftermath is that the building has had to be
closed because of yahooism and the savagery of vandals. The
closed doors should be a rebuke to the city fathers whose coop-

eration could make the house available to the public and safe if they could come to the same appreciation of their treasures as marks the city of Salem—and that, heaven knows, is little enough.

❧ 14 ❧
The Old World on Cape Ann

Cape Ann, particularly Gloucester, Rockport and Ipswich, has been a melting pot of nationals from various countries in the tradition storytellers like to dwell on. In the nineteenth century and the early decades of the twentieth century it was the fashion—nay, almost a phobia—to drive for assimilation and to submerge not merely ethnic differences but even ethnic traditions. In a more enlightened period we are putting value on the various strains that make up America, and efforts are being made to preserve folklore, language, traditions, and customs, and let them add their piquancy and substance to America's uniqueness.

The city of Gloucester has had three great immigrations of non-English-speaking races: the Portuguese, the Italians and the Finns. Gloucester never had the Jewish immigration from Russia and Poland as did Boston and New York. It has never occurred to the school authorities of Cape Ann to have courses in Portuguese, Italian or Finnish history, and even the citizens from those backgrounds probably are indifferent. It is, however, a lack of educational imagination that Finnish or Italian or Portuguese is not taught in any high school on Cape Ann. This indifference no doubt stems from the same educational theory that insists on teaching French to Negroes in New York's ghettos, which is quite useless to them, while Spanish might not only be more practical but could help encourage a neighborly rapport with their Puerto Rican neighbors. You can still hear Portuguese, Italian and Finnish spoken on Cape Ann, but if you wish to study those languages you must either organize a night school class or seek private instruction.

The immigrants from Portugal or the Azores, from the Italian mainland or from Sicily, or the Finns from that far northern country and their descendants, happily, maintain some of their unique customs. In Ipswich, French, Polish and Greek immigrants set up their separate churches and their halls. All three languages can still be heard there. Everywhere the racial groups are intermarrying and the homogenization process is under way. With diligence, Cape Ann can encourage the best of both worlds.

One of the first landmarks caught by the eye of the mariner as he returns from the sea to the port of Gloucester are the twin blue late baroque towers of the Church of Our Lady of Good Voyage with the figure of the Mother of Christ standing between them holding in her arms not the Infant Jesus but a sailing vessel. That figure is the theme of the church; Mary of Nazareth, whose son sailed on Galilee, is the patron saint.

The first church on the site was erected by the Portuguese of Gloucester in 1893. The port of Gloucester was at the height of its prosperity and fame, and the immigrants who could handle a sheet, a halyard, an anchor line or a dory were welcomed. The Portuguese had been sailing the Atlantic before Columbus reached the West Indies; and indeed, it is likely that Portuguese fishermen had been along the shores of the New World as early as the Vikings. They are still fishing today out of Portugal as they fished in 1893, but in 1893 the Portuguese immigrants were a substantial group in Gloucester and were prosperous enough to build their own church. In twenty years' time it burned down, and the present one was built in 1915, long devoted to the spiritual welfare of the Portuguese people of Gloucester under a line of distinguished pastors. Attractive stained-glass windows, featuring again the Mother of Christ and the sea, are the work of a Cape Ann artist, Nicola D'Ascenzo. On the walls are paintings of the city of Gloucester and Rome. Throughout, blue is the predominant color, and the decoration is unique. At the rear are ship models, lined up like votive candles. The church is now a national shrine, an active religious center, as well as one of the city's major tourist attractions.

Portuguese still go to sea, but most have entered other businesses. There was a time when the Cardinal-Archbishop of Boston would journey to Gloucester to bless the Portuguese fleet, and his auxiliary would come to bless the Italian fleet in colorful summer ceremonies that filled the harbor with small launches, sailboats and other sea craft to make a holiday. The ceremony continues today, but there is only one blessing, preceded by a procession and followed by uproarious celebrations.

At the Church of Our Lady of Good Voyage there is one unique annual ceremony dear to the hearts of the Portuguese-Americans—the crowning ceremony. The custom is five hundred years old, originating in the fifteenth century with one of the Iberian Isabellas, and was brought to Gloucester in 1902 by Captain Joe Mesquita, one of the most respected of all Portuguese skippers. His purpose was one of thanksgiving to God for saving his life in a particularly perilous passage, and he looked upon it as an annual act of consecration to the Lord. Each year on Trinity Sunday until his death in 1933, he was crowned in the Church of Our Lady of Good Voyage with a crown of solid silver with five arches curving to join a ball surmounted by a dove. The ball is, of course, a traditional symbol of the world, and the dove of the Holy Ghost as well as peace.

While his daughter Mary played the carillon in the church

steeple—the first such carillon in the country, by the way—
Captain Joe went in procession to the altar, where with choir
and congregation chanting "Veni, Creator Spiritus," the crown
was placed on his head. Flags, flowers, wine and resquillas—
round sweet Portuguese bread—were distributed, eaten and
praised. The ceremony persists to this day. Each year a candidate is chosen by lot, and the crown rests at his house. The custom is charming and inspiring, and the carillon thrilling.

When the carillon was dedicated in 1922, Anton Brees of
Antwerp came over to give the concert. Other famous carillo-
neurs have also played at the church. The instrument is unique,
like the organ at the Hammond Castle half a dozen miles away.

While the Portuguese came to fish, the Finns came to quarry stone, shape it and lay it. They constitute a unique colony on
Cape Ann, and even though the quarrying is gone, they have
not lost their identity as their descendants turn to clerking,
schoolteaching, and other work. The Finns were on Cape Ann
as early as 1870, but the bulk came between 1890 and 1912.
They were an independent, isolated—both by language and
location—uproarious, hard-drinking, political-minded group.
They settled in Lanesville, a section of Gloucester known as
"down back," on the shores of Ipswich Bay, separated from Pigeon Cove in Rockport by another village known as Bay View.

Some of the early hard-drinking Finns carried the traditional puukka, a knife strapped to the waist, which in barroom
brawls around the world have given their seamen the reputation
of being the most formidable knife fighters in the world. Consequently, the Lutheran church and the temperance society were
always big factors in the Finnish community. Despite such
wholesome efforts, when streetcars encircled Cape Ann the Saturday night ride on the last car from Gloucester Harbor to
Lanesville could be a nerve-racking adventure for a sober,
peace-loving man.

The local newspaper considered the Finns a dangerous element on the Cape in the nineties, and the earnest socialists and persistent nucleus of Communists among them did not add to their general popularity. They worked as hard as they drank; kept to themselves; read Finnish papers; heard Finnish preachers; and persisted even after the quarries went bust in the 1920s, and the Great Depression hit them a decade later.

They came in when the quarries were prospering. Ben Butler, the Civil War general whose name is still one to provoke rage in anyone from Louisiana, established the Cape Ann Granite Works at Bay View in 1867. He was living in a tent on the shore of Bay View with his two sons when he ran for Congress, was elected and went on to be governor of Massachusetts. Political influence was important to the granite industry because so many of the contracts were Federal or state deals. The General's partner on one occasion was awarded a contract for three million paving blocks for Boston over thirty-four other bidders. It must never be thought that politics was foreign to Cape Ann and its businesses.

The Finns took the toughest jobs in the quarries, and they prospered. The going was not easy. They formed unions, drove out a gang of Italian scabs in one strike, planted a bomb in another, and generally made their politics felt. The invasion of Finland by Russia in 1939 disillusioned those among them who had sympathy for the Soviet experiment, and today their radicalism is a memory. The majority of their sons and daughters vote Republican.

One monument the Finns brought to Cape Ann is the sauna bath, the traditional steam bath of Finland, which operates on the shore of Lane's Cove and does a steady business. It is opened three days a week; a bath costs $1.50, and is well worth it. Water is poured on heated rocks to provide hot steam, and the bathers sit on benches in the rooms. The benches are in tiers, and depending on what degree of heat one wishes, the bather moves up or down. Traditionally, after such a bath, the bather goes out and rolls in the snow. At Lanesville, a cold shower is substituted.

Another big factor in the Finnish community on Cape Ann was music. Church choirs and musical groups in the temperance halls or the socialist center were popular, and Sylvester Ahola, a distinguished trumpeter, was one of several noted musicians who came out of those centers. Ahola is mentioned because his jazz performances on records have now become collectors' items among aficionados.

The Italian community is the dominant one in Gloucester today, occupying almost entirely a section on the harbor front known as The Fort, manning most of the draggers that sail in and out of the port, and currently spreading into various businesses on the Cape. They are peerless and fearless sailors, with a traditional instinct for finding fish, although today sonar, radar and other electronic devices make it a scientific puzzle rather than an art. Then, too, where business conditions have made fishing uneconomical, Italians economize by fishing in family units.

The names of the draggers lined up at the Gloucester wharves today could tell a sharp observer the extent of the Italian influence: the *Holy Family, Villanova, St. Joseph, Salvatore and Rosa, Gaetano S, Cigar Joe.*

The Italians, like the Portuguese, were almost wholly a Roman Catholic community, but had no Italian church in Gloucester; they attended instead Saint Ann's and Saint Peter's, for they arrived after the late Cardinal O'Connell had banned establishment of any more "national" churches. The blessing of the fleet is one of their major religious occasions, and their great patron is Saint Peter, patron of fishermen. Each year with solemnity his statue is carried through the streets of the city on June 29, the feast of Saints Peter and Paul, and installed in a niche in a garish reredos, 40 feet high, violent with color, bristling with electric light bulbs, behind an altar, the whole raised against one of the three-story dwellings on The Fort.

For three days a carnival is held, and for two nights it is well-nigh impossible to find a parking space in that end of the city. A traditional midway with merry-go-round, a ferris wheel making its creaking way up to the stars, a "whip," hot dog stands, portable pizza stands, cotton candy machines, crowd a parking lot, making it day-bright with their neon lights, and loud with amplified carrousel music. Vendors peddle balloons, pinwheels that spin on the end of a stick as you carry them along, and a mad variety of hats made of cheap felt or straw, of numerous shapes and styles, some boasting pert feathers, others dangling ribbons. If you want, you can have your name stitched on. Boards of buttons catch the eyes of the youngsters: "I am an alcoholic, in an emergency administer beer," "Kiss Me, I won't tell," and the like.

From the midway, which stands at Duncan and Commercial Streets in Gloucester, all along Commercial to where it reaches the harbor shore, runs an arcade of lights on graceful arches, from one curbing to another. In many of the houses it is "open house," and Saint Peter's Men's Club, particularly in its new quarters on Main Street, is a humming social center for the week end.

During the evening Saint Peter looks down from his pedestal on two bands alternating their tremendous brass statements in a battle of music. Temporary six-banked grandstands are thrown up so grandparents can sit and watch the fun while the children and the young parents move around. The breeze carries in the smell of the sea. One sign reads "Giladi and Spumoni." A fire truck stands by for the emergency that fortunately does not come. The bandsmen take a five-minute break and

walk off to get a drink. The bass drum discloses that this year the "Italian Colonial Band of Lawrence, Mass." is one of the two. The canned music on the two carrousels—one of them with a blue canvas covering is for toddlers—never stops. The crowd comes and goes. For the Fiesta the whole city turns out, and its neighbors pour in from all the Cape Ann communities.

The Mafia has no role here, although in the past there were always rumors that one of the best hideouts in the world was a dragger ten miles off the coast, and many an immigrant is said to have come into the country by stepping from one fishing vessel to another far out to sea.

The Italians, too, are being absorbed into the Gloucester society. They have contributed a mayor, councilors, priests, labor leaders, bankers, artists, writers and businessmen to the community. They dominate several of the major fish companies. Like the Greek community in Ipswich, the Italians show a gift for business beyond that of the Portuguese and the Finns.

Neither Cape Ann nor any other part of New England is likely to see again such ethnic communities spring up in response to the demands of one industry or another. That sort of development seems part of an age that is past. Aside from Puerto Ricans coming in from their island, there is no such substantial immigration today, and the Puerto Ricans are in no significant numbers outside such major cities as New York and Boston.

Fishing brought the Portuguese and the Italians to Cape Ann; quarrying brought the Finns; factory work brought the French and the Greeks and the Poles. Their absorption is under way, and their contributions to the culture of Cape Ann significant. Their presence gives Cape Ann the distinction of offering haven in a manner analogous to the great American tradition, enabling us to see the Cape as a microcosm of the American experience—an experience which the Plymouth colony, of course, escaped.

What we see also are the immigrants brought to the New World for a particular trade—for instance, the Finns and quarrying—now turning in the second, third and fourth generations to the whole spectrum of opportunity and development offered by the United States. Through all this, we find Cape Ann's character such that it is able to absorb the shock of these ethnic intrusions without either altering its nature or losing its force, and the future assimilation, with increased intermarriage, interbreeding, and mutual exchange of cultural inheritances, can only promise more strength for the region which is, and will continue to be, dominated by the sea. "The unsoilable sea," poet Oliver St. John Gogarty called it; and while man has soiled it here and there, in Gloucester Harbor, for instance, and on many a beach, nevertheless the sea, with its increasing number of allies in the human race, will win the fight. It was washing the shores of Cape Ann before man came, and it will probably still be there when the last of our strange breed have fled to another solar system.

≽ 15 ≼

Cape Ann on Canvas,
or Space and Light—
The Artists of Cape Ann

"I take SPACE to be the central fact to man born in America, from Folsom cave to now. I spell it large because it comes large here. Large, and without mercy." Thus Charles Olson, Gloucester's most significant poet, not native to the city, but from childhood a summer resident. In his mature years he made Gloucester his home, electing The Fort, an all Italian-American section overlooking the harbor which is the pulsating heart of things, now as in the days of Champlain. The quotation is from his *Call Me Ishmael*, bearing the subtitle "A Study of Melville," which has been called "one of the most knowing books about Melville, his times and his influence, ever written."

Serenity and space are the two things we are most conscious of when we study the paintings of Fitz Hugh Lane (1804–1865), Gloucester's great painter, a native of the city, who pursued his trade in Boston for a while, even as Winslow Homer did, but for triumph and fulfillment returned to the city of his birth to put it, and himself as well, immortally in paint on canvas. In the Fitz Hugh Lane paintings, as in those of all distinguished artists, we have the man; and this man out of a life of physical suffering and physical handicap, a life marred by domestic strife, found serenity in the vistas of the harbor that he loved, and with his genius tamed the space that comes on large and without mercy.

For space in Gloucester is not plains, or valleys, or deserts, or savannas, or mountain peaks towering beyond mountain peaks, but the sea which is indeed SPACE with all capital letters. Perhaps it is not surprising that the two nations that have most suffered space and most dealt with space are the two most concerned with outer space. For Fitz Hugh Lane space was the sea and the sea was cruel. No one who grew up in the port of Gloucester in the days of the schooners, or even today, thinks otherwise. To be sure, the worst years, measured in terms of loss of life, came after Lane had gone, in the post-Civil War period. During his most prolific period—say from 1850 to 1864, the year before his death—Gloucester fishermen drowned at the rate of two score each year, and more than ten vessels a year were lost.

Lane knew the cruelty of space all right, and, if we may judge from the brooding expression in the only photograph we have of him, he knew also the terror of those interior spaces that can be darker, running on as they do toward infinity and doubt. All that is true, but in his paintings serenity rules and space is tamed.

He was born Nathaniel Rogers Lane on December 19, 1804, and so christened. Like Nathaniel Hawthorne and Henry David Thoreau, he had to tinker with his name. Perhaps it was the romanticism of the nineteenth century that was in every young man's bones. He took to calling himself Fitz Hugh Lane and so signed himself. In the summer of 1806, when he was not two years old, he was stricken with an infantile paralysis which we today would guess to be polio. He was never tall, and he never walked. His legs were useless, and he dragged himself on two crutches.

His father, Jonathan Dennison Lane, was a sailmaker, and in the mid-nineteenth century in Gloucester that was an important trade. There were three other children. Fitz Hugh was apprenticed to a shoemaker, but it was seen that his talents lay elsewhere. He had been drawing and sketching from childhood. A local lithographer brought his work to the attention of William S. Pendleton, whose Boston firm was well known. Pendleton offered Lane a job. Lane was twenty-eight years old when he went to work in Boston.

Lithography was new, changing and developing. European artists brought to this country the latest techniques, and the products were extremely popular. The demand ran high, and Lane had work aplenty. He made himself a reputation as a competent draughtsman, with a particular talent for portraying "naval architecture." After he had been at it ten years, he formed his own partnership with a John W. A. Scott, and he was soon known as a "marine painter."

He was well past forty years of age when he stopped entraining for Boston, and remained in his Gloucester studio painting. For fifteen years he was to produce prodigiously, and to win a sound reputation for his painting. His paintings sold, but he supplemented his income with sign painting and decoration. In 1853 his mother, Sally Lane, died in her eighty-sixth year. For Lane it was a heavy loss because he had become estranged from his sister and her husband, Ignatius Winter, in a dispute over the famous house that he built which still stands, the massive, gray, gabled granite pile long known to Gloucesterites as "The Stone Jug." The house naturally overlooked the harbor, and much of Lane's best work was done in it.

As we have remarked before, many artists who have been drawn to Gloucester's superb shore line or to the rough reaches of Dogtown Common and other uplands have also been drawn to the State of Maine, which was part of Massachusetts, not becoming a state until 1820. The shore is much the same, although there is a striking gradation of coloring as one pushes farther north, and the conifers increase in number and their deciduous brothers decrease, and the sea grows darker, and the whole a little wilder, and certainly more spacious. Space is again at the heart of it, and standing before many of Lane's finest paintings, we find ourselves moving off into space, toward a horizon that is low and distant, and through a sky that is large. Man is diminutive in these pictures, but he is not insignificant.

None of Lane's paintings is more popular, and none gives us a greater sense of space, than his *Ships in Ice Off Ten Pound Island, Gloucester,* a small canvas (12 inches by 19 ¾ inches) now owned by the Museum of Fine Arts in Boston, part of the famous M. and M. Karolik Collection. Five boats are in the picture: three schooners, a three-masted square-rigger and a shallop, in a masterful composition. More than two-score men are on the ice, and four or five barely visible aboard the ships. The prows of two schooners, both with all sails furled, point toward a rigged schooner in the center of the picture, half hidden behind the three-master, some of the sails of which are only half furled. Its bow points toward the horizon and sends the observer's eye off into infinity. The men are more or less indistinguishable, but we are certain that they are working.

In that note we have another distinguishing feature of the bulk of the Lane paintings, which tells us a good deal about the serenity that pervades his pictures. Almost without exception when we find persons in his paintings, they are working. This is not merely a matter of his reproducing what he saw before his eyes in Gloucester Harbor; it is a matter of his selecting what he wanted in his paintings. At the heart of the serenity he knew, which was hard-won, was work, the wholesome, laborious work of tending, repairing, sailing ships, before the gasoline engine polluted the waters of the harbor and the air above it, before the fish plants swilled their gurry into the harbor, before the seaside became so crowded that a man could not walk where he wanted without fear of breaking the law.

This was before the fish plants changed into packaging factories, when work done in unison was done to a chantey, before the brutalization of the mass production line where billingsgate even among the women packers would today shock any quarter-deck hand of a century ago. What Lane caught in his paintings was not merely Gloucester Harbor, but an age; and not merely an age, but the quiet glory of it. He was a romanticist, to be sure, but he was a great one; and he was his own man, as independent of the Hudson River School as he was of Europe, whatever he may have learned from either. It is no surprise that he was neglected after his death, although he was far from being without acclaim during his life. His revival must be recognized as in part due to our sudden awareness of what we have lost in America, and what is still threatened: our space and our reaches of unspoiled nature, not wilderness but open space that shows the concern of man, his order and his care, rather than the blistering and blight that can follow in his wake.

In her study of nineteenth-century American painting, Barbara Novak calls Lane "a paradigm of luminism," and sees a parallel between his art and the Transcendentalism of Ralph Waldo Emerson. The Concord philosopher visited Cape Ann many times, recording his comments on the countryside, and lectured in Gloucester, though it is not known if Lane heard him. But the parallel supports itself. From Lane's paintings one gets an immediate impression that the serenity of the pictures, the magic moment caught by Lane's smooth brushwork and his unique perception of the light, rested on a confidence in the spirit, its pervasiveness and its indestructibility. For his own spirit had been indestructible under the crush of polio, and while never as blatant as W. E. Henley crying out against "the

fell clutch of circumstance," Lane's grasp of reality, his sense of realism, was firm. He knew the men who manned the schooners, God-fearing, and he had sailed as rough a voyage of life as any of them, although he seldom left shore. In his great pictures, it all shows in their subtle effulgence, which must ever remain one of the qualities of great art.

What he had seen also was that the light on Cape Ann was unique, as perhaps it must be for every locale, but here endowed with a splendor that brings revelation. That light was to play its part in the development of a more celebrated artist than Lane, Winslow Homer, and before or after him, William Morris Hunt, Childe Hassam, Edward Hopper, John Sloan, Maurice Prendergast, Marsden Hartley, and Stuart Davis. For all these men, Cape Ann was a stage in their artistic development. For Lane it was fulfillment.

Whence the light? It is the light, if you will, that is common to islands, for the sea, the great reflector and refractor, is on all sides, and throws back to the sun and shore all that it takes from them. To it, also, the rocks contribute, for their moist, steely surfaces catch and play with the light, to the extent that it seems almost a palpable thing and carried on the wind. In this ever-changing refulgence, this lambent air, moments come which only art can distill. This Lane did, and we relive those moments in his paintings in the Cape Ann Historical Association's museum, where the serenity and composition match and complement his paintings.

Winslow Homer took to water colors to catch those fleeting moments when the Cape Ann light set the colors of the world in a pattern that tears at the emotions. John Wilmerding, chairman of the art department at Dartmouth College and author of a *History of American Marine Painting,* has written more on Lane than any other man, and his book *Fitz Hugh Lane, 1804–1865: American Marine Painter* was published by the Essex Institute of Salem in 1964. He has also written with great insight on the lure of Gloucester and Cape Ann to distinguished artists.

Art connoisseurs and collectors live in hope that additional paintings by Winslow Homer, that greatest of nineteenth-century American artists, will turn up in Cape Ann homes. Lane died in 1865; Homer then was wandering through the South sketching scenes of the Civil War, and his great days were ahead of him. Some of his finest paintings would be done on Cape Ann, including *Breezing Up*, which hangs in the National Gallery of Art in Washington, D.C. In that magnificent picture, in such contrast with the serene sweep of the Lane paintings, three boys and a man sail a broad-beamed catboat on a port tack through a choppy sea. On the transom of the boat is the word "Gloucester." The painting tells us as much about the wonder of boyhood as it does about the delights of sailing, but then, what better place for a boy to grow up than at the seaside where boats are as familiar to him as people?

One of Wilmerding's most interesting articles on Cape Ann was printed in the Historical Collections of the Essex Institute in January, 1967. In it he contrasts the work done in Gloucester by William Morris Hunt, Winslow Homer, Maurice Prendergast and Marsden Hartley, and makes the point that "there may be something preeminent about American artists' contribution in the watercolor medium," even as there is something pre-eminent about the Oriental artists' contribution to ink drawings and that of the artists of Northern Europe to etching. "The new medium," he writes, "demanded a boldness of execution and economy that in turn permitted a frankness and intimacy of statement." He then goes on to discuss at length *Children Playing Under a Gloucester Wharf* by Homer, which hangs in the Museum of Fine Arts in Boston.

These Gloucester beginnings of water color are apt to be overlooked by critics and connoisseurs. In a recent volume entitled *Winslow Homer Watercolors* by Donelson F. Hoopes, Homer's Gloucester days are forgotten, and the paintings are all from the West Indies, Prouts Neck in Maine, and Tynemouth, England. *Children Playing Under a Gloucester Wharf* belonged in the book, if only to show his beginnings as a water colorist.

In what paintings has the miracle of boyhood been caught with more exactitude than in Homer's six woodcuts: *Snap the Whip; Gloucester Harbor; Sea-Side Sketches—A Clam Bake; Ship-Building, Gloucester Harbor; The Nooning;* and *Dad's Coming?* As Homer's place in the pantheon of American painters has grown ever larger and more secure, interest has been drawn to his magazine illustrations and his numerous woodcuts. In 1873 he was in Gloucester and lived on Ten Pound Island in the Harbor with the family of the lighthouse keeper. He was on assignment from *Harper's* magazine, in effect, for although he was a free-lance artist at the time, he had an assured market with *Harper's.*

Critics maintained that his woodcut *Snap the Whip* is superior to the painting he later did of the same scene. But apart from such judgments, the six sketches done in August and September of 1873 are of a piece and constitute a magnificent sequence. In *The Nooning*, three boys with their hound loaf in the sun, but we are sure that they are planning the afternoon's activity. In *Sea-Side Sketches—A Clam Bake* with the sun from the west ten boys have a fire going on a rocky beach: one is bringing more wood, two others carry a large can no doubt filled with seaweed, the rest are gathered around the fire. *Snap the Whip* gives us a group of children at the game in a Gloucester meadow. *Gloucester Harbor* shows seven youngsters in two dories on what is again a lazy afternoon, although there is some wind, for the schooners are moving past them. In *Ship-Building, Gloucester Harbor*, tykes too small for clambakes or for dory handling sit in the foreground of the picture, two of them making ship models, the others with baskets to gather shavings. Behind them is the hull of a schooner under construction, with a dozen or more men working. *Dad's Coming* is the most poignant of the six. A young boy perches on the upswung bow of a dory drawn high on the beach and resting on a great timber. His eyes are on the horizon and perhaps the small white sail heading for the harbor. Behind him stands his mother holding his younger sister. These and other studies complement both Homer's other work in Gloucester and the paintings of Fitz Hugh Lane. The Cape Ann Historical Association deserves a Homer painting to stand beside the Lanes, or the series of the woodcuts, just as the cause of art would benefit if the Association should acquire some of the works of Sloan, Davis, Hartley, Hassam, Hopper, Prendergast and other greats who were caught up in the magic of Gloucester's sea and shore, life and light.

Boyhood was something special for Winslow Homer as it never was for Fitz Hugh Lane. But so was the terror of the sea. Homer sailed to the Grand Banks, probably out of Gloucester, watched the tides on Ten Pound Island, and became so enamored of the sea that he settled at Prouts Neck in Maine and died there. No one has ever caught the Gloucestermen as has he in his famous oils: *The Herring Net,* which is in the Art Institute of Chicago; *Eight Bells* at Phillips Academy in Andover; and the *Fog Warning,* which hangs in the Boston Museum of Fine Arts. In this last painting, a single bearded man in a dory has been tending a trawl and has a great halibut, perhaps two or three, in the stern. Far on the horizon stands his schooner, and rolling in over it is a dark menacing fog bank. The doryman is gauging the distance, alert to the peril. He has paused a moment to assess the situation and will, undoubtedly, soon pull for his ship. The painting is magnificent and tells much about the life of the doryman in the day of sail. In Lane, man and nature are one, man part of the landscape; and in no picture do we find man threatened, although we may see a ship burn or a storm at sea. In Homer, man is pitted against nature; there is a terror at the heart of things which was finally to show its face whole in *The Gulf Stream*. Gloucestermen knew that terror when the fog did close in, when the blizzard caught them away from their ship. Blackburn knew it. But they met it. Joseph Garland might have been speaking of any bank off the coast of North America when he wrote, "The Georges in Winter was only for men who could stare Death down."

Fitz Hugh Lane is the great native painter of Gloucester, and Homer the great visitor. But other great visitors came: Maurice Prendergast and John Sloan and Edward Hopper. They turned their eyes from the sea to the shore, and Sloan painted automobiles (so rare) where others painted schooners and draggers. Four years after Homer died in 1910, Sloan was in Gloucester on his first visit. Sloan wrote of it, "My first summer in Gloucester afforded the first opportunity for continuous work in landscape, and I really made the most of it. Working from nature gives, I believe, the best means of advance in color and spontaneous design." Like many an artist after him, and like too many artists today, Sloan painted the rocks on the *Back Shore*.

In 1916 he painted *Evening, Rocky Neck*, one of his finest pictures done in Gloucester. He subsequently wrote of it, "A mere handful of people of East Gloucester lives on Rocky Neck but in summer the artist colony was quite numerous. Such a fishing village atmosphere as is shown in this picture [*Evening, Rocky Neck*] creates a longing to see it all again. But it is probably all messed up with automobiles in various stages of decay, exhaust odors fighting the fishy ones." He wrote that thirty years ago, and it was all too true then and is worse now. There is no John Sloan on Rocky Neck. Some of the worst painting in New England is displayed at a common center, and various artists have shops where they offer their daubings, enough of which sell to

the uninitiated to keep the painting going. The best painting exhibited on Rocky Neck today is that of Mary Bryan, an artist of
distinction, whose husband, Alden, paints and exhibits with her.
Emil Gruppe, whose ready oils of Gloucester Harbor scenes are
very popular, is the son of an artist. We find there what we find
in Rockport, the blight of commercialism. If Gresham's Law applies to anything else besides money, it surely applies to art.
Given any art colony with a string of shops, bad painting drives
out good.

On Cape Ann, however, there is that lure in the nature of
things that brings the good men in, some to stay for a short
while only, others to stay longer. Like Prendergast and Homer
and Sloan, Marsden Hartley came to Gloucester to see and to
paint and to go away a better painter. He, like Homer, was
drawn to Gloucester's uplands, and his painting of Dogtown
Common with its intrusive, somehow threatening, boulders is famous. Like Homer, he loved to paint Maine, where he was born,
and he is no doubt best remembered for those paintings. He was
also a poet aspiring to a literary career of sorts, and it would be
interesting to gather his fugitive pieces and poems into a book
of reproductions of his paintings.

Hartley is not so well known as Prendergast, who came to
Cape Ann after Homer. Prendergast, who, like Homer, was born
in Boston, was the leading American pioneer of postimpres-
sionism. With Sloan and Davis, he was a member of "The
Eight," and an exhibitor in the famous Armory show that turned
the history of American painting. Prendergast's paintings of
Cape Ann beach scenes with gay parasols and the nineteenth-
century beach costumes are America's loveliest.

Less celebrated than Prendergast—indeed, almost forgotten,
but a major figure in bringing the message of impressionism to
American shores—was Philip L. Hale, the father of author
Nancy Hale and husband of Lilian Westcott Hale, the cele-

brated portrait painter, whose reputation at last eclipsed that of her husband. Philip L. Hale—not to be confused with the music critic Philip Hale, who also loved Cape Ann—was the son of Edward Everett Hale, and taught painting for years at the Boston Museum School. His first (and only) New York show was a success, and helped educate the public to impressionism. The Hales kept their studio at Folly Cove just over the Gloucester line in Rockport, and to it each summer Nancy Hale comes with her husband, Fredson Bowers, dean of the faculty at the University of Virginia.

Childe Hassam came in also to paint the Gloucester shore, and Edward Hopper immortalized the tawdry main street in *Early Sunday Morning*. Like Sloan and Homer they went elsewhere to achieve their greatest fame, but the eerie lure of the city and its shore and its rocks and its light had entered into their psyches.

As the popular interest in American art rises, so the Cape Ann period of these men heightens, and so in turn will the reputation of the lesser figures on the Cape as they are discovered by critics and connoisseurs. In Rockport there are half a dozen members or associate members of the National Academy of Design.

If the ambiance on Cape Ann today is all in favor of the traditional, the representational, the conventional, there are distinguished craftsmen working, such as Don Stone, whose paintings catch something of the spirit of Andrew Wyeth. Wyeth's favorite painter, by the way, is Fitz Hugh Lane, and there is no man working in black and white whom Wyeth regards more highly than Stow Wengenroth, whose home is in Connecticut, but who is a member of the Rockport Art Association, and whose drawings of Cape Ann shores are among his finest work.

Between Gloucester and Manchester, incidentally, there were three sculptors, all of whom were members of the prestigious

National Institute of Arts and Letters. They were Walker Hancock, who did the inauguration medals for President Dwight D. Eisenhower; the late Paul Manship, whose magnificent sculpture at the Bronx Zoo has delighted millions; and Katharine Lane Weems, whose animal sculpture surely equals that of Manship and who is regarded by many as America's foremost woman sculptor.

Gloucester's unique light, to be sure, has not made much difference to the sculptors, who like the presence of the granite even if they don't work it. Besides those mentioned, there are George Aarons, Richard Recchia, and Franz Denghausen, all of whom have done exceptional work. Nor has the light particularly entered into the work of the poets who have found inspiration on Cape Ann, although there is a long, curious and charming poem by the Reverend Samuel Gilman, a native of Gloucester, and Class of 1811 at Harvard, entitled *History of a Ray of Light*, in which the ray recounts to us its 6,000 years of existence (from chaos to the nineteenth century), during which time it got to just about everywhere, from the Burning Bush that Moses saw through Greek mythological history to the age of science, helping out artists and writers from Raphael to Thomas Moore. Forgotten today, the poem is not without interest, but most of all, no doubt, owes its inspiration to the singular behavior of light on Cape Ann.

Of Gloucester, Stuart Davis, who has moved to the West Coast, said that it had "the brilliant light of Provincetown, but with the important additions of topographical severity and the architectural beauties of the Gloucester schooner." The schooner has gone, and the less attractive diesel-powered dragger has succeeded it. But the light is the same, and the topographical severity—and variety—are the same. But several things have happened: too many artists have turned inward and paint the hallucinations of their neuroses; too many are no longer concerned with light, except it be artificial light; and Gloucester lacks an organized or semiorganized intellectual life to encourage the experimental. What Gloucester has, however, is that organic strength that inheres in the authentic, the power of self-renewal. Commercial artists may abound in Gloucester, or some sound ones like Ken Gore, master of the palette knife, but the natural strength of the city itself is once again luring young and powerful painters to its harbor, for it has that charm of any land's end—it is a taking-off place for the infinite.

﹋ 16 ﹌
Men and Women of Letters

Dear as Cape Ann has been and is to the artist, the fabricator in oils or water colors or caseins or acrylics, or to the sculptor with his clay and wood and stone, it has been equally a mecca and a haven for the man of words, the writer, the poet. From Anne Bradstreet and Nathaniel Ward to John Updike and T. S. Eliot, this sea-bitten, inlet-gnawed littoral has nurtured novelist and versifier, playwright, critic, essayist and scholar in a manner as signal as the ineffable, almost tangible, exchange between the region and painter.

Almost immediately we must pass over the peripheral cities and towns because they—Salem and Newburyport and the communities in between—have too rich a literary history in themselves. One can digress too easily. If we chose to discuss only Nathaniel Hawthorne and John P. Marquand, two of America's great novelists—the one a native of Salem, the other a long-time resident of Newburyport—we could offer interminable literary considerations. Today Truman Nelson, a revolutionary writer, makes his home in Newburyport, because of his affinity with William Lloyd Garrison, to fulminate against the social injustices of the age. In Salem, Daniel Foley, one of the country's leading writers on gardens and landscaping, has his desk; and Ernest S. Dodge from the Peabody Museum re-creates the history of the Yankee in the South Pacific, with the historian William Hickling Prescott, who was born in Salem, as one of his inspirations. In Marblehead there are Harry Kemelman, whose rabbi-detective is taking a deserved niche in whodunit literature; and Fanny Howe, heiress to an eminent literary family tradition, whose *Forty Whacks,* a collection of short stories, was acclaimed by the critics. Each of the towns can boast its poet or writer. Beverly has John Beecher, poet, and Theodore Vrettos, novelist. Essex has its native-born Arthur D. Story, shipbuilder and storyteller, and in the past had Rufus Choate, the greatest trial lawyer of his day, whose addresses and speeches were textbook oratory for the nineteenth century.

We must take special notice of Lucy Larcom, a poet and editor of the nineteenth century, whose little volume *A New England Girlhood,* telling about the Beverly of her childhood, has become a classic, and is likely to live forever because of its simplicity and charm. Quoting a passage from it can in no way catch the flavor of the book, but perhaps will help give something of the picture of the conditions in the Cape Ann-side communities in the first decades of the nineteenth century, and show us the omnipresent influence of the sea:

"The sea was its nearest neighbor, and penetrated to every fireside, claiming close intimacy with every home and heart. The farmers up and down the shore were as much fishermen as farmers; they were as familiar with the Grand Banks of Newfoundland as they were with their own potato-fields. Every third man you met in the street, you might safely hail as 'shipmate', or 'Skipper', or 'Captain'. My father's early sea-faring experiences gave him the latter title to the end of his life.

"It was hard to keep the boys from going off to sea before they were grown. No inland occupation attracted them. 'Land-lubber' was one of the most contemptuous epithets heard from boyish lips. The spirit of adventure developed in them a rough, breezy type of manliness, now almost extinct." Lucy was born in 1824, and the excerpt could apply to any city or town on Cape Ann. The sea is all-encompassing.

Some writers are born on Cape Ann and go off to make their fortunes; others are born there and remain; and still others, born elsewhere, come to the Cape to find strength in the secrets of the sea and the rocks. Some of these remain to the end; others move on, as did T. S. Eliot and William Vaughn Moody. Because Cape Ann is a summer colony par excellence, many come and go and a number return regularly. Russel Crouse, playwright and wit whose *Life with Father* brought down each house and raised him to fame, made his home in Annisquam, and as host entertained not only his collaborator Howard Lindsay and Lindsay's lovely wife, Dorothy Stickney, but dozens of other stars of stage and screen. Helen Hayes summered close by, and Ruth Chatterton. Elliot Norton, Boston's distinguished drama critic, summered for years at Annisquam.

Among the natives of Gloucester who have sought their literary careers elsewhere are the poet Jeremy Ingalls, author of the narrative poem *Tahl*, who went west to a teaching post shortly after her graduation from college; and after her Hilton Kramer, who went to New York to be an art critic on the *Times*. One of his predecessors was William Winter, who took a law degree at Harvard in 1857, but turned to literature instead. He was drama critic for the *New York Herald Tribune* from 1865 to 1903, his work marked, according to Ludwig Lewisohn, by a "smug and strident limitedness." His biographies of Edwin Booth and other figures of the theater were his best work.

For many years William Rose Benét made his summer home in Gloucester, and at his death most of his library went to the public library in Gloucester. Many a reader has been thrilled to find the book he borrowed inscribed with the poet's name. His presence brought many writers, friends or admirers, to the Cape.

The first summer writer-in-residence, so to speak, was Richard Henry Dana, whose *Two Years Before the Mast* has all the persistence of a masterpiece. Dana came into Manchester when it was still a sleepy village devoted to fishing and woodworking. He bought a large tract of shoreland and gave his name to a beach there. John Leggett, the novelist, whose winter home is New York City, summers not far from Dana's Beach, and the second of his three novels, *The Gloucester Branch*, took as its locale a town not unlike Manchester, somewhere north of Boston, obviously on the Gloucester branch of the Boston and Maine Railroad. His first novel, *Wilder Stone*, was written while he was living in Manchester year-round. His latest, *Who Took the Gold Away*, was hailed by critics as an excellent novel of manners of the 1930s. Peter Davison, chief editor for Atlantic Books-Little Brown in Boston, found himself writing poetry about this hunk of shore line and then lured to make his home in West Gloucester overlooking the marshes running down to the sea.

A regular summer visitor not far from William Rose Benét was the late Charles W. Morton, who was associate editor of *The Atlantic* (whose editor emeritus Edward Weeks has his home in nearby Hamilton) and author of *How to Protect Yourself Against Women and Other Vicissitudes*. Morton arranged the most literary of tennis matches on the Cape. We have mentioned Nancy Hale, who has great admiration for the sturdy people of Cape Ann, immigrant and native alike. She loves to tell the story of the Finnish woman who came in to help clear out the Hale studio after the death of her mother.

"It's a nice house," said the woman.

"Yes," replied Nancy. "My mother built it."

The woman looked around appraisingly.

"She must," she said, "have had a boy to help her."

Percy MacKaye loved Cape Ann, and wrote one of his most famous poems on Dogtown Common. Here, too, S. Foster

Damon has come to muse on William Blake, but not so abstract-
edly that he was not able to write a prize-winning play dealing
with the witchcraft hysteria that remotely touched Cape Ann.

No poet writing on Cape Ann has better caught the countryside than William Vaughn Moody in his poem "Gloucester
Moors," of which we quote two stanzas:

> A mile behind is Gloucester town
> Where the fishing fleets put in,
> A mile ahead the land dips down
> And the woods and farms begin.
> Here where the moors stretch free
> In the high blue afternoon,
> Are the marching sun and talking sea,
> And the racing winds that wheel and flee
> On the flying heels of June.
>
> Jill-o'er-the-ground is purple blue,
> Blue is the quaker-maid,
> The wild geranium holds its dew
> Long in the bowlder's shade.
> Wax-red hangs the cup
> From the huckleberry boughs,
> In barberry bells the gray moths sup,
> Or where the choke-cherry lifts high up
> Sweet bowls for their carouse.

In Annisquam, of course, they point out the house where Rudyard Kipling wrote *Captains Courageous*, a story, like *Kim*, that
is somehow best for boys. If you want to know how the Gloucester fleet operated, what life as a fisherman was, then you must
read James Brendan Connolly or Joseph Garland. If Connolly
cannot be trusted on historical fact, he can be trusted on the
way a schooner sailed, the way a line was hauled, the way the
men of the fleet faced danger or death, and the way they walked
and talked ashore. His tales may be cornball today, his charac-
terizations without depth, and his prose style short of Garland's,

but he has preserved the age of sail in Gloucester for us as no one else has, and was much more of a writer than Cape Cod's Joseph C. Lincoln, who won a similar popularity for his tales of the southern cape of the Commonwealth of Massachusetts. Garland is not only himself a sailor, a man who can handle a halyard or a tiller, but he is also a prose stylist who, at his best, can make a page ring with vitality, and whose research is impeccable. Connolly was an immigrant to Gloucester; Garland is a native whose grandfather was mayor. Both of them have the appreciation of the solid-day heroism of the men they have celebrated in their writings.

Connolly is dead and gone; Garland very much alive, his home on the shore of the harbor on Eastern Point Road, looking out at the breakwater and the light. Not two hundred yards away is the summer home of Catherine Drinker Bowen, whose biographies of Edward Coke, John Adams, Oliver Wendell Holmes, and Francis Bacon have all been best-sellers. Nearby as well is her brother-in-law, Samuel L. M. Barlow, composer and author whose *Mon Ami Pierrot* was long the only opera by an American given in the Opéra Comique of Paris. Barlow has written novels, short stories and poetry, but his best piece of prose must remain *The Astonished Muse*, in which, from a vast range of reading, he advances the theory "that artists have provoked those revolutions whereby civilization has made progress. The artist, who sustained the spirit in times of transition and ultimately selected for commemoration the beneficent residues of history, cannot be far from the heart of our tradition." Despite inaccuracies of instance rooted in haste, the book is a marvelous panygeric on behalf of the role of the creative artist in history, and hence the role of Cape Ann. Peter Viereck, poet and historian, who lately took up residence on Cape Ann, said of the book that it was the most brilliant discussion of the "ever-de-

batable link between private creativity and social responsibility"
that he had read.

Mrs. Barlow, who was Ernesta Drinker, sister of Catherine
Drinker Bowen, has been noted for her beauty from childhood
and was painted many times by Cecelia Beaux, whose home,
too, was on the Gloucester Harbor shore. Between Garland and
Barlow is the home of John Coolidge, long-time curator of the
Peabody Museum at Harvard University. His successor is Agnes
Mongan, who lives at Pigeon Cove on the other side of the
Cape with her sister, Elizabeth, one of the world's authorities on
prints.

A former resident of Eastern Point, and one of the most prolific of Cape Ann writers, was Elizabeth Stuart Phelps Ward
(1844–1911), who began writing for *Youth's Companion* shortly
after she left the seminary where she was educated. Her numerous books appeared with regularity throughout the later half of
the nineteenth century, and her husband, Herbert Ward, also a
writer, became her collaborator.

Such a proliferation of artists and writers generates a cultural
situation which might have been common to the intellectual aristocracy of the eighteenth century, but in the main is lost
today. It puts cross-disciplines to work on Cape Ann. Sculptor
Franz Denghausen writes music and poetry and also carves and
models in clay. Alan Davidson is at once a painter and a publi-
cist. Kitty Parsons Recchia is poet and painter, whose lines have
graced the national magazines and whose paintings are displayed by the Rockport Art Association. There are any number
of artists who do not exhibit. Some, such as Cheslie D'Andrea,
are book illustrators; others, such as Frank Kempton, are commercial artists.

Ruth Holberg and Lee Kingman Natti are authors of scores of
children's books. Paul B. Kenyon, a long-time editor for the

Gloucester Times, is also author of a children's book, *Driftwood Captain.* So, too, Gurdon Worcester, author of *The Singing Flute.* Mary Shore, an artist who works best in abstractions, has written critical essays on art.

Any number of journalists live on Cape Ann and work from there, or have retired there. The late Samuel T. Williamson retired from New York journalism to write some of his best essays and book reviews from Rockport. John Kieran is another refugee to Rockport from *The New York Times,* as is his neighbor Victor Lawn. Jeremiah V. Murphy of the *Boston Globe,* whose writings have been compared to those of Jimmy Breslin, lives here and wrote a recent column on the charm of such living.

One could list endlessly writers and other artistic folk who have sought momentary refuge on Cape Ann. Edward A. Moseley, for instance, was a resident of Newburyport; from 1887 until his death in 1911 he was secretary of the Interstate Commerce Commission, a forgotten public hero who, however, was an intimate of the poet John Boyle O'Reilly. Their favorite recreation spot was Loblolly Cove in Gloucester. It is not significant that comedian-actor Jackie Gleason loves to come to Gloucester for a lobster dinner. More significant is the fact that David McCord, poet, essayist and painter, journeys to Cape Ann to water color; that Carlton Coon, one of the nation's leading anthropologists, but a novelist as well, has made his permanent home in West Gloucester, having fled Pennsylvania because there was "nobody to talk to"; that Robert Frost loved winter strolls on Crane's Beach or in Ravenswood Park; that the late Jack Kerouac would journey from Lowell to Gloucester to visit the late Charles Olson, who died, alas, while this book was in progress. The meeting brought together two men deemed "King of the Beats" —Kerouac for his prose, Olson for his poetry—but that title narrows their accomplishments, which are broader in their scope and profundity than the "beat" subculture.

Horace Gregory came to Cape Ann as the summer guest of William Rose Benét, and wrote "Seascape at Evening: Cape Ann."

> What is that sound, what is that blue and golden light
> Between the rocks, running through grasses,
> And at night walking beneath Orion and the moon?
> Its colors are in cornflower and honeysuckle,
> And wherever one turns, morning or evening,
> It is the sea.
>   It is the presence
> Everywhere: the invisible weeping face
> Between the branches of the trees, the ancient
> Wild sound between sun and moon, the Doric
> Greek return of rock and island:
> Voice of the sisters who walk the tide,
> Who speak the fortunes of the dead
> In salt wind lifting
> The pale arms of the sea.
>   Even the innocent
> Blue flower at our feet stares at us
> Through the bright glass of sea and sky,
> Speaks to us of the veined rock and the grey forest
> Hidden in roots and moss: what does it say
> Of lives that have turned to stone?
> I hear their voices in the wind, in the waves, in the cries
> Of the white-breasted and great-winged
> Birds of the sea.

John Malcolm Brinnin, a Bay State teacher and poet, wrote for *The New Yorker* magazine a Cape Ann poem in which he too was caught by the sea and the birds:

CAPE ANN: A VIEW

> Tropic of ice—
> the sea a razor-line toward Spain.
> This house I rented on the first of June
> already hums with bees about their pueblos,
> and from a bare deck rotted by the sun

I see bird islands and the snow-patched slopes
where sea gulls hold their raucous councils.
In single file,
as if they had pried apart the whaleback rock
that shoulders my front door, late irises
shuck off their thin rag-paper wrappings
and stand like roosters while their petals blow.

Again the fond summer comes to a grim edge
off which, this morning, one gray lobsterman
goes trolleying from float to float
and stops at each, his bubbling motorboat
adrift, to rake the sea.
Becalmed, he hauls a shower to his knees,
measures his catch in ounces and in inches,
and, patient, throws out almost everything.
He swings about,
steadfast, his motor muttering, as if with hope,
and fades like a dead soul, still standing up.

A rusty lilac knocks against a shingle;
the old GE refrigerator champs and snores.
When echoes echo in too many rooms,
I go downstairs, compelled to open doors
as if someone stood waiting there . . .
Cold sun steps in. There's little to surprise
a stranger in this neighborhood.

Whoever lives here must be gone for good;
his lavish water colors bleed and sag,
his breadbox is unhinged, his tacked-up wall map
of the zodiac's washed brown with rain;
his pantry shelf keeps one white plate—on it
someone once painted a high-buttoned shoe;
upstairs, there's a wan piece of art nouveau
and a black sweater gone in the right sleeve.

My relics, fallen among his,
lean on the shelves of a long afternoon.
A trapezoid of light goes crabwise on the floor,
the bees with Yo-yo spoolings lift and sink

on the still air, and, in a thrust of gold,
a spider's little partly finished net
abstracts the heart of treachery.

The evening, at first screened in clear pastels,
soon washed out in a romantic clamor.
Gulls on a fishhouse roof,
spaced perfectly, a wing apart, observe
these last annunciations of the visible.
The stars come thick; and as I move
toward sleep within the sleep of walls
that may recall my tenancy, fish, lion,
scorpion and ram climb the important track
from whose solicitous and shining grace
a name descends on the anonymous.

T. S. Eliot, who knew Cape Ann better than either Brinnin or Gregory, gives the title "Cape Ann" to one of the poems from his "Landscapes." He, too, was taken by the birds; for, as we pointed out in an earlier chapter, to live on Cape Ann is to live with the birds and to be conscious of their struggle with the environment, and the maintenance of beauty in the midst of peril.

CAPE ANN

O quick quick quick, quick hear the song-sparrow,
Swamp-sparrow, fox-sparrow, vesper-sparrow
At dawn and dusk. Follow the dance
Of the goldfinch at noon. Leave to chance
The Blackburnian warbler, the shy one. Hail
With shrill whistle the note of the quail, the bob-white
Dodging by bay-bush. Follow the feet
Of the walker, the water-thrush, Follow the flight
Of the dancing arrow, the purple martin. Greet
In silence the bullbat. All are delectable. Sweet sweet sweet
But resign this land at the end, resign it
To its true owner, the tough one, the sea-gull.
The palaver is finished.

❧ 17 ❧

The Poets and the Cape

Charles Olson feared that by the year 2000 the people of the United States of America would have lost all sense of heritage. That was one of the reasons he incorporated so much of Cape Ann's history in his poetry. Part of that history—part of that heritage—is the legacy of T. S. Eliot, as well as the legacy of Charles Olson.

From 1895 to 1909 Thomas Stearns Eliot spent his summers at Eastern Point, East Gloucester. The house, on Edgemoor Road, lies between Eastern Point and Bass Rocks, beside the mysterious, beautiful Gloucester moors. When Eliot went there, the view from the house to the ocean was unimpeded, and one looked across the waste of the moors to the waste of the water. The poet came first when he was seven and annually until he was twenty-one years old. His memories of it were fond, and shortly before his death he came back to the house and was delighted to find the area still bustling with children. He himself had been one of seven.

Eliot's poetry echoes with the memories he carried of Cape Ann. We have already quoted his poem "Cape Ann," with its knowledge of the bird life of the region. As a boy he had watched the birds in the brush on the moors and in the rocks by the sea, and along the tidal flats. This was different country from St. Louis, and when he was in St. Louis he pined for the sound of the sea and the shore birds of the Northeast. The rose garden looms with mystery in his poetry, much of which is the mystery of childhood and the wild roses of Cape Ann. A brook near the house rambles through clustering wild rosebushes before tumbling into the sea. In "Sweeney Erect," we read:

> Paint me a cavernous waste shore
> Cast in the unstilled Cyclades,
> Paint me the bold anfractuous rocks
> Faced by the snarled and yelping seas.

In "The Love Song of J. Alfred Prufrock," we come again to the sea, to the beach, to the "ragged claws/Scuttling across the floors of silent seas," and in "Rhapsody on a Windy Night" to "an old crab with barnacles on his back, / [that] Gripped the end of a stick which I held him."

All the detail of the shore and the sea burned into his sensitivity, and could be reconstructed with precision in the brown fog of London. Yet, we know that much of it went on paper while he was still summering in Gloucester, and the notebooks in which *The Waste Land* and other poems were inscribed were purchased at Procter Brothers stationery on Main Street, Gloucester. Here are a few lines from "Marina":

> What seas what shores what grey rocks and what islands
> What water lapping the bow
> And scent of pine and the woodthrush singing through the fog
> What images return. . . .

Memories, too, of granite islands, culminating in "The Dry Salvages." At the opening he explains that the name rhymes with "assuages," and then gives the definition of a "groaner," the Cape Ann term for a whistling buoy. The one off the Reef of Norman's Woe carries on the wind to Manchester, and can be heard on Eastern Point. The whole of that third section of the *Four Quartets* is redolent of the mystique of Cape Ann.

Eliot sailed off the craggy shore in his older brother's sailboat. He learned nomenclature of the sea, and could write the line, "The garboard strake leaks," and drive the landlubber to his dictionary.

When he raises his eyes, he sees what Olson sees and what returning seamen have seen for decades:

> Lady, whose shrine stands on the promontory,
> Pray for all those who are in ships, those
> Whose business has to do with fish, and
> Those concerned with every lawful traffic
> And those who conduct them.

He is recalling the Church of Our Lady of Good Voyage, which Olson catches in his "Maximus Songs":

> (o my lady of good voyage
> in whose arm, whose left arm rests
> no boy but a carefully carved wood, a painted face, a schooner!
> a delicate mast, as bow-sprit for
> forwarding

One cannot read Eliot's poetry, and particularly *Four Quartets*, without sensing that the sea stirred in the depths of his being and stands as a major symbol in his work. His vision of the sea, like his vision of time, can be terrifying, for who can fail to see such a headland as Cape Ann as a ship breasting the ocean and breasting time? It is no surprise that he went the way the ship was pointing, to England, to track along the roots back to pure beginnings.

Charles Olson, with similar vision, turned the other way to restate the beginnings of Cape Ann, the beginnings of America. Both saw the waste land: both were afraid not for themselves, but for Western civilization: and both list its promises. Where Eliot went to re-establish the connection between America and

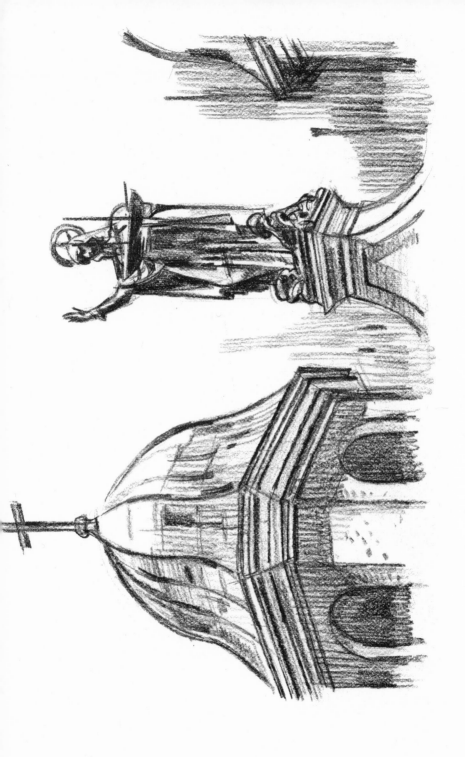

England, Olson remained on the American shore to clear the lines once again, to find the Elizabethan man.

For Olson, Gloucester was a charismatic city in the history of man, a terminus, where something ended as the glacier did, something as massive and nearly as old, and something began that could be everything.

"I regard Gloucester," he said, "as the final movement of the earth's people, the great migratory thing, which no longer is interesting at all. Migration ended in Gloucester; the migratory act of man ended in Gloucester, and I think the migratory act of man is the fillet of the rose, is the fires of the energy pattern. And Gloucester began this continent, in any interesting fact."

For him Gloucester had "primacy" and an "originatory nature," a similar but more terminal role than Venice or Tyre, both of which he looked back on as climacterics along with Greece in the migration of man, his movement over the seas to the last frontier.

"Man today," he cried, "must either rediscover the earth or leave it."

He thus addressed his poetry to the city of Gloucester and its people, taking as a persona Maximus of Tyre. For him Maximus was a figure of speech, and Tyre a symbol. Olson stood better than 6 feet 8 inches tall, and he was not an elongated animal such as we see on the basketball courts, but a large man, thick in the shoulders and chest, with a large head, leonine in a way. Some persons thought that he chose the title Maximus because of his size, and others, less charitably, because he thought of himself as "the greatest." He chose Maximus of Tyre in his vision of history and because Maximus, centuries ago, gave one of the finest expressions we have in definition of the autonomy of art. Origen is buried in Tyre, and that early Christian philosopher, with his love for learning and the centrality he gave the classics (as opposed to the anticlassicism of Gregory the Great), meant much to Olson. So Maximus he was, and as Maximus he addressed the city of Gloucester in his letters and songs, asking the city and its people to wake up to their heritage, to relish what they had been given. Gloucester, he tried to tell them, is a climacteric, a true polis, a city with a place in the linear destinies of man.

He wound his own lyricism into the history of the city, to its soil and sand and rocks under his feet, and to its buildings and artifacts and topography.

In "Maximus, to Gloucester 11," he wrote:

The rock reads
  the rock I know by my belly and torn nails, the letters on it
  big enough I sat in triumph arriving,
  by a head start,
  run up the face, grab the stone emboss
  anchor rope
  carved from it) get onto
  the bronze plaque:
          "In the Early History of,
A Notable Exemplification of
Arbitration"
          And the Short Chimney
wld have died right there, been plugged by a fisherman if
Conant had not ordered Capt Hewes to lower his gun, to listen
to what the little man from Plymouth had to squawk about

Mister Standish
wld have been the first to lie in the cemetery where my father
    does,
            at least where I say he does,
            where I wanted him to, either that
            or load him in a dory, row him
            beyond the Breakwater, and set fire to it, let him go, so
            to sea.
That a man's life
(his, anyway)

is what there is
that tradition is

at least is where I find it,
how I got to
what I say

He got to what he said by a circuitous route. He was born in Worcester, summered in Gloucester, and went to Wesleyan University, where he took his A.B. and M.A. degrees. He then went to Harvard, where he took his Ph.D. degree in American Studies, and made a significant contribution to the body of scholarship surrounding Herman Melville. His book *Call Me Ishmael: A Study of Melville* was published in 1947 when a Guggenheim award enabled him to finish it. Not until thirteen years later were *The Maximus Poems* published. In those thirteen years he worked chiefly for the Office of War Information, and taught at Black Mountain College, where he, in a way, created himself and a school of poets, disparate perhaps in style but devoted to him and to their art.

What went on between those years is not so important as his return to Gloucester. With his second wife and his son Charles Peter, he made his home at 28 Fort Square in the Italian-American Fort section to burrow into the marrow of his historic city. His mammoth figure in rumpled, and often ragged, clothes, a sweater sometimes tied around his waist, grew familiar to the life of the city. His conversations turned everywhere, seeking more and more meaning in the city. Hours on end were spent in Salem, at the Essex Institute, the Registry of Deeds, and the Superior Court, poring over the earliest records to find out who bought the land from the Indians (and for how little) and resold it (for how much).

All the time he sought, through the Maximus letters, which continued to appear (the last volume in 1968), to call the atten-

tion of Gloucester "to what is has been given," to its heritage, to
its role in history, to its past greatness.

He had not been back in his native city for long when he
sought out Vincent Ferrini, a maker of picture frames for liveli-
hood, but a dedicated and not widely read poet. Olson had read
a poem by him, knew him as of Gloucester, and went to his
door to form a friendship that lasted to death. Ferrini and his
wife were among those persons who went to the deathbed of
Olson in New York to wish him recovery.

He knew that death was near. "If I only had ten more years,"
he said. The last word he breathed, Charles Boer, his fellow
professor at the University of Connecticut and his literary exec-
utor, tells us was "wonderful." It was an affirmation of life,
something he made often. He knew that Gloucester was fading
into history, unable or unequal to revitalization, and that the
days of glory would not return. What could be the city's future?

"An image," he said, "of creation and of human life to the best
of the life of the species."

However, for him Gloucester was not being run by "the best
of the life of the species," but by "the junior chamber of commerce." He felt that the entire country had been delivered over
to the Junior Chamber of Commerce. Yet he could be euphoric.
"What's wrong with things as they are?" he asked. And he tried
to stop the dissolution: "Have I not fought for every building,
every stone, every blade of grass?"

When a venerable old building was about to be torn down,
Olson wrote a "scream" to the editor of the *Gloucester Daily
Times,* who gave over most of a page to it. When another significant building was threatened, he asked to buy it. No terms
could be arranged. He had no liquid assets of the necessary sort.

The failure of the people of Gloucester and of the United
States to preserve, cherish, improve, utilize what they have sick-

ened him. He jeered at the attempt to find a new home on a new planet, and welcomed "every new ash heap."

"What's wrong with what is?" he asked of men trying to find a new world.

One of the things wrong with what is, of course, is the popular disdain of art and artists, or poetry and poets. Olson was more celebrated in England than in Gloucester, more welcome on campuses than at City Hall. He was translated into German and French, while the bulk of the people of Gloucester never read him.

This was the result of a number of things; among them, a faintly Marxist flavor to some of his writings (some called him Fascist); the references to him as the father of the Beatnik poets or the dean of the Beatnik poets, a title he brushed away (not that he scorned them, but because his work lay elsewhere); and the obscurantism or hermetic quality of much of his poetry. Much remains difficult, but most yields itself to effort once one grasps his method and familiarizes oneself with the history of his beloved Gloucester. Some critics dismissed his poetry as prose oddly arranged on the page. Even though it may not maintain the traditional standards of poetry, *The Maximus Poems* makes interesting reading in itself. Wise critics long ago pointed out that a certain friction was a necessary part of poetry, and G. K. Chesterton put it more humbly when he said that, while it should not be unintelligible, it should not be an after-dinner cigar. It may be that the future will read Olson with more ease than do his contemporaries.

He earlier had distinguished a type of poetry which came to be called "Projective Verse," and which was in many ways a protest against the academic slickness of the New Criticism. "Projective or Open Verse," he wrote, was "at all points a high-energy construct and, at all points, a high-energy discharge. . . ." In it, "form is never more than an extension of content," and "one perception must immediately and directly lead to a further perception." James Dickey scoffed at it, and other poets may have been unimpressed. William Carlos Williams was very much excited, and the illuminations of Olson's famous essay led a number of younger men into the making of poetry. Olson was relatively old when he began.

He gave new life to Ferrini, who had been struggling for years with little acceptance, bringing out his works with small publishers, in avant-garde magazines, or under his own auspices. Ferrini, too, loved and loves Gloucester, although his poetry never gave it the role in history which Olson saw.

Ferrini's first works were poems of social protest, proletarian poetry, circulated in Lynn when the unions were organizing at the General Electric Company (largest payroll in Massachusetts) and the effects of the Depression were not only felt in most homes but burning most souls. The verses were not gathered and published until the 1940s. Among his books were *No Smoke,* a series of portraits of the people of Lynn, reminiscent of *Spoon River Anthology,* followed by *Injunction,* and *Blood of the Tenement,* the titles of which indicate the nature of the content. His style was imagistic touched by surrealism. As with Olson, so with Ferrini the touchstone of things was not Marxism or politics, but art, or, in both their cases, poetry. With his proletarian years far behind him, Ferrini was still viewed with suspicion by the people of Gloucester, who put politics ahead of poetry and fed on the past. Olson the Ph.D. and Ferrini the picture-framer were from different literary worlds, but their poetry brought them together. Ferrini published an avant-garde magazine, *Four Winds,* to which Olson (and Denise Levertov, among others) contributed. For Olson, Ferrini was a demonstration that poetry still lived in the rocks of Cape Ann, and that the struggle lay outside the academies.

When he needed money, Olson went back to academia to

teach. He was a brilliant teacher, for his breadth of knowledge was formidable and his fancy was kaleidoscopic. It also amused Olson that while Harvard, Brown and Buffalo Universities were collecting the works of Ferrini, his adopted city was pretty much ignoring him—although lately the local newspaper has published Ferrini's poems on several occasions, including a eulogy for Olson.

Olson always claimed that his inspiration to become a poet traced to the day when, crouching behind a stone wall, he heard two fishermen talking together. The vivacity, the profundity of their language caught him up, young as he was. He was four.

"Those men," he said in an interview shortly before his death, "had that fantastic condition of the human race where everything mattered. Today nothing does; that's what's so poor. I know men for whom everything matters still, who see, feel and know that everything that they run into does matter, and then they retain it, and then they have it, and they have it forever. And when they are buried, they are bigger than those who don't, even if they look the same and fit the same box."

Did all Gloucester fishermen have that?

"Not all, but qualitatively the container had a better chance to have a better content."

Olson sought to attain that condition himself. He sought to remain alert to every nuance of the sounds of Main Street, Gloucester, of the politics of the city, of the movement of the fleet, of the aspirations of the people. He eschewed political activity; for him culture was the hope of the world and might yet be revived. In his avant-garde, or dragon world, as Pound might have called it, his detractors called him a "culture imperialist," a "fantasist of history." Let the argument rest among them. He was alert, sensitized to the significance of Cape Ann, to the men who had been the world's music makers, and to an age that was dying.

"I know men for whom everything matters still. . . ." He read the records of the Gloucester fleets and dwelt on the nobility of the men who sailed them. He could argue about the value of this type of schooner or that, fret about the "clipper ship" bow schooner that took too many men to their deaths off Georges Bank near Sable Island. He could evaluate James B. Connolly better than other critics: "in a funny way, the greatest writer of Gloucester, the only trouble is he chose to write in that goddam stage Irish, which ruins the thing. But the fact is that Connolly knew Gloucester at the height of the industry, of the fishing, of the machine, of the schooner, and his work is so dependably the story at the date you can't touch it." Typically, somehow, of Gloucester, Connolly's works are in collection at Colby College in Maine. No one in the city knew more about Captain Joseph W. Collins, one of the most literate of Gloucester skippers, who ended up an executive of the Smithsonian Institution in Washington, D.C., and wrote so penetratingly on the fisheries.

"When Gloucester celebrated its two hundred and fiftieth anniversary," Olson could say with indignation, "this man, Collins, who did this fantastic logging job on flogging in the navy, who designed the schooner that replaced the schooner that cost the lives, who wrote with as much authority as Melville, this man came to the celebration of the two hundred and fiftieth anniversary, and nobody knew him."

What went out of Gloucester when the men of sail went out of the city?

"One big thing," Olson could reply, "Nature. It was like as though you didn't have to hunt for your food. They were still fishermen as hunters for food, because of the condition of the vessel, the danger to the vessel, it was like Indians and white men as hunters. There isn't any danger in fishing any more. The ships today are factories, like the Soviet factory ships. We're talking about something that went out in our lifetimes. I can remember the days when a man went to work—he was in danger. My father's job was to replace brick chimneys with iron; he had to go onto a staging; it was high steel, or like it. It relates to our nature of perception; our body is our soul; that is crucial; if we lose our sense of perception, we have lost our soul.

"The horror today is the limpness, the slackness, laziness, the lack—you don't need attention any more, you don't need perception. It is all taken care of for you by the environment of your automobile, of your house, of the economy, of the money system. We don't need money, only credit; it works. It is a crazy sort of a post-natural thing that the species has got into. So who cares. Let's have another species. I just happen to have liked that species that's called man. And I therefore thank God it was interesting because of man. I still think creation is crucial and if you don't stay close to it you lost everything. That's all. Just everything."

The city that he loved, that he believed central, he also saw falling farther and farther away from creation—or grace, as he sometimes called it. Remember, of course, that he considered the rest of the country even farther away—in the main, that is.

"Every day," he said, "I have to go further from my house, a further distance, to find what I believe, to get in touch with those things which I consider necessary."

What were they? Well, the sight of a red-winged blackbird or a weed that interested him, or a fresh movement of air, among other things. And the people.

Great orators, it has been said, arise to defend dying causes. Olson was not unlike Demosthenes warning against Philip. He was warning against a future that was likely to forget its heritage, and, indeed, so far as he was concerned, Gloucester and Cape Ann had all but forgotten it, while America had forgotten Cape Ann.

➤ *Epilogue* ⤦

What we have tried to delineate is a lost heritage, one that is slipping away from the people of the United States, who do not know their past very well or understand the symbiotic link with Europe which not only established this country but has continued to regenerate its vitality. Without being pessimistic about it, we must resign ourselves to a decline in popular interest in our early beginnings and the organic twisting through time which has brought us where we are, and is making us what we shall become. "Tomorrow is upon me today," cries out Ferrini in one of his poems. "They never knew how good they were," James B. Connolly said in his old age of the Gloucester fishermen he knew and admired. The same could be said of much that exists on Cape Ann today—its residents don't know how fortunate they are in their natural heritage, which some are fighting to save and too many are destroying in their pursuit of riches.

The layer upon layer of history on Cape Ann and the historic communities that border it could be translated into a series of volumes to match in size the *Encyclopedia Britannica*. I have left out too much and have, no doubt, included some of the wrong things. I have, for instance, all but ignored the handicrafts of the region, the ethnic dancing, the square dancing, the discussion clubs, the gardeners who have produced rare orchids and other exotic flowers to top annual competitions, for the English habit of gardens and the grace of Irish gardeners are common on Cape Ann.

The amount of folklore that does not appear in this book is larger than the book itself. When James T. Fields, Boston's most famous publisher in the golden days of its literary leadership, would write from Manchester to Oliver Wendell Holmes who was in Beverly, Fields would give his address, "Manchester-by-the-Sea," and Holmes would respond, "Beverly-by-the-Depot." Today children chant, "Manchester-by-the-Sea, Gloucester-by-the-Smell."

We have not mentioned the newspapers of the region, or its leading publisher, Philip S. Weld, except to remark on his advocacy of the catamaran. One of his papers, an offset weekly, brings to Cape Ann with each edition some portion of the story of its heritage.

We have hardly mentioned the music that is played and composed there. There is first of all a Cape Ann Civic Symphony Orchestra, although the population figures would not seem to justify it, which plays brilliantly. Dr. Gardner Read, whose Fourth Symphony was recently performed—a premiere—by the Cincinnati Symphony Orchestra, makes his home in Manchester on part of the estate of the late Chalker Walker. Several composers on the Cape are experimenting with poetry set to music, with total theater and the dance. In Beverly, a cultural center, with, sadly, too little support from surrounding communities, is nevertheless establishing itself, the North Shore Music Theater. The top layer of history on the Cape is quick with the life of the intellect, persons drawn to the region not by the natural surroundings alone but by the noble beginnings of the place, the romance of the sea —the decency, if you will, of the life of the fisherman in those days when he was a hunter, risking his life to feed a continent. That life is being lost even to those who want to pursue it.

A letter to the editor of the *Gloucester Daily Times* by a young man eager to catch up that tradition recently appeared: "Every day it gets bad to worse. The Gloucester fishing boats need men to work the boats and now the Gloucester High School wants to close the fishery shops. In Gloucester 70 percent of the fishermen are over 40 years of age. One out of every 20 has a high school diploma, and they still want to close the fishery shops. In ten years there will be no men to go fishing. Boats cannot catch fish tied to the docks. Gloucester needs this shop. Let's help to keep it going."

The syntax and the vocabulary are not equal to the passion, but the message is clear: Does Cape Ann see? If there was a schooner museum in Gloucester, it might inspire someone to remember, as the *Constitution* in Boston inspires tens of thousands each year. In Mystic, Connecticut, such a schooner raises its masts proudly to receive visitors. Another sails out of Maine, and some assemble each year for the historic convocation and race. Just as in Monaco Errol Flynn's schooner, the *Zaca*, recently rotted at the piers, so Gloucester has allowed its schooners to disappear. The fish companies and the city are indifferent. Gloucester has no schooner. If one is ever restored, it will be by private citizens, ship-minded and enthusiasts.

Each year the people of the city assemble at the Cut—the popular name for Blynman Bridge—to memorialize the dead of the fishing fleets and strew flowers on the water. The ceremony has moved the hearts of man, poets as well as mourners. Some lines of my own try to catch the significance of the ritual:

AT A GLOUCESTER MEMORIAL SERVICE
May I call attention to the flowers?
Ten sleeps down I dreamed a blackness

Striped by the tooth-white tops of waves
Shuttling over the whale-rib graves
Of men who died in their matter-of-factness
Working out their eight hours.

They had shopped a square dance with their wives,
Barked at their children and filled their pipes,
Tumbled statistics into the books
Where eyeless scholars drag their hooks,
Juggled their laughter and their gripes
Then went off and laid down their lives.

Our petals drop on the crown of the sea
That hugs their bones and their dungarees,
Half-way heroes without a war,
All too sure what they battled for,
Bread, home, children, liberties,
The orchids of life's monotony.

You can see them only in a dream
Too shining for man's single sight,
Statistical records and town reports
These all too credible cohorts
Fishermen brought to the naked night
By the wind's rude snare and the sea's last scheme.

The following two pages show reproductions of a Gloucester
memorial service program:

Fishermen's Memorial Service

SUNDAY, JULY 14th, 1963, at 7:00 P. M.

WESTON U. FRIEND, Officer of the Day

AT STATUE

BAND—"Holy, Holy, Holy."   John B. Dykes

LAYING OF WREATHS

Capt. Colin Powers
Representing Master Mariners' Association

Capt. Lemuel R. Firth
Representing Gloucester Fishing Masters' and Producers' Association

Alphonsus F. Hayes
Representing Atlantic Fishermen's Union

Leslie F. Yelland
Representing Gloucester Fishermen's Institute

BAND—"Abide With Me"   W. H. Monk

MARCH TO BLYNMAN BRIDGE
EXERCISES AT THE BRIDGE

BAND—"Eternal Father Strong to Save"

INVOCATION   Father Francis Andreoli
Our Lady of Good Voyage Church

DUET—"Hark, Hark, My Soul"   Rev. F. W. Faber
Mr. Robert Churchill and Mrs. Ronald Maciel

BAND—"Faith of Our Fathers"

ADDRESS   Mr. Norman C. Ross
(Lt. Comdr., U. S. Naval Reserve)

DUET—"O for Peace that floweth as a River"   Jane Crewdson
Mr. Robert Churchill and Mrs. Ronald Maciel

BAND—"What a Friend we have in Jesus"   C. C. Converse

MEMORIAL PRAYER   Rev. Gordon W. Lind
St. John's Episcopal Church, Gloucester

SINGING BY THE AUDIENCE   Leader - Robert F. Churchill

"SCATTER FLOWERS ON THE WAVES" (Mary Brooks)

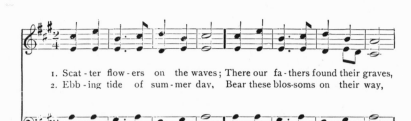

1. Scat - ter flow - ers on the waves; There our fa - thers found their graves,
2. Ebb - ing tide of sum - mer day, Bear these blos-soms on their way,

Broth-ers, sons and hus-bands sleep; Strew your gar-lands o'er the deep.
North and east to bank and coast Where they lie whom we love most.

FLOWER CEREMONY

READING OF THE ROLL of local men lost during the past twelve months
Mrs. Harriet Hayes

In memory of all the seamen who through all the years, have found a last resting place in the waters that wash every shore, we lovingly strew these flowers.

WREATH from the FISHERMEN'S INSTITUTE WOMEN'S AUXILIARY
Mrs. Harriet Hayes

WREATH from the CITY OF GLOUCESTER
and REMARKS   The Hon. Ralph B. O'Maley, Mayor

WREATHS FROM NEXT OF KIN, and others

ANNOUNCER—Mr. Kyle Ulch   Resident Fisherman

Mrs. Martha Hill   Mrs. Mary Pereira
Mrs. Veronica Naves   Mrs. Elaine Pina
Mrs. Helen Parisi

MASTER MARINERS' ASSOCIATION   Capt. Colin Powers, V.P.

FISHING MASTERS' AND PRODUCERS' ASSOCIATION
Capt. Lemuel R. Firth

SEAFARERS' INTERNATIONAL UNION OF NORTH AMERICA
Mr. Michael Orlando

ATLANTIC FISHERMEN'S UNION   Mr. Alphonsus Hayes

FISHERMEN'S INSTITUTE   Mr. Adelbert Hines, Resident Fisherman

PARTICIPANTS STANDING ALONG THE WATERWAY ARE INVITED TO CAST THEIR BOUQUETS OF FLOWERS UPON THE WATERS.

BENEDICTION   Rev. Wm. Ralph Stayton
Baptist Church

TAPS

BAND—"Anchors Aweigh"

This custom itself is modulating into simply another aspect of the Memorial Day service in the city. There was a time, of course, when the fishermen who died at sea outnumbered the other dead in the city. They are now a minority, but it seems somehow unsuitable to forget the past and let such a distinctive service become an appendage.

Perhaps this book, with all its omissions, may help to refocus and emphasize the significance of Cape Ann in the history of America, and its suitability as a microcosm of the United States of America today, justifying in a way the title *Cape America*, which is of my own devising, and a result of the reflection prompted by the theme set forth in this book.

To set foot on Cape Ann is not to sense immediately its thick texture of history and culture. No doubt too many of its inhabitants never revert to its historic past, but it is there, around them, and to a small extent they cannot escape it. Flesh and bone absorb it; it can strengthen the spirit. If the study of history can enlarge us, so can living in its midst, but only if we can recapture the sensitivity of an ancient helmsman, alive every minute—alive to everything, and above all to the American heritage—and so make every Cape Ann a Cape America.

❧ *Index* ❦